"No one understands the importance of the oceans and their impact on today's security better than Admiral Jim Stavridis. He is a leader and a sailor who stands out in every way. This is a must-read book."

—Senator John McCain

"Stavridis strikes a perfect balancing tone between the theoretical and the personal; he's read widely in the annals of naval history, and he's also seen years of that history in the making. . . . *Sea Power* is clear-eyed about the dangers of the modern nautical realities, but it doggedly retains this tone of hope throughout. And hope or danger, on one point the book compels agreement: the oceans are still the crucial theaters of this water world."

—*Christian Science Monitor*

"Admiral Jim Stavridis served as a combatant commander for nearly seven years, as NATO Supreme Allied Commander for four years, and knows the world well. In *Sea Power*, he turns his intellect to helping us understand the maritime world in clear, sharp strokes—vital analysis in this turbulent century."

—Robert M. Gates, Secretary of Defense, 2008–2011

"Marvelous and essential . . . [Stavridis] not only describes what his subtitle promises—the history and geopolitics of the world's oceans—but also seeks to accomplish something far more elusive, sophisticated, and significant: to show how service at sea in one of the world's great global navies simultaneously expands tactical, operational, strategic, and policy knowledge and skills in an officer and—most important—develops insights in him or her regarding myriad possible interconnections among those levels of conflict. . . . This is a book for all sailors and policymakers, and especially for those who are both." —*Proceedings Magazine*

"Admiral Jim Stavridis has sailed the world's oceans and has distilled the journey into a sharply observed geopolitical take on global affairs in the maritime sphere. This is a sailor's view of this turbulent nautical world, and it is a voyage worth taking."

—Admiral Mike Mullen, USN (Ret.), seventeenth
chairman of the Joint Chiefs of Staff and
twenty-eighth chief of naval operations

"Stavridis, a retired U.S. Navy admiral, summons the collected knowledge of his extensive career as an operational commander to provide insight into navies' routine functioning.... It's a stimulating and provocative work . . . a timely reminder that oceans may seem tamed—but that's only true on the surface."

—*Publishers Weekly*

"Fellow Admiral Jim Stavridis spent nearly four decades as a U.S. Navy sailor and is well known as an important geopolitical thinker. In *Sea Power*, both of those attributes come together to create a must-read for anyone seriously thinking about the world's challenges in the twenty-first century."

—Admiral Bill McRaven, USN (Ret.), chancellor,
the University of Texas system, and former commander,
U.S. Special Operations Command

PENGUIN BOOKS

SEA POWER

Admiral Jim Stavridis, USN (Ret.), spent more than thirty years in the US Navy, rising to the rank of four-star admiral. He was Supreme Allied Commander at NATO and previously commanded US Southern Command, overseeing military operations through Latin America. At sea, he commanded a Navy destroyer, a destroyer squadron, and an aircraft carrier battle group in combat. He holds a PhD from the Fletcher School of Law and Diplomacy at Tufts University, where he recently served five years as dean. He received fifty medals in the course of his military career, including twenty-eight from foreign nations. He has authored or coauthored nine other books, including *2034: A Novel of the Next World War* with Elliot Ackerman.

ALSO BY ADMIRAL JAMES STAVRIDIS, USN (RET.)

Sailing True North
The Accidental Admiral
Partnership for the Americas
Destroyer Captain

COAUTHORED BY ADMIRAL JAMES STAVRIDIS, USN (RET.)

2034: A Novel of the Next World War
Command at Sea
The Leader's Bookshelf
Watch Officer's Guide
Division Officer's Guide

SEA
POWER

THE HISTORY AND GEOPOLITICS
OF THE WORLD'S OCEANS

Admiral James Stavridis, USN (Ret.)

PENGUIN BOOKS

PENGUIN BOOKS

An imprint of Penguin Random House LLC
penguinrandomhouse.com

First published in the United States of America by Penguin Press,
an imprint of Penguin Random House LLC, 2017
Published in Penguin Books 2018

Map illustrations by Jeffrey L. Ward unless otherwise credited.

ISBN 9780735220614 (paperback)

THE LIBRARY OF CONGRESS HAS CATALOGED THE HARDCOVER EDITION AS FOLLOWS:
Names: Stavridis, James, author.
Title: Sea power : the history and geopolitics of the world's oceans /
Admiral James Stavridis, USN (Ret.).
Description: New York : Penguin Press, 2017.
Identifiers: LCCN 2016056758 (print) | LCCN 2017021421 (e-book) |
ISBN 9780735220607 (e-book) | ISBN 9780735220591 (hardback)
Subjects: LCSH: Sea power—History. | Naval history. | Geopolitics—History. |
BISAC: POLITICAL SCIENCE / Political Freedom &
Security / International Security. |
HISTORY / Military / Naval. | HISTORY / United States / General.
Classification: LCC V25 (e-book) | LCC V25 .S73 2017 (print) |
DDC 359/.03—dc23
LC record available at https://lccn.loc.gov/2016056758

Printed in the United States of America
ScoutAutomatedPrintCode

DESIGNED BY MEIGHAN CAVANAUGH

For all the sailors on distant voyages.

And for Laura, Christina, and Julia,
who waited patiently for their sailor
to come home from the sea.

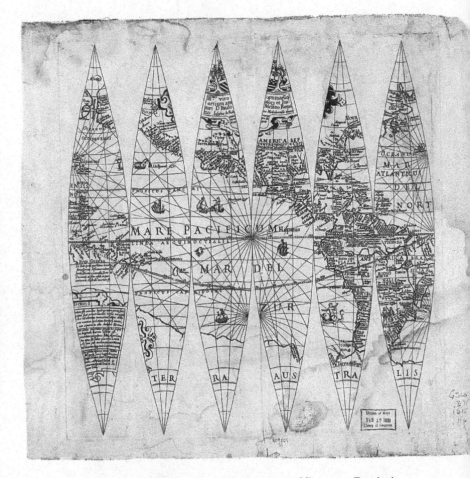

Jodocus Hondius's 1615 map showing the world's oceans. Despite its
impressive detail, cartography has come a long way in 400 years.

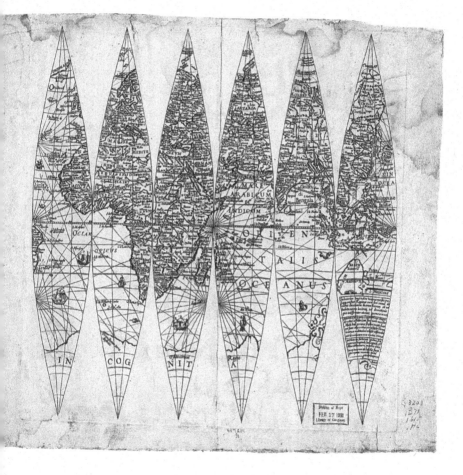

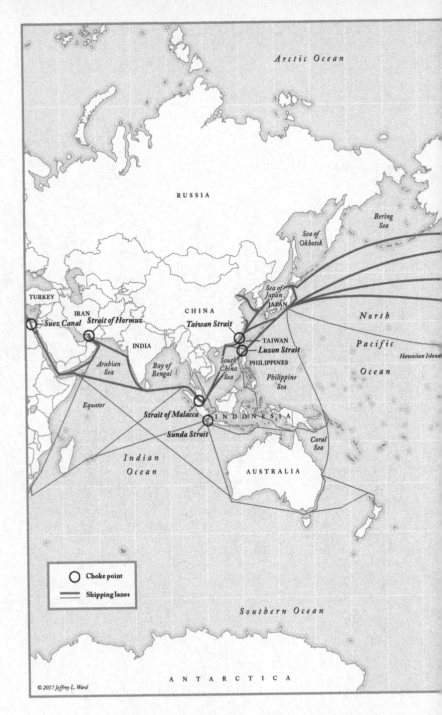

The world's major shipping routes, ports, and choke points.
These routes are the lifeblood of our global economy.

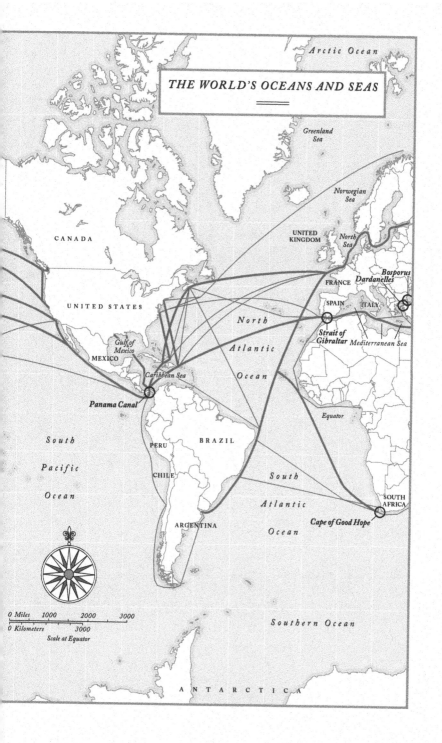

THE WORLD'S OCEANS AND SEAS

CONTENTS

SEA
POWER

THE SEA IS ONE

S hakespeare, in his immortal sea drama *The Tempest*, said, "We are such stuff as dreams are made on, and our little life is rounded with a sleep," referring to the small and confined dimensions of our individual lives. It is a haunting passage, and one I have thought about a great deal. The play opens with a massive storm at sea, and the line has always had profoundly nautical implications for me. In my nearly four decades as a Navy sailor, when all the days I spent on the deep ocean, out of sight of land, are totaled, they add up to nearly eleven years. The endless vistas of the open ocean, upon which I gazed for more than a decade of my life, provide quite a setting for such dreaming. And in those days, when I looked at the ocean, I always felt a sense of seeing the same view that millions upon millions of other deep-sea mariners, coastal sailors, and even land dwellers close to the ocean saw. Like the fishermen, traders, pirates, harbor pilots, and indeed sailors of every ilk who went down to the sea in ships of all kinds, we have all seen the same ocean views. In a way, it is like looking at eternity; to gaze upon it for an hour, a day, a month, or a lifetime reminds us gently that our time is limited, and we are but a tiny part of the floating world.

In addition to simply warning us not to overimagine the importance of our own small voyages on this earth, Shakespeare's line also makes us consider quite literally what we are indeed made of. It is worth remembering that each of us is, essentially, largely made of water. When a human baby is born, it is composed of roughly 70 percent water. It has always fascinated me that roughly the same proportion of the globe is covered by water—just over 70 percent. Both our planet and our bodies are dominated by the liquid world, and anyone who has sailed extensively at sea will understand instinctively the primordial tug of the oceans upon each of us when we look upon the sea.

I still dream about being on a ship, and part of why I wanted to write a book about the oceans is in response to those dreams. It often happens as I nod off on my now landlocked bed that I dream of the faint rumble of a ship's engines and feel the rolling of the waves pushing and rocking the hull of my ship. When I rise and head up to the bridge, it is always on a bright day, with the clouds hanging in front of the bow and the ship pushing through the sea. I never know exactly where the dream will take me but I always end up approaching the shore, and when I do, I feel a pang of regret to leave the ocean. The approaches to land are always difficult in my dreams, and the ship often finds herself running out of deep water and becomes rapidly in danger of foundering on a beach or up a river or upon a reef. I always wake up before the ship finally impales herself ashore, and I always wish I had stayed farther out to sea.

The British navy, which dominated the world's oceans for so many years, truly and deeply understood the interconnected character of the global waterways. "The sea is one" is an expression you will hear from a Brit. I heard it first when I was eighteen years old and a second-year student, called a midshipman, at the U.S. Naval Academy in Annapolis,

Maryland. My navigation instructor was a crusty British lieutenant commander, who seemed incredibly old and salty—he was probably in his mid-thirties, and who could imagine being so ancient? This Old Man of the Sea was a crack hand with a sextant, a nautical almanac, and a tide table to be sure, but what he really taught me was the way in which all the world's oceans are at once connected—obvious enough given the continuous flow of water around the continents—but also separate. He would painstakingly discuss each of the great global bodies of water—the Pacific, the Atlantic, the Indian, and the Arctic oceans—as well as the major tributary bodies: the Mediterranean Sea, the South China Sea, the Caribbean. The lieutenant commander could talk for an hour about a particular strait between the Indian Ocean and the Pacific Ocean, and how the water looked in the winter, and why it was a crucial passage. I learned a great deal from him, not only about the science and art of navigating a destroyer, but also about oceanography, maritime history, global strategy, and how the tools of empire so often were dusted with dried salt, like the taffrails of a sailing cutter. You could drop a plumb line from my days as a teenager at Annapolis through the arc of nearly four decades as a Navy officer and finally end up on the pages of this book.

The oceans were the place I spent much of the early years of my career. I sailed through them all, validating the lessons he taught me, improving my own ship handling and navigational skills, and learning to lead men and women at sea. As my understanding and appreciation of the international system increased—accelerated by a PhD at the Fletcher School of Law and Diplomacy of Tufts University, where I am now a very deskbound admiral—I came to understand the influence of the sea on geopolitics. It is no coincidence that so many of the great national enterprises of the past two thousand years were influenced by sea power, and that continues to be true today. The sea is one indeed, particularly as a geopolitical entity, and will continue to exert an enormous influence on how global events unfold—from the high tension of the South China Sea, to the cocaine smuggling of the Caribbean, to the piracy off the coasts of Africa, to the unfortunate reemergence of a new cold war in the Greenland-Iceland–United Kingdom gap in the North Atlantic. Some observers may not be interested in the geopolitics of the oceans, but they will haunt our policy and our choices in this turbulent twenty-first century. The oceans will matter deeply to every aspect of human endeavor.

When we go to sea—whether in a warship for a nine-month combat cruise, or a week on a Carnival cruise liner, or just a day sail out of sight of land—we are launching ourselves into another dimension altogether. The world shudders and shakes beneath us, the wind cuts more sharply with nothing to slow its pace, the weather skims by our unprotected hull, the dolphins sometimes swim alongside for hours—it is a very different world. In a primal sense, we are "an ocean away" every time we go to sea and can no longer see the land. When you are on a hull, however large or small, and come up on the deck and slowly pivot around to see nothing but the ocean stretching away from you, stop and measure the moment in the passage of your life: you are seeing the same view, the same endless ocean that Alexander the Great saw as he sailed the eastern Mediterranean, that Napoleon gazed upon on his long, sad voyage to exile in the South Atlantic, and that Halsey saw as he lashed his Fast Carrier Task Force into combat in the western Pacific. In that sense, as a sailor, you are at once an ocean away from the world of the land, but also connected to a long, unbroken chain of men and women who have set their course for the open ocean.

It is those two important aspects of the oceans that I have tried to capture in this volume: the personal experience of a mariner at sea, and the geopolitics of the oceans and how they constantly influence events ashore. Only by understanding both the individual and personal experiences of sailors and trying to pour that distinct nautical culture into the larger questions of how the oceans drive the international system can we fully appreciate the value and the challenge of the sea. In that sense, this is a book that could have been written by many different sailors at any point in the long, long history of our collective human voyages both over the ocean and through time. Writing it now, in this century, is simply an attempt to take a vivid snapshot of those two tendrils of human experience—a sailor's life at sea and the strategic impact of the oceans—upon the vast water world we call earth.

Let's get under way.

1.

THE PACIFIC

MOTHER OF ALL
THE OCEANS

Ortelius's 1589 map showing what was then the
Western world's best understanding of the Pacific.

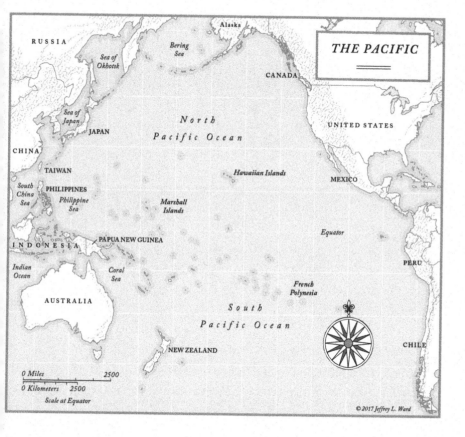

I vividly remember the first time I sailed into the Pacific. It was in 1972, on a U.S. Navy cruiser, USS *Jouett*. She was a beautiful and modern warship of around 8,000 tons, with a length of about 550 feet, depth of 29 feet, and beam of 55 feet—a lot of ship as a general proposition, but not so much space internally when you considered there were nearly five hundred officers and men manning her.

At the time, I was seventeen years old and a very green midshipman, the lowest officer rank in the Navy, on my so-called youngster cruise out of Annapolis, which is what midshipmen did after their first year of academics instead of taking a summer break. Having grown up in a Marine Corps family (my father would eventually retire as a full colonel of Marines after combat service in Korea and Vietnam), I went to the U.S. Naval Academy with every intention of becoming a Marine infantry officer like my father. And so I went grudgingly to San Diego in the summer of 1972, grumpy about having to go to sea—like many Marines, my father's motto in service was "don't go near the water" (or the Pentagon either, but that's another story).

. . .

JOUETT SLIPPED HER LINES from San Diego's naval station and headed out to sea, past the beautiful shiny buildings of downtown San Diego, perhaps the nicest sea detail (the voyage from a pier to the open sea or the reverse) in the world. We passed under the Coronado Bay Bridge, passing the city skyline of San Diego to starboard and the large island of Coronado to port. I had been given the august responsibilities of "line handler, fantail," which meant that I was to report to the back end of the ship and help haul in the wet, heavy lines after they were slipped off the bollards on the pier. Immediately thereafter, I had been told to report to the bridge of the ship to take a turn learning how to handle the helm.

It was a sunny early summer's day, relatively early in the morning, a crisp Southern California day with a temperature in the mid-seventies, and by the time we were secured from the fantail, the ship was nosing out past Ballast Point and into the Pacific Ocean. Fortunately for my landsman's stomach, the seas were very calm, and as we pointed the bow due west, I made my way up several stories and stepped onto the bridge. As I emerged from the relatively dim passageways of the ship, I was simply stunned by all the sunshine and salt air and the vast ocean in front of me. Like Saint Paul on the road to Damascus, I had an epiphany: I wanted to be a sailor. In all my life, we had not been a family particularly oriented to the water, but the Pacific grabbed me by the throat and said quite simply, "You are home." I've never looked back.

We tend to think of the Pacific as the mother of all oceans because of its size. The Pacific is massive, and I do not use that word loosely. Even the people living along its periphery, from Canada to Chile, from Russia to Australia, and everywhere in between, appreciate only a small aspect of its size. A simple Google search will show a surface area of nearly 64 million square miles. But such a large number obscures its meaning unless you measure it against other benchmarks. The Pacific Ocean alone is greater than the combined landmasses of the entire Earth. In our country, where geography is no longer a widely studied discipline (if at all), it is hard to appreciate that a traveler flying from Washington, D.C., to Honolulu will spend no more time flying to her connecting flight in California than she will from California to her final destination. And perhaps more impressively, there is not a great deal of landmass *inside* the Pacific Ocean. All of the nations that border the Pacific—and there are many— think of the ocean as a kind of endless back porch. The sea dominates the geography of the Pacific more than anywhere else on earth.

But throughout this gargantuan maritime expanse, it is worth remembering that there *are* small and not-so-small islands of all shapes and sizes, both inhabited and uninhabited, each with a distinct culture and often racial group, representing thousands of years of habitation— Tahiti, Fiji, New Caledonia, New Guinea, New Ireland, New Georgia, on and on, an area of the world that is often referred to not by the names of the islands but by the term "Oceania."

In many ways, it is remarkable that these isolated pockets of life have human beings on them at all. To be initially colonized, someone in a distant past had to set sail, cross enormous distances, make landfall, and survive. Conquering such distances requires ingenuity, courage, and an inhuman amount of will. It would have been incredibly impressive if these islands were settled using the technology of a few hundred years ago: large-hulled ships with massive sails and complex navigation equipment like sextants—think of the HMS *Victory*, Lord Nelson's flagship in the 1800s. Instead, humans found a way to conquer these distances *ten thousand years ago*. Using nothing but outrigger canoes with oars, the erratic currents, and the stars, mass migrations from Southeast Asia spread people throughout the saltwater expanse. These Austronesians, the Polynesians, Micronesians, and Melanesians who still inhabit the islands to this day, journeyed as far as Hawaii, more than five thousand miles from what most historians believe was their point of origin on the coast of East Asia. The migrations took many years as Austronesians island-hopped as far as their oars and the sea itself could take them, a drama that would unfold in reverse during World War II as Allied forces followed the island chains back toward the Asian heart of the Japanese Empire.

Soon after I was commissioned as a young ensign out of Annapolis, those primitive voyages were much in my mind when I first crossed the Pacific in the late 1970s. Indeed, what I remember most about my first crossing was simply the length of the voyage. Luckily I wasn't in a *Kon-Tiki*-like boat modeled on the ancient Austronesian vessels. It takes a week to get from the West Coast of the United States to the Hawaiian Islands, and that is merely the front door. From Pearl Harbor on the island of Oahu in 1977, I sailed south to Fiji, New Zealand, and Australia—a long, long haul. We were in a small, three-ship squadron—just two new *Spruance*-class destroyers, *Hewitt* and *Kinkaid*, and a supply ship, the *Niagara Falls*. Crossing the Central Pacific from Hawaii south to the equator was a long, lazy sail with very little to do. There were basic chores in terms of maintaining the equipment and engineering plant on the ship, plenty of drills and practice events, underway replenishment wherein the smaller destroyers come alongside the larger supply ship and receive hoses to refuel—quite exciting at just a hundred feet between the ships. It was calm, hot, and flat, day after day after day.

Although we had access to some rudimentary electronic navigation systems, our principal navigation was done by sextant and paper charts. As the youngest ensign on the ship, I was expected to shoot the stars daily, as well as drive the ship, learn about the engineering plant, and mind my division of sailors (I had charge of the high-tech sailors focused on antisubmarine warfare, who had exactly zero to do in that vast submarine-less expanse). The most exciting thing we had to look forward to was the ceremony of "crossing the line," the day we would finally go past the equator and "enter the Kingdom of Davy Jones."

When U.S. Navy ships crossed the equator in those days, it was traditional to have a pretty rough hazing ceremony conducted by those who had crossed before (Shellbacks) at the expense of those who had not yet crossed (Pollywogs, or usually "slimy Wogs"). The ceremony consisted of being awoken well before dawn and herded up to the forecastle (the forward part of the ship) and sprayed with fire hoses and strewn with garbage. After a few hours of crawling around the rough decks of the ship (called nonskid, very abrasive), knees and palms are quite chewed up. It ends up with a crawl through a few canvas chutes full of very ripe garbage, dosed with this and that, before finally being made to kiss the well-greased stomach of a fat sailor dressed up as "Davy Jones" and being dunked (baptized) in salt water pulled up from the equator. It was quite a memorable day. Luckily for me, my commanding officer had never been across the equator before, so the hazing was sort of adjusted to a more gentlemanly level in his vicinity. I stayed close by his side.

Fiji is an interesting place, and as our ships pulled in, I was struck by its multicultural quality. At the time, about 50 percent of the population were Melanesian islanders, about 40 percent of Indian descent (from the indentured Indians brought by the British to work the sugar plantations more than a century earlier), and 10 percent East Asian or Anglo. The Melanesian percentage has gradually increased over the years, but it remains a multicultural society today. We arrived in the mid-1970s, shortly after Fiji had declared independence from the British crown.

I REMEMBER THE CLUSTERS of islands as we approached Suva, the fairly primitive capital, where we spent several easy days on the beach and playing tennis on the grass courts at the governor general's palace.

Of note, today Fiji has an uneasy political climate, having just emerged from a military coup undertaken by a commodore, of all people (normally it is an army general who takes over a country, not a senior navy officer). But a recent election—largely deemed credible—seems to have put this small, beautiful archipelago back on a relatively stable footing, much to the relief of the Australians, who keep a close eye on the region and worry about refugees streaming out in the case of real violence.

We sailed on to New Zealand, spending time on both the North and South islands. The New Zealand of the 1970s was a lot like the United States in the 1950s—quiet, kind, sensible, and slightly boring but in a very nice way. The two islands that constitute the country are both spectacular and beautiful, ranging from the tropical reaches of the North Island to the high Alps of the South, where the *Lord of the Rings* films were made by Kiwi director Peter Jackson.

After a week or so of liberty and saddled with a colossal hangover from drinking New Zealand's spectacular Sauvignon Blanc at a wine bar, I was given the job of junior officer of the deck, driving my ship, *Hewitt*, out of Auckland's harbor in a hard-blowing squall. It was pitch black and raining sideways, and the conning officer, a lieutenant junior grade who was even greener than I, was noticeably seasick, which did not enhance his already minimal ship handling skills. Our increasingly nervous captain watched us nearly swing the stern into a channel buoy in a too-tight turn and snapped at me to take the conn (drive the ship). That sobered me up swiftly, and with the help and oversight of the ship's operations officer (a very experienced and skilled mariner) we somehow got out of the channel and into the open sea without further incident. The Pacific was hardly pacific that night, let me assure you.

We then pushed on to Australia, thus completing a crossing of both the equator and the Pacific from San Diego to the incredible natural harbor of Sydney. We were all in our dress whites and the sun was shining, with the iconic Sydney Opera House, whose gorgeous architecture to me conjures up white sails at sea, gleaming across the harbor as we tied up on Garden Island, a naval dockyard on a promontory jutting into the harbor. The Pacific Ocean seemed far behind us as we fell into the warm arms of the Australians, who maintain a keen sense of gratitude to the U.S. Navy for our efforts in the Second World War to keep the Japanese from finding their way south. In those days it was a good idea to wear a uniform ashore, perhaps not so much today. But it is worth noting that the Australians continue to be very close to Americans, and in the military context have stood alongside us throughout our missions to Iraq and Afghanistan. I encountered no better fighters than the Aussies in Afghanistan, for example, and they are a serious part of the coalition against the Islamic State today.

After the delights of Sydney, we began to work our way up the Australian coast, stopping over for a few days in Townsville on the Great Barrier Reef. Situated at the foot of the spikelike peninsula on the northeast coast of Oz, Townsville is a laid-back town of around 200,000 today, far smaller those decades ago. It is a gateway to the reef and a significant tourist destination. Drinking a Foster's Lager and looking across the perfectly gorgeous waters of the reef out toward the barrier islands and the Pacific was extremely relaxing, and I felt I was close to the end of the Pacific crossing. Then I remembered what was ahead: the Torres Strait.

The good news about the Torres Strait is that it is relatively wide as international choke points go. It is the body of water between the northeastern tip of the continent of Australia and the big island of New Guinea, and, as a result, one of the busiest sea passages in the world. But the bad news is that it is unusually shallow and filled with a maze of small, nearly submerged islands and delicate reefs. In the mid-1970s it wasn't particularly well marked with navigational buoys, and no one on

Hewitt had ever been through it. Given the risky nature of the passage, the captain elected to take the conn and drive the ship himself, a quite unusual decision. As the sea detail junior officer of the deck, I was supposed to provide tactical navigational advice based on radar sightings, while the ship's navigator used traditional plotting of visual landmarks. Fortunately, we passed through in good weather on a bright day with relatively light traffic, and everyone breathed a sigh of relief as we headed fair from the Coral Sea of the western Pacific into the Arafura Sea of the eastern Indian Ocean.

Thus ended my first crossing of the Pacific, a voyage I have since duplicated many times over.

The first European to cross the Pacific, Ferdinand Magellan, ended up far worse than I did.

To appreciate the voyage of Magellan, you have to look at the globe with eastern Australia and Indonesia at the bottom left part of the circle. It is a water world indeed: you would see only slivers of western North America and Northeast Asia—the rest of the enormous circle is essentially water. Yet despite the long voyages of the Austronesians, there was no real sense of what existed west of the Americas from a European perspective until the beginning of the 1500s, when Vasco Núñez de Balboa crossed the Isthmus of Panama, stood atop a high hill, and both discovered and claimed the Pacific "for God and Spain." The discovery set off a maritime version of the scramble for land colonies in the Americas, and for the next three centuries the Europeans gradually mapped the vast stretches of the Pacific.

It was Magellan, an irascible Portuguese sailing on behalf of the Spanish crown, who actually named the Pacific, deciding that the waves were gentle and calm (which they are decidedly *not* much of the time, by the way) as his ships sailed into the deep South Pacific. He was the first European to sail across the Pacific Ocean, and the five-ship expedition under his command was the first to circumnavigate the globe. (Although Magellan himself did not complete the voyage and was killed in the Philippines in 1521.) Until Magellan, most of the voyages to Asia (in search of spices and gold, principally) were conducted by passing under the tip of Africa; he reasoned that it would be possible to reach Asia by sailing west, particularly as he reputedly thought the Pacific was only six hundred miles wide—he was off by more than ten thousand miles, not to put too fine a point on it. He persuaded the Spanish crown to finance his voyages and they provided him with five ships in 1519.

Magellan's flotilla, consisting of about 250 men, sailed down the coast of South America looking for a gap to sail to the Pacific. Naturally, the weather got worse and worse and the southern winter set in, destroying one ship and requiring the remaining four ships to winter over before finally discovering what would become known as the Strait of Magellan at the bottom tip of South America. The weather continued to be challenging, and the crew of one of the ships refused to continue, but Magellan eventually broke into the southern Pacific after observing the natives along the southern coasts burning big fires—hence the name Tierra del Fuego, or "land of fire."

Getting to the Pacific was exciting, but quickly the enormous length of the ocean ahead of them dawned on Magellan and his men. The sailors gradually pushed themselves farther and farther west from the coast of modern-day Chile without finding themselves in Asia. Eventually, by early spring of 1521, they made landfall on Guam in the Mariana island chain. They worked their way farther west to the Philippines by Easter of that year, where a mass was celebrated on the island of Cebu. Magellan then foolishly became involved in interisland conflict, sailing to a nearby island called Mactan, where his party of fifty Spaniards was overwhelmed by natives and he was killed. His crew chronicled his end: "That [a spear wound] caused the captain to fall face downward, when immediately they rushed upon him with iron and bamboo spears and their cutlasses until they killed our mirror, our light, our comfort, and our true guide."

The two centuries after Magellan's death were consumed in building transpacific trade, with the Spanish Empire in the lead by virtue of its colonies in the Philippines. Spain's flag, the Cross of Burgundy, was the dominant flag, but the Dutch, Portuguese, British, and French were also at play in the Pacific. The Spanish built the first truly international oceanic conveyor of goods, carrying silver mined in the New World to Asia and carting back manufactured goods to European markets. Over time the Spanish influence weakened, reflecting events in Europe (including the wars of the Reformation) that bled the peninsular nation. By the seventeenth and early eighteenth centuries, it was the Dutch and British who were in the ascendance in the western Pacific. In 1743, one of the massive Spanish treasure galleons was seized off Manila by British navy commodore George Anson, striking another significant economic blow against the Spanish. The French explorer Louis de Bougainville was the first of his nation to circumnavigate the Pacific as the French belatedly made their way into the region. While there were many expeditions and increasing levels of trade, there were still vast parts of the Pacific that were completely unexplored. Enter Captain James Cook, perhaps the greatest of all the Pacific sailors in history.

James Cook was born in 1728 to a lower middle-class family from northern England that initially apprenticed him to a shopkeeper; fortunately for the Pacific Ocean, he was obsessed from an early age with boats, rivers, and the sea. He managed to secure an apprenticeship with a shipping firm and began to learn to handle awkward commercial ships in the difficult and constrained waters around Great Britain. Cook also began to develop a true specialization in charting and mapmaking. He was drawn into the Royal Navy by the Seven Years' War and emerged an officer with a series of commands under his belt.

As the British began to think in a truly global way by the mid-1750s, it became apparent that mapping and surveying the Pacific Ocean was a means to develop sea power and leverage global influence. Cook was given command of HMS *Endeavour*, a 106-foot bark—short and chunky, but with a shallow draft to get in close to small islands and over reefs. He sailed for the Pacific in the late summer of 1768. A crucial member of his company was the wealthy, handsome naturalist and scientist Joseph Banks. Together, the two men spent the next several years exploring the far reaches of the Pacific.

One easy way to cruise the Pacific without leaving the comfort of a library is to pull out an atlas and trace the voyages of James Cook. He went out three times on a variety of ships and covered more than 150,000 sea miles. His ships were named *Endeavour, Discovery, Resolution*, and *Adventure*—all names that quite accurately describe how he spent the years from 1768 until his death at the hands of natives in the Hawaiian Islands (he called them the Sandwich Islands) in 1779. To lay out the courses of the three voyages is to chart virtually every important Pacific port—Cook Inlet and Prince William Sound in Alaska, Nootka Sound in western Canada, the Kamchatka Peninsula of Russia—and all of the important islands: Hawaii, Marquesas Islands, Tahiti, Fiji, New Caledonia, Easter Island, Cook Islands, Friendly Islands, and New Zealand's North and South islands. He also sailed close by Antarctica, circled Australia, rounded Cape Horn at the tip of South America, and cruised both the Atlantic and Indian oceans. In a brilliant and highly readable memoir, *Blue Latitudes: Boldly Going Where Captain Cook Has Gone Before*, Tony Horwitz follows Cook across the many sea miles from Alaska to Tasmania and from Easter Island to Russia. The Pacific was still essentially unexplored and certainly uncharted before this Yorkshire farm boy arrived—his genius opened it up, and his legacy lives today in the hearts and minds of mariners who sail those waters.

The Russians too participated in the great opening of the Pacific to outside powers. Using their bases in eastern Siberia, Russian crews with minimal technology accomplished rugged journeys across difficult distances through what must have seemed to be simply a cold, watery void. They carved out claims to Alaska, of course, being so close to the Bering Strait, but their influence extended south throughout much of the Pacific as well. Lured by the same fur trade that enticed American and Canadian trappers, Russian ships operated from forward operating bases, such as Fort Ross, north of San Francisco, in the early nineteenth century. But overhunting drove down the number of fur animals and made the expensive expeditions less economically viable. The Russian toehold in the Pacific was transitory, retracting from Fort Ross in the 1840s as the weight of its large empire became too burdensome and the czarist façade began to crack. Famously, Russia sold its claims to Alaska to the United States in 1867, just a scant two years after the conclusion of the U.S. Civil War in a deal widely mocked in the United States at the time. Yet despite their transitory physical presence, the Russians made invaluable contributions to the scientific exploration of the region.

The United States came into the Pacific world in fits and starts. Ships from Boston had made the arduous journey to China since the days of the Revolution but never established a permanent presence until the 1840s with the acquisition of California after the Mexican-American War. The fortuitous discovery of gold at Sutter's Mill in 1848 kicked off the California Gold Rush and drove mass migrations west, either by land across the continent, or across the isthmus of Panama (in the days before the Panama Canal), or around Tierra del Fuego as Magellan had done three centuries before. Capitalizing on the use of whale oil, whaling became a boom energy industry that migrated from the Atlantic to the Pacific due to overexploitation. Additionally, the lucrative commercial China trade became more and more important as the decades went on. This mania of interest brought the Pacific world into the minds of those on the East Coast.

The advent of coal-powered ships in the 1860s changed how the United States interacted with its Pacific domain. Coal ships were faster and more reliable than their sail-powered counterparts, but coal is heavy and exhaustible. Ships could not carry an unlimited amount of coal without sinking into the briny deep. They needed dedicated coaling stations at regular intervals in order to maintain their impressive speed. Fortunately, the Pacific for all of its vastness was dotted with islands perfectly situated to serve as coaling stations. It was this impulse that drove the U.S. annexation of Hawaii in 1898, with the beautiful port of Pearl Harbor serving as the fulcrum for its Pacific presence.

In a geopolitical sense, an interesting question to consider is why Japan did not develop much as England did, essentially becoming the Great Britain of the Pacific. There are many similarities in their geopolitical trajectories: each is an island nation that faced threats of invasion early and often (with the British Isles succumbing far more frequently over their first millennia than did the Japanese); both are proud and capable societies with militaristic talent; they both produced skilled sailors and shipbuilders; and each had relatively few natural resources within their natural boundaries, theoretically necessitating a turn to the oceans. Why did the British come to create an empire that held sway over vast tracts of the earth while the Japanese turned inward for the better part of three hundred years, emerging aggressively only in the twentieth century after the opening of their world by the West?

.   .   .

THE ANSWER LIES AT LEAST in part in the geography of the Pacific Ocean as opposed to that of the Atlantic.

First and foremost, the Pacific is just so much larger than the Atlantic, and the nations on the coast of Asia sit astride a relatively small land littoral facing an enormous sea to their east. Vessels launched to the east would sail away and literally disappear more or less indefinitely given the tyranny of distance. Additionally, unlike the British, who were separated from continental Europe by only a very narrow strip of the English Channel, the Japanese had both a wider distance across which invasions had to be launched as well as fewer and less aggressive geopolitical rivals developing in their littoral. They also keenly felt the size of the Pacific at their back, providing a natural buffer to the east.

The Japanese faced early invasions from the Mongols in the thirteenth century, but defeated them relatively easily by surrounding the invaders on beachheads upon their arrival. Despite having significant internal rivalries, the Japanese were able to set these aside and defeat the Mongols twice in the late 1200s, assisted by the weather in the form of a typhoon (Kamikaze, or Divine Wind) that scattered the invading fleets.

After a long period of consolidation and relative isolation under the various shoguns, the Japanese invaded the Asian continent in the 1500s, attacking the Korean Peninsula around the turn of the seventeenth century. They were defeated by Chinese land forces and the Korean navy, and settled back into the home islands again. This was around the time of the Battle of Lepanto in the Mediterranean, and the change in naval technology in the Pacific was notable as well—the lightly armed galleys heretofore used for grappling and ramming were giving way to heavier platforms capable of carrying larger cannons. After two serious attempts to invade Korea in the final decade of the sixteenth century, the Japanese decided to essentially remain within home waters. Unlike the British, they did not attempt to cross the broad Pacific, but essentially stood watch, protecting their western coastline and relying upon the sheer distances of the Pacific to ensure that there would be no attacks from the east. This became official doctrine; going to sea was seen as "going outside," as one noted Asian scholar, John Curtis Perry, has described it.

Similarly, the Chinese faced resolutely to the west and to their land borders. Why? Because that was the threat vector for them, not from the Pacific. They correctly regarded the principal existential dangers to their civilization as coming from the barbarians of the Asian steppes (hence the building of the Great Wall of China) and to some degree from the infections of European civilization transmitted through trade and engagement. There were abortive attempts at oceanic domination during the impressive voyages of Zheng He in the fifteenth century. But these voyages went west to known entities in the South China Sea, Indian Ocean, and East Africa, resulting in only a transitory impression on the locals and the withering away of the Chinese fleet when political tides turned against exploration. Looking to the east at the enormous range of the Pacific did not engage the Chinese geopolitical imagination any more than it did the Japanese (or that of any other Pacific culture for that matter). In the end, it was the Europeans, ironically, who would well and truly cross the Pacific and seek to connect the two worlds in a fashion beyond episodic trade and missionary work. And no individual act of opening the Pacific world could have been more dramatic than the voyage of American commodore Matthew Calbraith Perry to Japan in the 1850s.

At that point, Japan had held itself more or less aloof from the world for more than 250 years. It had developed a deeply homogenous and intensely internally focused national culture, including limited trade and engagement even in the commercial sphere. But the United States was irresistibly pulled toward Japan. Pacific whaling operations, so crucial to the American economy, shifted from the South Pacific to the North off the coast of Hokkaido. The increasing trade with China made the home islands of Japan very advantageous as logistic bases to facilitate sea lanes of communication. U.S. president Millard Fillmore therefore produced a letter and directed Commodore Perry to deliver it, with the objective of gaining access to Japanese ports.

Although the use of force was authorized, Perry had studied Japan and decided to take another, more diplomatic approach. Sailing in paddle-wheel steamboats, he came loaded with gifts and did all in his power to act the part of imperial representative of a great power. He sailed into Tokyo Bay in July 1853 with the intent to communicate using what we would think of today as a "soft power" approach—sensitivity to culture, avoiding a resort to military force, using economic and diplomatic levers as a first choice, and laying out a compelling geopolitical case to other actors. His ships were deeply impressive to the Japanese, and he augmented the squadron size over the winter. By March 1854, he had managed to execute the Treaty of Kanagawa, the first such cross-Pacific instrument that provided for the rights of shipwrecked sailors and refueling rights at two Japanese ports.

It was the beginning of European engagement with Japan, involving most of the major powers—notably Russia and Great Britain. The internal Japanese debate over modernization crested with a two-year civil war and the return of the emperor in the so-called Meiji Restoration. Suddenly Japan was quite literally on the march—and more important, in terms of naval developments, sailing to sea. Japan's industrial base sprinted into the late nineteenth century, rapidly developing significant military capability in its army and navy. Midshipmen were sent to Great Britain and the United States for naval educations, and the dockyards of Japan began to produce very capable, large warships. The Pacific, after centuries of being seen as a vast empty buffer zone, started to loom on the Japanese geopolitical map as a potential zone of conquest.

In terms of naval strategy, the Japanese, unsurprisingly, began to think like Great Britain. Like the British, they were an island nation hanging off the coast of a huge continent, and they worried about China and Russia, the great land powers. Because Korea was essentially a strip of buffer zone between themselves and the Chinese, it became logical in their eyes that they should dominate and hold it as a means of putting space between themselves and the vastly larger Chinese Empire. This led to the first of two important wars for Japan—both of which had significant naval components—the Sino-Japanese War of 1894. It began when Japan's navy attacked a Chinese troop convoy heading to reinforce Chinese troops in Korea—*before* war was declared, by the way—demonstrating the propensity to seize on surprise that they would again use five decades later in attacking the United States at Pearl Harbor.

The war was short and sharp, and Japanese naval forces comported themselves well. Of note, the naval tactical debate of the period was about whether massive armor or heavy guns were most important in maritime combat, and the Battle of Yalu did not clearly demonstrate the superiority of either. What did emerge was the efficacy of using maneuverability and speed, as the Japanese did under Admiral Sukeyuki Ito. He split his force into a "Flying Squadron" of fast ships and a slower but still capable main squadron, and was able to rake the Chinese ships throughout the engagement with more rapid fire from faster ships. Over the next few months, the war became a rout, and ended in 1895 with Japan consolidating its possession of Korea, Formosa, and various other islands. In terms of geostrategic position, Japan was in the driver's seat in the eastern Pacific. Now it needed to shore up its northern flank, which led to war with Russia.

. . .

THE RUSSIANS WERE ACTUALLY the cause of the Russo-Japanese War. After Japan's victory over China, it was Russia that pushed against the Japanese Empire, demanding the demilitarization of the Korean Peninsula and taking Port Arthur as a warm-weather port. The Russians cooperated with other European powers and pushed hard against Japan's expansion. This led to a war in 1904 for which the Russians were unprepared both militarily and politically. Militarily, the Russian fleet was split all around the periphery of that vast state and needed time to consolidate its forces. Politically, the rumblings that would eventually lead to the Russian Revolution and the fall of the czar were already apparent, and the ruling claque in St. Petersburg could not fully focus on the external conflict that was brewing on Russia's Pacific coast.

The Japanese, although numerically inferior, were able to concentrate their forces and attack early, preventing the Russians from building up strategically to challenge them. Fresh off the defeat of the Chinese fleet, the Japanese fleet again launched its first powerful attack before war was declared—a night torpedo raid conducted by Japanese destroyers that damaged important Russian warships caught in harbor. Despite the arrival of a dynamic new Russian admiral, Stepan Makarov (who died in a mine strike shortly thereafter), and the long sail of the Baltic Squadron to Pacific waters, the Russians never gained the tactical upper hand, and with the help of the interior strategic position and relatively newer technology, the Japanese prevailed. The Russians ended up losing their Pacific fleet and the key base of Port Arthur in January 1905.

The final blow to Russia in the Pacific came when the Baltic Squadron was destroyed in May 1905 at the Battle of Tsushima, losing fifty of the fifty-three ships that had sailed from the Baltic beginning in October of the previous year. Faced with this complete loss of their fleet, the

Russians were forced to settle the war in an agreement negotiated by U.S. president Theodore Roosevelt—for which he was awarded the Nobel Peace Prize. The Russians lost the war because they were outfought tactically in each engagement, but mainly because they failed strategically to concentrate their forces and were defeated piecemeal.

This, by the way, constituted a crucial lesson for the United States on the importance of building a Panama Canal—otherwise the U.S. fleet would be essentially separated for months by the necessity to sail around the southern tip of South America to combine forces. An interesting side note was that the age-old principle of warship captains' "striking their colors" and surrendering their ships was practiced for the last time in the Russo-Japanese War by the Russians. When the commanders came home, they were court-martialed and sentenced to death, ending for all intents and purposes the idea of surrender. Today, in the U.S. Navy and most other naval forces, the philosophy is definitely not one of striking the colors in gracious surrender, but rather "don't give up the ship" and be willing to fight to the end.

It was the occupation and buildup of the Hawaiian Islands that truly vaulted the United States into power in the Pacific. Pearl Harbor, on the island of Oahu, is a spectacular natural harbor, and I can vividly remember the first time I sailed into it in the late 1970s. I was still a very inexperienced deck watch officer, and the captain decreed that I should take the conn into port. It was blowing hard, and the breeze worried me as I tried to line up the ship and glide into the berth, something I'd watched my very salty captain do several times. I had foolishly declined to use an offered tug, and didn't heed the advice of the experienced harbor pilot who was there to advise us: I wanted to do it all by myself, like a defiant toddler.

Unfortunately for me, I simply kept too much "way" on the ship (meaning we were moving too fast) and managed to bang the stern hard against the pier, scraping off a lot of paint and putting a small, insignificant, but deeply embarrassing dent in the after starboard quarter of the ship. My captain sidled over and offered an observation from Admiral Ernest King, the tall, hard-driving Navy leader during the Second World War: "The mark of a great ship handler is never getting into a situation requiring great ship handling"—in other words, use the tugs and listen to the pilot. Lesson learned.

After recovering my composure, I walked around the beautiful naval station later that day and realized that I was in America's gateway to the Pacific, and the heart of the U.S. Navy. So much of the Navy's modern ethos is tied up with the Pacific campaigns of World War II, and when I thought in those long ago days of the legendary officers who led the service through the war, I contemplated how comparatively small and circumscribed my own career would probably be—the cold war of the 1970s didn't seem to offer much chance of massive fleet combat. Admirals like Nimitz, Spruance, Halsey, Kinkaid, and the other giants of the Pacific War had a sense of the vast landscape of the ocean that permitted them to construct the enormous, sweeping, island-hopping campaign that ultimately defeated the Japanese Empire. So much of the Navy's mental map begins at Pearl Harbor and opens out from there to the endless distances of the ocean; so it was fitting and shattering at the same time to be attacked without warning in early December 1941 as war came to the United States.

In order to understand the severity and totality of the Pacific Theater of World War II, you need to imagine the vast scale of the region and pair it with the fact that for the first time in history, military operations would cover the far reaches of the Pacific north of the equator and a good distance south. As the late William Manchester illustrates clearly in his excellent biography of five-star general of the Army Douglas MacArthur, *American Caesar*, the area of operations "covered mileage equivalent to that from the English Channel to the Persian Gulf—twice the farthest conquests of Alexander, Caesar, or Napoleon"—a comparison the ego-driven general would have enjoyed. That vast emptiness, which had taken outrigger canoes decades and steamships months to cross, could now be traversed in weeks. Technology did not just increase the power of ships but added new dimensions to war. Above the water, aircraft and radar altered the calculus of range. Below the surface, submarines could menace military ships and civilian shipping alike with little to no warning. The Pacific Ocean's first experience as an arena of total war came at a time when war at sea was suddenly profoundly different from ages past.

The early morning hours of December 7, 1941, on Hawaii were punctuated by the sound of airplane propellers and air raid sirens. Japanese naval aviation launched what was the largest air attack in history at that time. Planned by the brilliant and colorful Admiral Isoroku Yamamoto, a graduate of Harvard and lover of American culture, the Pearl Harbor raid devastated both the U.S. fleet in harbor and its ground-based aircraft. But the jewels of the U.S. fleet, the aircraft carriers that were the primary target of the raid, were, by a stroke of dumb luck, out of the area when the attack happened and spared destruction. The battleships *Arizona*, *Oklahoma*, *West Virginia*, and *California* were not so lucky—caught in port on a quiet Sunday with much of their crews ashore, they were pounded by the Japanese and sunk.

My wife, Laura, is today the "ship's sponsor" for a new Navy destroyer, the USS *John Finn*, named for a Pearl Harbor Medal of Honor recipient, a high honor of which she is justifiably proud. She christened the ship in 2015 and will be part of the ship's commissioning as well, continuing to have a relationship with the captain and crew throughout the life of the vessel. As a result, we have spent a fair amount of time learning about those terrible hours as an unexpected strike literally blew up the gorgeous harbor before the unbelieving eyes of Navy sailors. Chief Petty Officer

John Finn organized a machine gun nest and returned fire with a "pickup" crew of sailors, receiving many shrapnel wounds in the process. He fought proudly through the rest of the war, and lived to be more than one hundred years old, always remembering the way the world changed forever on that quiet Sunday morning.

That same day, on the other side of the Pacific, 5,500 miles away from Pearl Harbor, Japanese forces assaulted the United States in the Philippines. Just as in Hawaii, ground-based aircraft in the Philippines were devastated by the Japanese air assault. Unlike Hawaii, the Philippines were not one of the world's most isolated island chains. Their proximity to occupied Indochina meant that Japan's air assault could be followed by a ground invasion. Despite valiant resistance by American forces in the mountain redoubt of Corregidor on the Bataan Peninsula, the islands fell and would remain occupied until 1945. The Japanese war machine was churning in high gear and had not lost a battle. Things looked bleak in early 1942 for the United States and its Pacific allies.

American fortunes turned upward at the Battle of Midway in June 1942. The Japanese war plan conceived of surprise attacks across the vast Pacific in order to dislocate American efforts and put Japan in the best position possible to deal with America's demographic and industrial superiority. But in the waters around the small island of Midway, the United States was victorious despite having far fewer ships on hand in the early days of the war. Through another stroke of luck (just as at Pearl Harbor), the American carriers remained hidden from the Japanese because a mechanical failure delayed the departure of a Japanese reconnaissance plane by fifteen minutes. Unsure of the exact location of the U.S. fleet, the Japanese commanders nonetheless decided to switch the weapons carried by their planes from bombs (to target the American fortresses on Midway Island) to torpedoes (to target the American fleet).

The cat-and-mouse game came out in the Americans' favor as the

Japanese aircraft were caught on the decks of their carriers in mid-transition between armaments thanks to the fifteen-minute delay. These aircraft were nearly defenseless and were largely destroyed on deck. The result was a catastrophe for the Japanese as four of Japan's carriers, the same ones that had participated in the Pearl Harbor raid, were sent to the bottom of the Pacific along with Japan's hopes of holding out against America's numerical superiority later in the war. As one of the Japanese combatants at Midway, Commander Masatake Okumiya (later a lieutenant general in the Japanese Air Self-Defense Force), said in the book *Midway: The Battle That Doomed Japan*, "The Pacific War was started by men who did not understand the sea and fought by men who did not understand the air."

With the victory at Midway, the Americans could begin to advance across the Pacific in two prongs. The first prong, led by the Navy under Admiral Chester Nimitz, went across the Central Pacific by hopping from island to island, using the islands once coveted as coaling stations as refueling points for ships and aircraft. Meanwhile, the South Pacific campaign was led by the Army general Douglas MacArthur, pushing up from his exile in Australia back toward the Philippines. The people fighting under his command found conditions as brutal as their compatriots in the Central Pacific; the jungles of Indonesia and New Guinea bore deadly traps and virulent diseases. Those same passages of water like the Torres Strait, which one day I would be so nervous about navigating, were then full of Japanese defenses that posed a vastly more lethal threat than simply submerged reefs. The going was hard for both campaigns. But the slow, methodical pace yielded fruit, resources were cut off from the Japanese, U.S. industrial might began to tell, and Japan's strategic options were increasingly foreclosed. Japan's eventual capitulation was inevitable, although the island-by-island defenses were at times fanatical. The prospect of a land invasion of the home islands was pre-

dicted to cost enormous casualties on both sides—leading to the decision
to use nuclear weapons against Hiroshima and Nagasaki. The long war,
culminating in the two atomic bombs, the firebombing of Tokyo, and
the subsequent psychological impact of the occupation, headed up by
General MacArthur, devastated the Japanese home islands. For Japan, it
would be a long period of rebuilding and a withdrawal from global military and security affairs for many years.

It is worth remembering the other two admirals who led the fight in
the Pacific, serving under the iconic Nimitz: Admiral William "Bull"
Halsey (although he hated the nickname) and Admiral Raymond Spruance. Halsey's life was wonderfully captured in *Admiral Bill Halsey: A Naval Life* by Thomas Alexander Hughes, and Spruance's equally well in
The Quiet Warrior by Thomas Buell. The two men could not have been
more different: Halsey impulsive, tempestuous, and loud, while Spruance
was quiet, cerebral, and deeply reflective. But Nimitz harnessed their different personalities and skill sets and together they led the grandest naval
campaign in history, equal to the challenges of distance, time, and determined resistance. Their names remain irrevocably bound to the Pacific
Ocean, and will remain so as long as sailors go to sea in warships.

Sadly, conflict would not disappear from the region as the Korean War
would break out several years after the end of World War II, and of course
the U.S. war in Vietnam would follow just over a decade later. But on the
vast expanse of ocean itself, the Pacific once again became peaceful. To be
sure, there were cold war tensions above and below the waves. The Soviet
navy, under the long tenure of Admiral Sergei Gorshkov, expanded its
presence in the Pacific for the first time since Russia's defeat in the Russo-
Japanese War. Submarines armed with nuclear warheads prowled the
oceans to provide a stealthy nuclear deterrent while surface ships on both
sides tried their best to find and track their opponents. But the islands and
the peoples themselves were largely untouched. The period of U.S.

trusteeship over the islands it seized from Japan in the western Pacific morphed into the Compact of Free Association, an agreement with the Marshall Islands, the Federated States of Micronesia, and Palau, which continues to this day. The return of peace, the economic revival of Japan, and the emergence of new economic powerhouses in Taiwan, Korea, Singapore, and Hong Kong led transpacific trade to overtake transatlantic trade for the first time in the 1980s. That trend also continues.

Are we living in a Pacific Century? It is hard to say. Certainly the Obama administration thought so, announcing a "pivot to the Pacific" several years ago that ended up being more sound than light given events in the Middle East, the resurgence of Russia, and the ideological direction of the Trump administration. But the Pacific region still boasts most of the world's largest and most powerful countries, and economic power is moving inexorably that way. The United States, China, Japan, Russia, and even France all frequently call themselves Pacific powers, and the region is home to a host of other vibrant countries as well, including Australia, Korea, Canada, Mexico, Indonesia, Colombia, and Chile. Almost half of the world's trade happens along the Pacific Rim. And this is just the beginning, especially as India begins to engage in the Pacific in more significant ways. Countries across the Pacific Rim are developing ways to spur economic development of the region, whether through the Trans-Pacific Partnership (an agreement that, after the United States withdrew in 2017, continues to be discussed between the remaining parties) or China's Asian Infrastructure Investment Bank (which I hope evolves into a responsible actor), to unlock the region's potential.

Although the Pacific has a great deal of potential, it is still a region of great risk. Overfishing remains a dangerous strain on the sustainability of global fish stocks, as does the continued increase of illegal, unreported, and unregulated (IUU) fishing. Human pollution is taking a toll on the region's ecosystem with a Texas-size island of plastic circulating both above and below the surface of the Pacific. On the environmental front, the Pacific Ocean experiences terrible typhoons that menace the region, particularly the areas on the front lines such as the Philippines, Taiwan, and Vietnam. The increasing frequency of these storms (regarded by many scientists as the result of global climate change) will be a source of untold suffering and economic backsliding unless the players in the region make sensible investments in humanitarian assistance and disaster relief (HA/DR) capabilities. Military and civilian agencies around the region need to work together to ensure that they are equipped to deal with these challenges.

On the geopolitical and security front, one powerful indicator worth watching closely is the increasingly tense state of the ongoing arms race around the Pacific—which is real and growing. It will have a tendency to increase the possibility of open conflict in the region, and will require delicate diplomacy as military options tempt nations to use the military forces upon which they have spent a great deal of national wealth. And the vast majority of the systems are designed to be used either on, below, or from the sea to attack neighbors around the rim of the western Pacific.

Data from 2013 to the present reveal a preference to modernize systems rather than simply increase the size of the active force within a country. The trends in the macrodata are striking. According to *The Military Balance*, defense spending in Asia broadly (including India) rose 9 percent, from $326 billion to $356 billion from 2013 to 2015. As points of comparison, defense spending over the same period of time in the United States fell 6 percent, from $633 to $597 billion, and in Europe fell 12 percent, from $281 billion to $246 billion. How do we temper this arms race and ensure the security of the Pacific Rim?

North Korea, the most unpredictable and dangerous nation on the Pacific Rim, has more than doubled its military spending to about $10 billion from 2013 to 2015. While it is notoriously difficult to assess the actual spending inside this isolated nation, recent nuclear tests combined with long-range missile testing and road-mobile launchers are obvious causes for concern. The North Koreans will continue to prioritize high levels of defense spending, even in the face of harsh new sanctions and a weakened economic environment—the young leader, Kim Jong-un, knows that only through military might will he retain his grip on power internally and maintain some level of influence in the region.

China is the source of a disproportionately large portion of the increase in Pacific Ocean defense spending. China increased its defense spending by 26 percent to almost $147 billion between 2013 and 2016—and these numbers tell just part of the story; actual defense spending may well be more than $200 billion. The most visible display of China's aggressive approach is the construction of artificial islands that serve as a handful of "3,000-acre aircraft carriers" (a U.S. 100,000-ton aircraft carrier is only 7 acres, by the way) on permanent station in the disputed regions of the South China Sea. This policy decision puts China at odds with many nations throughout the region. Building radar and missile systems as well as airfields on its artificial islands is another key investment.

Other Chinese technological and strategic advances can be seen in China's investment in advanced fighters such as the J-20 and the J-31, the DF-21 antiship ballistic missile known as the "carrier killer," and its own nascent attempts at building an aircraft carrier fleet. These advances, when combined with its focus on offensive cyber, will enable China to push past its current so-called antiaccess/area denial (A2/AD) strategy to a more active defense, which would improve its ability to project offensive power. This will be a game changer in the region.

Strategically, China is by far the biggest military spender in the region, but must also cover more territory both ashore and at sea than other Asian nations. The shift from "peaceful development" to the notion of "active defense" is likely designed to mask internal problems and attempt to shift the focus of its population away from its own contradictions to external challenges. Capable missiles like the DF-21D alter the risk calculation for the United States, especially for carriers. Finally, there is quite a bit of focus on China's aircraft carrier program. Chinese carriers are not competitive relative to those of the United States. However, as a "prestige platform," they are symbolically important and conceivably useful in maritime combat against smaller powers in the region. The irony here is that China's carrier is threatened by the very same A2/AD technologies it champions as Japan, South Korea, and Vietnam all up their game in that regard. Strategically speaking, the Chinese carrier program is not a game changer, but it will unnerve many smaller neighbors.

Given all of this, it is important to think about American capabilities and potential responses at sea. The United States, with its six heavy nuclear-powered carriers and dozens of sophisticated air defense cruisers and destroyers plus long-range bombers operating from Guam, still has a powerful maritime position in the region. The construction of artificial islands in the South China Sea plus the increased capability of the long-range ship attack missiles by China shift, but do not fully reverse, the balance of power in Asia, especially given the strength of U.S. allies such as Japan and South Korea.

Other nations in and around the Pacific are likewise ramping up spending, including Japan, which announced an increase to its 2016 defense budget, the first such increase in more than a decade. The stated policy focus of Japan's drive for security is "seamless integration" with the United States. Japan is adding significant missile defense, airborne surveillance, and advanced aircraft to its already highly capable forces. Another ambitious capability acquisition includes the desire to field an Amphibious Rapid Deployment Brigade by 2017. This capability will integrate ground, naval, air, cyber, and space domains.

Japan's technological edge makes it the second most powerful navy in the world, and its air force and army are quite capable as well. Ensuring that its security policy matches its defense capacity and capability enhances its importance to the United States in a collective defense scenario. Although Japan's record defense budget of $42 billion in 2016 is relatively low when compared with China's, its focus is clear and local and will reduce operational seams to complement its most important treaty ally: the United States.

Japan has reduced spending for its Ground Self-Defense Force and increased both Air and Maritime Self-Defense Forces—clearly showing that its priorities are aligned with its policy shift to support collective defense. These investments are relevant in a confrontational scenario with China. On the other hand, China's spending on defense must cover more territory and focus on internal security. While the exact ratio of external-to-internal defense spending is unclear, we do know that internal defense concerns will continue to act as a brake on its external ambitions.

South Korea continues to invest in technology while increasing the quality (as opposed to quantity) of its personnel. Although the South Korean defense budget increased 6 percent from 2013 to 2015, it shed 4 percent of its manpower in the same period. It is acquiring major systems: upgrading its fleet of F-16 jet fighters, seeking an F-X program to develop a sixth-generation fighter, and developing a new unmanned airborne vehicle for its army and marine corps. While still reliant on the United States for air and missile defense, South Korea continues to pursue a Korean-operated air and missile defense in light of the threats it faces from Pyongyang.

Meanwhile, Australia, another staunch ally of the United States, has increased defense spending by about 7 percent and focused on combat aircraft and ships, including upgrades to its diesel submarine force.

While beyond the far reaches of the Pacific Ocean, India is notable as the only country, besides China, that increased the size of its active military personnel roster between 2013 and 2015 (2 percent, the same as China). This came in tandem with a significant increase to its military budget. A central focus of this increase serves to drive defense production within India's borders in line with Prime Minister Narendra Modi's "Make in India" initiative. New procurement runs the gamut across sectors: new tactical helicopters, new Rafale fighters (despite continuing issues in the negotiations between France and India), and additional heavy airlift transports—with a significant uptick in spending on American systems. Vietnam, South Korea, Taiwan, and other actors are likewise stepping up their defense spending with a focus on a potential war at sea.

This maritime arms race in Asia comes from each state's perception of external threats. A worst-case scenario would see the region falling into the so-called Thucydides trap, where miscalculation of intentions leads to armed conflict—either between the United States and China globally, or possibly between China and Japan in the region.

The best chance we have to avoid conflict rests in maritime diplomacy. This must begin with a continued high-level U.S.-Chinese conversation about points of friction, from artificial islands (and the resultant "freedom of navigation" patrols by the United States) to cyber intrusions to balance of trade disagreements. The United States should encourage cooperation between its allies in the region (i.e., Japan, South Korea, the Philippines, Australia, and others) in a way that does not create an Asian cold war between China and a U.S.-led bloc of nations.

Additionally, Pacific Rim nations should be encouraged to use their militaries for exercises, training, and other confidence-building measures—like the U.S.-organized RIMPAC annual exercise, which has seen solid Chinese participation. This helps build confidence and military-to-military cooperation. And the nations of the region can also work together on soft-power projects using their militaries for disaster relief, humanitarian operations, and medical diplomacy in the coming decades.

The Pacific Ocean arms race is real and it is dangerous. Transparency, cooperation, and diplomacy can mitigate the potential for open conflict. Now is the time to put such mechanisms in place—before nations are tempted to reach for the military instrument and exercise hard power in addressing their geopolitical concerns.

Despite the tensions and the risks in our modern Pacific Rim, the odds are better than even that the region will develop peacefully. None of the societies have a long tradition of imperialist behavior, and most have found ways to cooperate and collaborate in a variety of dimensions, despite the arms buildup. Other than North Korea, which is by far the most dangerous actor in the region, there seems little likelihood of any of the nations' moving to open warfare as an instrument of policy. There will probably be some flash points in and around the South China Sea, but the chances of nation-on-nation high-level combat are low.

The Pacific Ocean that I sailed into in the 1970s as a naïve, young, and unformed officer as the cold war unfolded was a more dangerous place. Today's major actors—Japan, Korea, China, the United States—all know well the devastation of a Pacific war at sea. The strength of commerce, depth of culture, and quality of human capital of the nations in the region all point to the potential for a positive trajectory of growth. While the South China Sea and the Korean Peninsula present challenges and tension, hopefully the Pacific will live up to its name as the twenty-first century sails along; much will depend on the willingness of the actors around its vast littoral to work together around the ocean that binds their fate together in so many ways. On the other hand, the potential for an explosive war—perhaps on the Korean Peninsula, or between Japan and China—looms on the horizon like a tempest headed our way. The twenty-first century in the Pacific has many unexpected twists ahead.

2.

THE ATLANTIC OCEAN

THE CRADLE OF COLONIZATION

Pascoal Roiz's famous 1633 map showing the Atlantic world.

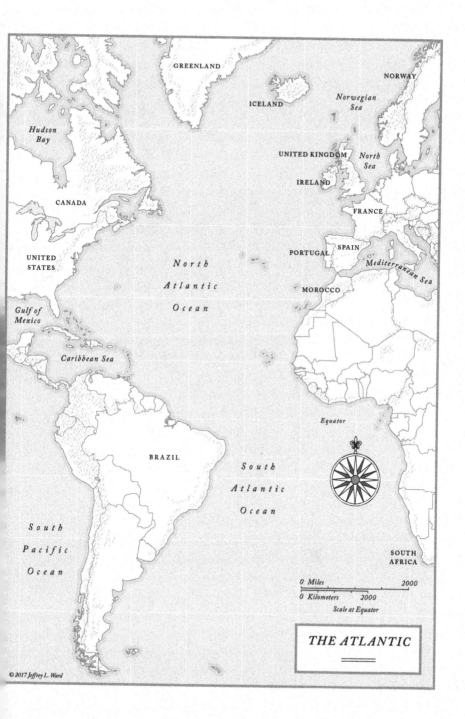

THE ATLANTIC

*M*uch has been made about the twenty-first century being the Age of the Pacific. And indeed, many metrics would suggest that the Pacific—especially when considered as the Indo-Pacific, to include the waters surrounding South Asia and the Indian subcontinent—will be the dominant sea space of this unfolding century. The Obama administration's famous "pivot to the Pacific" (now tempered as a "rebalance to the Pacific" in the wake of events in the Middle East and Europe) seemed to validate that concept. Recent actions by the Trump administration seem intent on shelving that policy in favor of greater isolation.

Yet no matter where the world is headed in terms of the importance of the oceans relative to one another, there is one inescapable fact about the Atlantic: it will always be the cradle of our civilization as we know it, especially when the Mediterranean is included in its broad remit, and also when we consider that it formed the nexus of exchange between European nations, newly formed North American states, Latin American civilizations, the Caribbean, and Africa.

When I think of the Atlantic Ocean, I am occasionally reminded of Louis Malle's small masterpiece of a film, *Atlantic City*, which came out in 1980. Set in that city, it features an aging Burt Lancaster as a fading mobster named Lou seeking to help a young Canadian on the run, played by Susan Sarandon. Musing on the beauty and power of the Atlantic Ocean when he was a young up-and-comer, Lou says in all sincerity, "You should have seen the Atlantic Ocean back then." Somehow I doubt the Atlantic had changed a great deal over the few decades of Lou's life, but its power to impress has been with mankind for centuries.

The Atlantic Ocean is the world's second largest, after the Pacific, covering more than 40 million square miles (more than ten times the size of the United States*) and about 20 percent of the earth's surface. The name derives from the ancient Greek mythological character Atlas, who in legend supported the world on his shoulders. The ocean is really composed of two distinct regions, often referred to as "basins," one on either side of the equator, and overall forms the letter *S* if viewed from space. Any casual observer looking at the west coast of Africa and the east coast of South America would quickly guess that the two continents drifted apart at some point in prehistory, the space between them creating the landscape of the ocean's sea bottom.

The Atlantic has two key tributary seas—the Mediterranean and the Caribbean, as well as an important strategic gap to the north (the Greenland-Iceland–United Kingdom gap), which was a nautical zone of competition and near conflict in the cold war. To the south, it is connected with its two sister oceans, the Pacific and the Indian, by a relatively small strait, the Drake Passage to the Pacific, and by a broad expanse of ocean water to the Indian Ocean in the east. Including the two tributary seas, it is bordered by nearly a hundred nations and territories,

---

* Common estimates place the United States at 3.8 million square miles.

ranging in size and economic power from the vast scope and scale of the United States and Brazil to tiny countries like Belize and Montserrat.

MY OWN FIRST IMPRESSIONS of the Atlantic are from the early 1960s, when, as a very small boy, I sailed with my family from New York to Athens, Greece, where my father—an active-duty Marine officer—was headed for an assignment at the U.S. embassy. Sailing in those days on a large cruise liner was a throwback to the great liners of the twenties and thirties—terrific food, small but elegant staterooms, and plenty of open bars. We were on SS *Constitution*, which offered many programs for children, but all I wanted to do was watch the ocean roll by. I was endlessly fascinated by the way the surface of the ocean could form at one moment a smooth skin like a trampoline, and the next be full of chopped white-caps, and as quickly turn into long but smooth ocean waves. It was the show that never ended, full of colors and light and high-flying seabirds in shades of gray and white. For a very small boy, it was mesmerizing. On the way, we stopped at Lisbon then sailed through the Mediterranean, making a port call near Rome before arriving in Piraeus Harbor, the gateway to Athens in our ethnic homeland of Greece.

I returned to the Atlantic in a serious way just over a decade later, in the early 1970s, when I sailed in the then brand-new aircraft carrier USS *Nimitz*. As a midshipman just over twenty years of age, about to enter my final year at the Naval Academy, I sailed from Norfolk into the rolling, dark blue waters of the Gulf Stream, one of the most distinctive features of the western Atlantic. This current, which forms itself originally off the west coast of Africa, travels across the Central Atlantic as a sort of river within the ocean. It bounces off the northeast coast of South America, splits into two parts, then reforms and heads north through and beyond the Strait of Florida.

The Gulf Stream is typically about sixty to seventy miles wide and almost four thousand feet deep, with a high velocity near the surface, approaching five miles per hour in places. Colonial navigators became very aware of it in the eighteenth century, although mariners argued over the best way to use its speed and pace to best advantage. It has figured in many works of literature and films, and the sense you have of it as a mariner is one of relentless flow and power, moving everything in its path deeper and deeper into the North Atlantic. In a famously long and pedantic sentence, Hemingway laid out a comprehensive if somewhat tedious description of the Gulf Stream, one that would probably require drinking a Papa Hemingway–size daiquiri to get through. It is a feature of the Atlantic that continues to fascinate writers.

THE FIRST EUROPEANS TO VENTURE into the Atlantic were probably the ancient Greeks, although the extent of their travels beyond what is today called the Strait of Gibraltar and was known to them as the Pillars of Hercules is shrouded in legend, myth, and mystery. A central part of the mystery involves the reputed existence of the mythical city of Atlantis. To get a sense of how the Greeks envisioned the physical world, go back to ancient mythology, much of which I learned from my father while a small boy in Greece in the 1960s. According to the myths, the titan Atlas held up the world with arms that never wearied, standing at the very end of the earth before the Hesperides—a collective name for a blissful group of nymphs who resided in a garden at the edge of Oceanus, the ocean that encircled the world. Not exactly precise mapping.

A variety of early explorers began to penetrate the mystery of the Atlantic as early as the sixth century A.D., including an Irish abbot, Saint Brendan, also known as "the Navigator." The voyages of this ecclesiastical character were supposedly in search of converts, few of whom would have been found at sea. Some records indicate his voyages took him to the rest of the British Isles (Scotland and Wales) and possibly across the English Channel to Brittany. The extent of the legends of Brendan the Navigator have him making it to icebergs off the coast of Greenland and possibly the south shore of Iceland. None of what such early explorers managed to learn was made widely available to others, and the Atlantic continued to reflect real mystery and danger to the European world. On the Atlantic's western coast, the widely scattered indigenous settlements in the Americas did not appear to move beyond minor coastal voyaging—leaving a vast tract of unexplored ocean.

Not until the time of the Vikings in the period from A.D. 800 to 1000 is there evidence of recorded voyages into the open Atlantic. The first real settlements in Iceland were probably Viking, perhaps in the late 800s. There are recorded voyages in the late 900s, including one by Bjarni Herjolfsson, who was evidently driven west by fierce storms from the relatively known waters around Iceland and Greenland and reported seeing heavy forests to the west. This voyage has led some observers to credit the Vikings with the first sighting of the New World, linking Europe and North America by the maritime highway that continues to matter so deeply today. By the tenth and eleventh centuries there appear to have been settlements in present-day Canada—Labrador and Newfoundland. Some reports exist of "Viking relics" that supposedly have been found as far inland as Minnesota and the upper Midwest, although the vast majority of serious scholars discount those as urban legends run wild. It is hard to imagine what a Viking would have thought about the fact that in today's world more than $4 trillion passes annually between the two continents, reflecting the largest trading relationship in the world economy.

There is a bit of an academic debate over whether all of the Viking activity constitutes actually "discovering" the New World or merely reaching it. In his seminal work on this topic, Daniel Boorstin makes a distinction between such voyages of exploration and the act of discovery, in the sense that discovery implies providing feedback to European civilization that would cause a real change in its worldview.* What is clear is that the early voyagers like the Irish and Vikings opened the Atlantic world as we understand it today—a maritime bridge of enormous importance. In the end, they were more sailors at sea than colonizers ashore. It was the warmer-weather voyagers in the fifteenth and sixteenth centuries—led by the intrepid Portuguese—who not only explored but also discovered and colonized the Atlantic world both at sea and ashore. In a way, this is the difference between the oceans themselves—which are but glittering passages across which the world's trade, commerce, research, and security are conducted—and the riches of the vast lands that the world of the seas connects.

MY FIRST TRIP ACROSS the North Atlantic as a ship captain was in the mid-1990s. My ship, USS *Barry*, was a brand-new *Arleigh Burke*–class guided missile destroyer with a crew of about three hundred and a huge array of missiles for air defense, land attack, and killing submarines—a so-called multimission warship. Given that the ship was named for Captain John Barry, a Revolutionary War hero of Irish descent, we were sent across the North Atlantic in the early summer of 1994, bound initially for goodwill visits in Ireland. After a brief stop there, we would head into potential combat operations in the Arabian Gulf.

As we sailed across the broad expanse of the rolling Atlantic over that Memorial Day, I was struck by the differences and similarities we experienced compared with early voyagers. We had all the comforts of home—

* Daniel J. Boorstin, *The Discoverers*, 1st ed. (New York: Random House, 1983).

good hot food and showers, pleasant bunk rooms, communications with family and friends back home (although limited compared with today), plenty of fuel brought out to us at sea by wide-ranging oilers (ships designated to act as at-sea gas stations). While our accommodations were not luxurious, compared with a Viking long ship we were living like kings at sea, sailing in a well-heeled palace—a very different world.

But the impetus was the same: we sailed on a mission for our country, left our families for a long, seven-month voyage, faced real danger in our ultimate destination—the volatile Arabian Gulf in the time of Saddam Hussein—and felt between us the same bond that sailors have felt going back two thousand years or more. We were hardly Vikings, nor faced the sea in such a dramatic way, but we were in every sense part of the long story of the Atlantic Ocean. We knew where we were headed, but not what would unfold. In the end, that uncertainty and sense of adventure is a significant part of what draws many of us to the oceans.

THE FOURTEENTH AND FIFTEENTH CENTURIES saw key improvements in sailing technology. The frail, single-mast Viking ship—which was really a simple adaptation of what the Greeks and Romans used in the Mediterranean nearly a millennium earlier—gave way to multiple masts, a bowsprit to carry sail in front of the ship, and a handful of sails. The compass came into general use, as well as simple means of measuring speed using knotted ropes (hence the term "knots" for the speed of a ship). The necessity of "dead reckoning," which is using landmarks ashore to plot a course, was gradually resolved by using celestial means to navigate, which improved gradually. As trade goods—especially spices, gold, jewelry, perfumes, dyes, and gems—began to flow, the appetite for longer and longer voyages increased.

Whether or not we credit the Irish (or more likely the Vikings) with the first significant European voyages across the Atlantic, what is indisputable is the early and enormous impact of the Portuguese. The most iconic of these intrepid figures was Infante Henrique of Portugal, Duke of Viseu, who earned the sobriquet Prince Henry the Navigator. He lived in the first half of the fifteenth century and launched many expeditions throughout the early 1400s that sailed down the Atlantic and explored the coast of Africa. His taste for exploration and profit was whetted early in his life by a crusade conducted against the city of Ceuta, in what is today Morocco—there he discovered spices, gold, silver, and the other potential riches of the Atlantic coast of the massive continent to the south. He also gathered to himself many of the best navigators and sailors of the day in an informal "maritime court" in Sagres, on the southern Algarve of Portugal, which he presided over with enthusiasm. While there is a fair amount of scholarly debate over the degree to which Henry actually conducted regularized meetings of this "court," it seems reasonable to say that upon occasion he brought together maritime experts and drew from their collective wisdom.

Prince Henry sponsored many of the voyages that both solidified knowledge of the world to the south and permitted the expansion of new techniques of sailing and navigation. The caravel, a type of lightweight, lateen-rigged ship (sails fore and aft instead of squared up to the stern of the ship), was crucial to these explorations. While small, caravels could be operated in small flotillas and could sail not only down the coast of Africa, but, crucially, back up the coast by beating into the wind. The expression "sailing close to the wind," implying taking risk and going against the normal flow of events, comes from lateen-rigged sailing caravels.

The Portuguese navigators of the time also perfected the use of the various prevalent winds and currents in the Atlantic to sail first southwest from Lisbon and Lagos to ports on the equatorial coast of Africa, then north and west—actually away from home—but finally swinging back to the northeast around the vicinity of the Azores Islands and catching the so-called Portugal current for home. This huge triangular passage was called the *volta do mar* or the "turn of the sea." A smaller version of it consisted of sailing to a mid-distance port on the African coast, then heading northwest to the Canary Islands before turning for home. Taking advantage of both currents and winds (which were known as the Gyre of the Atlantic) allowed European explorations to unfold with increasing frequency. The technology of the caravels allowed for expeditions via these two routes that thoroughly exploited the vast northwestern coast of Africa, from the ancient port of Ceuta on the southern point of the Strait of Gibraltar down to the first major fort built by the Portuguese off the coast of modern Mauritania on the island of Arguin—which they held for two centuries, until the mid-1600s.

After the death of Prince Henry in the middle of the fifteenth century, the Portuguese voyages continued under a new generation of sailors who had literally grown up in the culture of exploration. Three of the key sea captains were Bartolomeu Dias, Vasco da Gama, and Pedro Álvares Cabral. Dias, for example, departed the White Tower on the River Tagus in the late 1480s and worked his way around the Cape of Good Hope (more or less accidentally, as legend holds it was a storm that blew him east) after a year-and-a-half voyage. Da Gama pushed farther and was the first European to touch the Indian subcontinent at the very end of the fifteenth century. In the first year of the sixteenth century, Cabral discovered Brazil, and continued on the first known voyage to touch four continents: Europe, South America, Africa, and Asia on the Indian subcontinent.

Taken together, the exploits of these and other Portuguese sea captains gradually opened the southwestern coast of Africa, helped build up trading routes, continued the search for the legendary Christian kingdom of Prester John (never found), and eventually rounded the Cape of Good Hope and sailed into the Indian Ocean. Their great voyages of discovery inspired Europeans, exploited Africans (often with extreme brutality), and created the connections between the Atlantic and Indian oceans over the fifteenth and sixteenth centuries. Some have called this the dawn of the Oceanic Age.

My first sea voyage into Lisbon and up the Tagus River was in 1962 on SS *Constitution*, while our family was headed to Athens for my father's three-year tour as the assistant naval attaché. An infantry officer at the time, he was not particularly enamored of sea voyages, but I remember loving the experience of being under way. Our first port after departing Boston was Lisbon, and we sailed up the Tagus on a hot summer day. Even as a seven-year-old boy, I was enchanted by the ships swaying on the waterfront, the wide and beautiful river, the gleaming white tower from which each of the Portuguese captains after the early 1500s departed on the voyages that opened the world. Decades later, I would return to Lisbon as a grizzled four-star admiral with many commands at sea and too many sea miles under my belt to remember—and the magic of that tower felt the same. As I toured the Portuguese maritime museum a few blocks from the waterfront, I was struck by the courage it must have taken to sail away from all you knew—a European and Christian world, a vibrant society, a loving family—to launch into an unknown void to the south. As they watched that white tower—by then known as the Belém Tower, recede from view, how they must have been torn between a longing for home and a thirst for the sea, like sailors everywhere.

COLUMBUS AND HIS FAMOUS VOYAGES of 1492 are discussed in more depth in the chapter on the Caribbean, but it is worth noting that he initially offered his services to the Portuguese and was turned down, finally winning the trust and financing (as well as the affection) of Queen

Isabella and King Ferdinand of Spain. He initially sailed south toward West Africa, but turned westward, taking advantage of favorable winds. In just over a month, he changed the course of world history with his landing in what is today the Bahamas. Eventually styled "Admiral of the Ocean Sea," perhaps the most pompous title in maritime history, he completed three more voyages to the "New World" that would bear his imprint for centuries.

By the sixteenth century, just a few decades later, voyages across the Atlantic were becoming more and more common. Of note, within twenty years of Christopher Columbus's "discovery" of the New World, Ferdinand Magellan, whose expedition would later circumnavigate the earth, sailed on a voyage that resulted in discovery of a passage connecting the Atlantic and Pacific oceans at the bottom of the world—the Strait of Magellan at the tip of South America. Ironically, Magellan was Portuguese by birth, but sailing under commission to the Spanish throne. As we've seen, he would not survive his circumnavigation of the world, but his deeds and the resulting changes in cartography influenced the rising mariners of France and England, who next began to sail the Atlantic waters, especially in the Northern Hemisphere.

While the Portuguese and Spanish led the way across the Atlantic to the Caribbean and South America, the British and the French concentrated on North America. By the end of the fifteenth century, John Cabot—ironically an Italian, sailing for the British crown—explored Newfoundland, but was subsequently lost on a follow-up expedition with five ships. This had a bit of a chilling effect on British exploration, and it was roughly a century before the Brits returned in numbers across the Atlantic. As the sixteenth century unfolded, both the French and the British established colonies in what is today Canada, as well as settlements along the Atlantic coast of the modern-day United States.

In Britain, a nautical tradition emerged in the 1500s under Henry

VIII, who commissioned the building of the first national warships. They featured heavy cannons that were muzzle loaded, and towers fore and aft to afford height from which to shoot down upon opposing mariners. The use of multiple cannons firing together became known as the "broadside," and was used to devastating effect in nautical warfare for the next five hundred years, until the advent of aircraft and long-range missiles in the mid-twentieth century. By the late sixteenth century, the battle for geopolitical supremacy between England and Spain was in full flower, exacerbated by the religious wars that came following the Reformation and Henry's decision to break with the Catholic Church and reject the authority of the pope. English sea rovers, who were essentially pirates formally authorized by the crown and called "privateers," became strategic weapons in the duel between England and Spain. Two of the most feared were John Hawkins and Francis Drake. Their ships, notably Drake's *Golden Hind*, ravaged the coast of South America in the late 1500s.

This led to one of the epic battles of the Atlantic—the attack of the Spanish Armada, sometimes known as the Grand Armada. A massive force for the times, it consisted of well over a hundred vessels, a thousand cannons, and nearly thirty thousand men. All of this was assembled while Spain was simultaneously fighting in the present-day Netherlands, which along with Germany was essentially ground zero of the wars of the Reformation. The English were able to muster more than thirty heavy men-of-war, and by dint of armed merchantmen eventually put to sea nearly two hundred ships. The crucial difference was that the English ships were smaller, lighter, and more maneuverable, and expert sailors manned them. The Spanish ships were heavier (with broadsides more than double in firepower) and had shorter-range cannons. The battle, which took place in the waters off the English coast, was notable for being the first significant clash between sailing fleets, as well as a pivotal moment in the confrontation between Catholicism and Protestantism.

The exchanges included firing many tens of thousands of rounds between the two sides, but without great effect because of the significant distances between the fleets. The Spanish reached their first objective, the French port of Calais, where they were to take on additional troops before crossing the Channel and invading England. Unfortunately for the Spanish, they had expended most of their heavy shot and could not be resupplied from distant armories in Spain, while the English, with the home court advantage, were able to reload. Despite this advantage, the English were not able to crush the Spanish fleet but rather chased them into the North Sea and eventually back to Spain—a voyage that was interrupted by terrible storms and bad navigation, which, between them, account for dozens of sunken Spanish ships. When the Armada limped back into Spain, it was half its original size. "God breathed and they were scattered" is inscribed on the English victory medals.

Over the next century, the remarkable Dutch began to emerge as a competing nautical power with designs on the Atlantic and other territory in the New World. In the 1600s, there were three wars between the English and the Dutch, which did not turn out well for the Hollanders— the British enjoyed a significant strategic advantage by sitting astride the sea lanes over which the Dutch needed to sail to make it into the open waters of the Atlantic. This was the period of the Commonwealth in England, and Oliver Cromwell had a deep distrust of admirals (I am sorry to report) and decided to send his generals (who normally commanded only land forces, of course) to sea in order to take command. This led, of course, to more orderly tactics of columns and the so-called line ahead, which competed with the "melee school" of simply putting your ship next to the enemy vessel with alacrity. By the 1700s, when

England and now France were engaged in Atlantic warfare, command had returned to the sailors—but the general approach of fighting in column and with precise maneuvers stayed central to maritime warfare.

The Seven Years' War in the mid-1700s can be regarded as the first truly global conflict, with France and England fighting in the Atlantic and its tributary seas, the Mediterranean and Caribbean, as well as in the Pacific, the Indian Ocean, and ashore in all of those locations. Britain developed a strategy that served it well for the next three hundred years of aligning with a continental European power to create a geopolitical balance against its major foe—in this case France. The English would hit at various points around the world, including a central campaign against French colonies globally and against France's fleet in the Atlantic, while holding French ships in port by blockading and counting on continental allies (in this case, Prussia) to threaten France ashore. Sometimes known as "Pitt's Plan" after the creative geostrategic genius William Pitt, who conceived it, some variation on this approach continued to be seminal for England for the next three centuries. France tried to respond by defending its colonies and threatening to invade England. In the end, British mastery of the seas was decisive, and Britain ended with possession of Canada and significant gains in the Caribbean Sea. The Seven Years' War demonstrated the power of a global naval force and control of the sea lanes of communication as the key to winning wars.

What is notable in the gradual progress of the Europeans across the Atlantic is the degree to which exploration led inexorably to transformation. In addition to the technical improvements in sailing technique, sails, rigging, and hull form that flowed from the requirement for longer voyages and the urgent need to sail opposing the wind, the other major transformation was the result of the discovery and return to Europe of new agrarian products. Diet began to change in Europe as a result of the flora and fauna hauled back, initially as curiosities, then increasingly as commercial products. This has been called the Columbian Exchange or the New World Exchange.

Just as the Europeans brought "guns, germs, and steel" to Africa and the Americas across the Atlantic Ocean (as writer Jared Diamond describes in his classic work of the same name), the New World sent products back. Tomatoes, potatoes, rubber, vanilla, chocolate, corn, and tobacco came from the New World, while Europe sent onions, citrus, bananas, mangos, wheat, and rice. Livestock sailed largely from Europe to the Americas, fundamentally changing lives there—horses, pigs, donkeys, dogs, cats, bees, and chickens were all introduced as a result of the Atlantic bridge. Discovery of the two new continents created new trade routes for the Europeans, including, over time, the flow of human slaves to the Americas to work plantations (notably sugar, cotton, and tobacco) with finished products then returning to Europe. This "Middle Passage" of human slaves was tragic and horrific, and indeed has come to reflect the worst moments of Atlantic history. Slavery formed but one part of an enormous migration across the Atlantic that has continued to this day, resulting in the eventual settlement of more than a billion people in the Americas today.

All of this helped create the basis in the eighteenth century for the Industrial Revolution, which was enhanced by the trade in raw materials and the flow of humans across the Atlantic. With the increase in trade and commerce, and the attendant rise in industrial capability, came great-power geopolitics. Gradually, the five imperial powers of the Atlantic Ocean—France, Britain, Spain, the Netherlands, and Portugal—embroiled themselves in a series of colonial wars that required the Atlantic to serve as a maritime battlefield, a logistic bridge to support military campaigns in the Americas, and a highway for the economic advancement that fueled the wars. Over the next two centuries, what might be termed the "Wars of the Atlantic" were fought both ashore in the

Americas and in Europe, as well as at sea. Essentially the competition was over the products of the New World—the riches that flowed from gold, silver, slaves, sugar, tobacco, fish, furs, manufactured goods, and the markets themselves. The imperial powers realized that what we would call today "sea control" was an essential element of national power. While a coherent theoretical framework to describe their strategies would have to wait another couple of centuries and the writings of Alfred Thayer Mahan, this was sea power at play on a broader scale than had ever been seen in human history. The rise of great oceangoing vessels—both commercial and warships—created the engine of sea control and power projection that came to dominate global politics for centuries and still exists today. All of that was birthed in the Atlantic Ocean.

In the United States, the relatively small region of New England began to develop as the first truly global maritime hub for the Americas. Rudimentary shipyards began to emerge in the decades leading up to the American Revolution, and the independence and wealth they generated were central to the ability of the colonies to eventually break away from the British crown. Naturally, the disputes at the heart of the revolution fell out of the Atlantic trade, from the imposition of taxation without representation to the growing sense of liberty and freedom owed to men and women who had sailed into the unknown and created a new political entity with increasingly different norms and behaviors. The trading routes grew increasingly complex, to include lumber, meat, grain, tar, resin, pitch, rice, and indigo by the middle of the 1700s; literally thousands of ships were engaged in this trade, with hundreds of warships protecting and escorting them, as well as fighting a series of skirmishes, battles, and wars at sea. Alongside this legitimate trade and military protection, of course, was a flourishing pirate culture centered in the Caribbean, an area that afforded many advantages to piratical activity, as we'll see: many small inlets and bays, tiny islands, temperate weather most of the year, and the natural geopolitical chaos resulting from five national entities competing in a relatively small space.

All of this trade, wealth, and geostrategic competition acted as a complex and combustible mix that was eventually ignited by the ideas of the Enlightenment. This helped create the conditions for the American Revolution, in which the Atlantic again played a major role. Following the French and Indian Wars (the North American portion of the Seven Years' War), the British crown was in a less advantageous position, caught between unrest at home, continued anger and resentment on the part of fellow imperial power France, and a sense in the American colonies that their burden and obligation to Britain was too high a cost to bear. Gradually increasing taxes and tariffs led to significant unrest in the colonies, catalyzed by the Boston Tea Party in 1773—an act that did not go down well in Britain and led to further restrictions on the colonies, including the closure of the port of Boston. By 1775, the northern colonies in particular were in a state of rebellion, and the battles of Lexington and Concord (essentially shootings and skirmishes) led to full-blown war.

No revolution in history has been embraced unanimously. About a third of the American population at the time of the revolution wanted to remain loyal to the crown, about a third were more or less ambivalent, and a third were strongly pro-independence at the outset. But once combat was joined in New England, the tide turned in the colonies and a revolutionary spirit strengthened. While the Americans hardly possessed a significant navy compared with Great Britain, they were aided by the French, still smarting from their losses in the French and Indian Wars and eager to weaken the position of their rival in the Americas. The colonists marshaled their small vessels and attacked British interests where and when they could—afloat on Lake Champlain and ashore into Canada. Surprisingly, they were also able to carry the war into British waters by deploying privateers and the first vessels of the Continental

Navy. Massive British troop deployments to the colonies as well as total control over the Atlantic seaways took a toll on the lightly armed American ships. Americans quickly realized that British control over the Atlantic was a key element they had to overcome to be successful. Only when France entered the war in 1778 were the Americans able to begin to establish some level of what we would today call sea control in the approaches to our shores.

By the 1780s, American naval officers, including the iconic John Paul Jones, had scored real victories at sea in the North Atlantic. Jones sailed into Irish and British waters, first in the *Ranger* and later in the *Bonhomme Richard*, conducting a *guerre de course*, or war against shipping. His small squadron of lightly armed ships attacked a British convoy and captured the heavily armed English ship *Serapis* in 1779. This was perhaps the most famous U.S. naval engagement of the revolution, in which the British captain asked Captain Jones—his ship nearly sunk under his feet—if he wanted to strike his colors (surrender to the enemy). His reply, "I have not yet begun to fight," has been memorized by generations of midshipmen at Annapolis (including a young plebe named Stavridis in the summer of 1972).

John Paul Jones, by the way, is probably the only famous American naval officer many citizens could name from the early days of the republic. He was quite widely traveled across the Atlantic. While he tends to be revered as the "father of the American navy," in fact he was a mercenary who fought for both the United States and the Russian Empire, rising to the rank of rear admiral in the Imperial Russian Navy. He wasn't particularly happy with the way he was treated (he was a prickly Scot) throughout the Revolutionary War and returned to Europe for better pay and larger commands, but was eventually outmaneuvered in court politics. In 1792, he died penniless in Paris and was buried in a French cemetery.

His star rose considerably after his death, however, when Theodore Roosevelt took an interest in him and had him exhumed, and in 1905 Jones sailed once again across the Atlantic, in the American warship USS *Brooklyn*, escorted by three other cruisers. Jones was then buried with enormous pomp and circumstance, first in Bancroft Hall (home of the Brigade of Midshipmen at Annapolis), and ultimately in a gorgeous black marble crypt under the massive chapel at the U.S. Naval Academy in Annapolis. He is probably the only person who crossed the Atlantic over the course of three centuries, from the late eighteenth to the early twentieth.

Luckily for the nascent United States, the French were trying to turn the tide of the battle by helping resupply American forces across the Atlantic, conducting harrying attacks on the British where they could, and drawing up plans for an invasion in the southern colonies. Ultimately, the French Marquis de Lafayette proved to be the reliable ally the colonies needed, conducting a decisive and vital campaign at Yorktown in southern Virginia. The battle—truly a campaign conducted over months—showed the value of sea power. First and foremost, it was enabled by sea control across the Atlantic; it also illustrated the strategic mobility that sea power can confer as the Americans, using French naval power, were able to shift forces smoothly and apply combat power at the point of maximum need. As forces converged via sea on Yorktown in the late summer and early autumn of 1781, the naval fight in the Atlantic turned into a tough, close-in battle between British and French warships. The French mauled the British and forced them to sail north to try to bring more troops to the embattled British general ashore, Lord Cornwallis. But time was against the British, and Cornwallis was forced to surrender as a result of superior sea power—in this case supplied by the French, our oldest and first ally. By 1783, the British had greater geopolitical challenges and turbulence at home, and the Treaty of Paris ended the war and recognized the independence of the new United States, stretching from the Great Lakes to Georgia. The Atlantic seacoast of the United States was our nation's first and most prominent geographic feature, and our doorway to the world opened through it as we achieved our first real degree of independence.

The next great series of campaigns in which the Atlantic played the central role was the long conflict unleashed in Europe by the rise of Napoleon Bonaparte. The long duel between Napoleon's France and the nations he conquered or persuaded to fight with him against the coalition led by Great Britain rumbled along through the end of the 1700s and the first decade of the 1800s. It was a geopolitical fight that ultimately turned upon Britain's use of sea power to maintain its independence, blockade French power, fight over distant colonies, and continue to function economically despite Napoleon's domination of the continent. Perhaps the most iconic sailor in history, Britain's Viscount Horatio Nelson, was a key figure in the long fight. He fought battles on all sides of the Atlantic—in the Caribbean, the Baltic, and the Mediterranean—and crossed it dozens of times in the course of the Napoleonic Wars. His two early successful battles against the French were crucial: in Egypt, the Battle of the Nile probably saved British India from French conquest, and in Denmark, he managed at the Battle of Copenhagen to force Napoleon to the bargaining table. His influence on the British navy is felt to this day.

It is worth knowing that in this age of transparency and political correctness, Lord Nelson would never have passed a U.S. Senate confirmation process. He was subject to violent seasickness and had various other medical challenges. He was a short and scrawny figure, standing well under five feet six inches, who eventually lost both an eye and an arm in combat. Nelson had a long-running affair with Emma Hamilton, who might charitably be called a courtesan, with whom he fathered a daughter out of wedlock. He consistently took delight in countering the tight, regimented tactics of maritime combat at the time, and his ability to weld together a "band of brothers" from among the various sea captains serving under him was instrumental in creating the best fighting force ever to sail the oceans up to that day.

What really mattered about Lord Nelson was his centrality to the fate of his nation in the latter part of the eighteenth century and the beginning of the nineteenth; as a continental land power, France under Napoleon sought to dominate the maritime power of the world, Great Britain. He was fundamental to Great Britain's ability to execute a classic maritime strategy of dominating the lanes of communication across the Atlantic and around the littoral seas of the European continent while maintaining economic vitality from colonies around the world.

By 1805, Napoleon was actively seeking an invasion force to attack Great Britain. Nelson pursued the French fleet (and its Spanish allies) vigorously, knowing full well that defeating it was the key to ensuring the safety—indeed, the sanctity—of the British Isles. The British knew that their strategic center of gravity (which has been described in war as "that about which all else revolves") was the English Channel and the ability to control it via sea power. This pursuit led ultimately to one of the most famous sea battles in history, the Battle of Trafalgar in October 1805. Fought off the coast of Spain in the eastern center of the Atlantic Ocean, it brought together two massive battle fleets. Tactically it was notable for the production of Nelson's memorandum on how to fight the battle, which he promulgated just before the fight.

Nelson knew that he would not have clear and instantaneous communication with his nearly forty major warships, and that the fog of war and the probability of heavy weather would make precise command and control impossible. As he said in the memorandum, "Something must be left to chance; nothing is sure in a sea fight." He lays out the basic direction and tactics of the fight, but then includes the most crucial line, one that is often quoted by sailors headed into combat: "In case signals can neither be seen or perfectly understood no captain can do very wrong if he places his ship alongside that of an enemy." That spirit of independence in command, and the resultant tradition of taking action with real initiative, lives on in the U.S. and British navies—and in those of many allied forces—to this day.

On that October morning, the normally roiling Atlantic was strangely calm. Nelson deployed his forces in two long columns, spreading the nearly thirty ships out and bearing down on the Spanish and French fleets, seeking to force them to fight. Nelson was able to drive into the center of the enemy's line. Just before the battle, Nelson wrote out a will and a prayer, which included the words, "May humanity after victory be the predominant feature of the British fleet." He then launched a signal that any British sailor can quote: "England expects that every man will do his duty." He certainly did, and tragically, he was killed by a sniper's bullet a few hours later while he stood on the quarterdeck of his ship, fully exposed to enemy fire and wearing all his medals and decorations, inspiring his men. He died in agony belowdecks in his flagship, HMS *Victory*, as it rocked on the unnaturally calm Atlantic. The battle was a tremendous success, resulting in the capture of fifteen of the French and Spanish fleets' most capable warships. Thus ended the attempts of Napoleon to invade the United Kingdom, demonstrating the "influence of sea power upon history," as the American naval historian Alfred Thayer Mahan described it decades later in his classic work of maritime strategy.

Ironically, the ultimate loser of Trafalgar, Napoleon, eventually ended his life deep in the southern Atlantic. After successfully escaping from his first exile to the Mediterranean island of Elba, he was defeated at Waterloo and sent far, far from Europe: to the tiny, volcanic island of

St. Helena. A vastly diminished figure, Napoleon's life closed in on him, dampening his exuberant demeanor and saddening his small retinue of loyal courtiers. A superb portrait of both the island and his final days is Julia Blackburn's book *The Emperor's Last Island*, which is as much about the island and the ocean as it is about Napoleon. Bonaparte died there in 1821 after six long years in exile on a tiny rock measuring five by ten miles. He spent much of his final years staring endlessly across the waves of the Atlantic, the one venue he could never conquer.

The next chapter of note in the geopolitical history of the Atlantic was the rise of the U.S. Navy, born of necessity in the turbulent years after the revolution. The two principal political parties of the time, Alexander Hamilton's Federalists and Thomas Jefferson's Democratic-Republicans (who, by the way, were *not* the fathers of today's Republican Party; that party devolved from the Whigs and other groups), were on opposite sides of the "big navy" issue. The Federalists wanted a serious seagoing navy, arguing that American interests would be expanding over time and that the simple existence of the Atlantic Ocean would be insufficient to protect the young nation. Jefferson felt that the real expansion of the United States would be to the south and west, and that agriculture, not nautical concerns, would be at the heart of the new nation's business. In essence, they were both right—and thus the U.S. Navy was grudgingly constructed in stops and starts over the several decades following the revolution. The Navy Department was created in the final years of the eighteenth century in time for an undeclared war with France (the so-called Quasi-War, fought largely in the Caribbean from 1798 to 1800).

Despite Jefferson's aversion to relatively big ships, a declaration of war against the United States by the Barbary pirates forced the by then president to launch a series of expeditions to the Mediterranean to deal with pirates preying on U.S. shipping in the first decade of the nineteenth century. In 1803, young, aggressive naval heroes like Commodore Edward

Preble and Lieutenant Stephen Decatur burnished their strong reputations through their campaigns in the Mediterranean, operating from a base on the island of Sicily. Eventually, this foray across the Atlantic ended in victory for the young United States.

Yet despite this outcome and the seemingly obvious lesson that real sea power was necessary to help guard the nation, the Republicans in office decided that a strategy of small ships—gunboats—and coastal forts could be used to protect the Atlantic coastline. Such forts still exist in a chain running all along the eastern Atlantic seacoast of the United States. They proved quite inadequate, of course, during the War of 1812 with Great Britain. It was lucky that the early construction program for six medium-size frigates—lionized in Ian Toll's brilliant book *Six Frigates*— was completed by this point despite the emphasis by the administration on the gunboat-and-fortress strategy.

Soon the Atlantic was again a battleground for the United States and Great Britain, in a war that stemmed from lingering resentments on both sides after the successful revolution and was catalyzed by the boarding of an American warship, USS *Chesapeake*, by sailors from HMS *Leopard* in 1807. The Brits came aboard after firing on an unprepared *Chesapeake* and forcibly removed four sailors suspected of being British deserters (only one of them was proved to be so). This enraged the American public and, coupled with trade restrictions levied by Britain on the neutral U.S. merchant fleet, led to a high level of tension between the two nations. By 1812, events had spun out of control and the United States—with a navy that numbered a grand total of eighteen seagoing warships—declared war on the British Empire, with hundreds of heavy warships and centuries of nautical warfare experience. Fortunately for the United States, the British viewed the War of 1812 as a sideshow, and never devoted a significant level of sea power to prosecuting it. The British executed largely by blockade, while American warships tried to conduct raids on British maritime shipping. A series of small-scale battles on the Atlantic had some surprisingly successful outcomes for the Americans, with battles coming out roughly a draw over the years of the war.

In the end, while good for American morale, the sea battles were not the drivers in determining the overall outcome of the conflict. The United States fared badly in the War of 1812 because of the combination of the effect of the British blockade on U.S. commerce and the successful invasion of the United States by British troops, who gleefully burned the capital of the young nation, Washington, D.C. While American maritime operations in the North were marginally successful, they did not sway the direction of the war. Fortunately for the Americans, the British had larger matters to deal with than their upstart former colonies. Eventually, given other pressing matters globally and war fatigue in Great Britain, the British were content to come to the negotiating table, ending the war and planting the seeds for the "special relationship" that continues to this day (albeit with occasional subsequent periods of tension between the Atlantic cousins).

From the end of the War of 1812 to the Civil War, the Atlantic was relatively peaceful, and the world saw a period of less conflict after the end of the Napoleonic Wars. Nevertheless, a different type of revolution (that of naval technology) was happening at sea, spurred by inventions and ideas flowing from the war years. Navies began the transition from sail to steam and started to apply serious levels of metal armor to the sides of their ships. Instead of smoothbore cannons that had to be brought to bear at extremely close range, rifled gun barrels led to great improvements in range and accuracy. The initial ideas of fire control, or the way in which guns are sighted using optical targeting systems, were developed and implemented. And instead of hammering home a charge with a muzzle loading system (a slow and ponderous process), the use of percussion-fired projectiles emerged—with significant gains in efficiency and rate of fire. Much of the testing and use of these new technologies happened on training ranges created off the Atlantic coasts of both Europe and the United States. While there were outbreaks of warfare in the littoral seas of the Atlantic—the Gulf of Mexico in the Mexican-American War, the Baltic and Black seas in the Crimean War—for the main part of this four-decade period the Atlantic was not the perennial battleground it had been for the preceding three centuries. However, that changed with the advent of the Civil War in the United States.

The Atlantic became a zone of real conflict again in the 1860s as two American battle flotillas, one from the North and the other from the South (quite small by European standards), squared off on the inland lakes and rivers, the littoral and coastal waters, and occasionally the deep waters of the Atlantic Ocean. The key tactic by the North was the immediate installation of a blockade, which it could put in place because it had the advantage of having inherited a preponderance of ships by virtue of the general loyalty of seagoing officers to the Union. As a result of the disparity in the number of ships between the two sides, the South never matched the North on a ship-by-ship basis. Instead, the South pursued a strategy of privateering and the offering of letters of marque, as well as commerce raiding on a selective basis. The Confederacy also tried to procure ships from a generally sympathetic Europe and attempted to convince other nations that the blockade existed only on paper—something that was true for a year or so before the North became more organized and systematic in enforcing it by putting its assortment of more than two hundred ships to sea over time. New technologies from the "ironclad" armored vessels on both sides (such as CSS *Virginia* and the oddly turreted, low-slung Union *Monitor*) and torpedoes (which are called mines today) were on display. Commerce raiding by the South had some impact (especially the morale-raising exploits of CSS *Alabama* under Captain Raphael Semmes), but could not in any sense turn the tide of the war. As was the case ashore, over time the vastly greater industrial might, employable population, and advanced technologies of the Union made the end more or less inevitable. The North prevailed at sea on the Atlantic as it did ashore, and the blockade was crucial in choking off the South's ability to resist. While it mainly supported the North's efforts on land, the Atlantic nevertheless allowed the North to implement a successful war strategy.

In much the same way that new technologies transformed the fight between the North and South during the Civil War, the Industrial Revolution of the nineteenth century also transformed Americans' relationship with the Atlantic. Advances in shipbuilding techniques expanded the zone of competition between nations beyond naval warfare; commerce in and of itself began to be a tool of statecraft. This was manifested at sea in the rise of various shipping lines and individual packet ships. SS *James Monroe* will sail into history as the first vessel to leave on a schedule regardless of wind and weather, and initial shipping lines included the Black Ball Line, the Red Star Line, and the Swallowtail Line, all of which began to become operational in the third decade of the 1800s. These were of course initially sailing ships, usually called clipper ships, and they competed for speed records. One of Donald McKay's clippers, *Lightning*, sailed 436 miles in a day, the single-day longest distance recorded by a sailing vessel, and a record that still stands.*

The net effect of these new technologies gave a certain psychological power to the growing sense that the seas in general were shrinking. This was especially true for the North Atlantic. As steam vessels became more

---

* Martin W. Sandler, *Atlantic Ocean: The Illustrated History of the Ocean That Changed the World* (New York: Sterling, 2008), 324.

commonplace by mid-century, the ocean appeared further reduced, facilitated by the advent of transatlantic telegraph cables that the increasingly big ships were able to place on the sea floor and operate with reliability by the 1860s. Before the cables became fully operational, normal communications had to be transported in a vessel, a voyage of generally ten to fourteen days. When telegraph cables became reliable, a message could flow across the Atlantic within minutes.

Queen Victoria sent a telegram of congratulations to President James Buchanan to open the line, directed to his summer residence in the Bedford Springs Hotel in Pennsylvania. She said that she hoped the link would create "an additional link between the nations whose friendship is founded on their common interest and reciprocal esteem." The president replied, "It is a triumph more glorious, because far more useful to mankind, than was ever won by conqueror on the field of battle. May the Atlantic telegraph, under the blessing of Heaven, prove to be a bond of perpetual peace and friendship between the kindred nations, and an instrument destined by Divine Providence to diffuse religion, civilization, liberty, and law throughout the world."*

Despite these advances, it is worth remembering how challenging the sea remained for mariners. Even a casual student of the Atlantic knows the story of the doomed *Titanic*, the "unsinkable ship" that was lost after hitting an iceberg. Leaving aside the fairly accurate film and its associated doomed love story paralleling the fate of the ship, the sinking remains a cautionary tale of the hubris of man and the capricious nature of the high seas. As I sailed across the north Atlantic in the mid-1990s, almost a century later, the story of *Titanic* was not far from my mind—even in a high-tech, solid-steel, brand-new U.S. Navy destroyer.

---

* "England and America United," *Christian Observer*, Aug. 19, 1858, 130; ProQuest, Web, accessed May 14, 2016, http://www.worldmapsonline.com/kr-1858-wotel.htm.

Following the short but bitter Spanish-American War, which saw a few naval engagements in and around Cuban waters, the next significant set of battles on the Atlantic were those of the First World War. The United States tried to avoid being pulled into the war, but eventually was drawn fully into the conflict. Fortunately, by that point in the nation's history our navy had improved dramatically. This was a direct result of the combined strategic thinking of Rear Admiral Stephen B. Luce and Captain (later rear admiral) Alfred Thayer Mahan and the energy and political advocacy of Theodore Roosevelt. Mahan and Luce conducted their collaboration at the Naval War College in Newport, Rhode Island, and Mahan produced a series of seminal books that used the prism of history to describe the importance of sea power. Mahan became a sort of intellectual mentor to Roosevelt, who became the youngest president in American history in 1901 when an assassin struck down William McKinley.

As president, Roosevelt drove a naval construction program that created a true blue-water navy of powerful battleships and cruisers. He pushed through the creation of the Panama Canal, intervened frequently in Latin America and the Caribbean, and used the emergence of new technologies to improve the sea power capabilities of the United States. Big battleships of 15,000 tons and more were able to speed through the waters at nearly 20 knots—a big improvement over sailing ships or more primitive steam-driven vessels that topped out around 12 to 15 knots—and were armed with massive eight-inch guns. Smokeless powder, greater range, and faster, more accurate torpedoes were also developed. The airplane was emerging in that first decade of the twentieth century, and the first flights in America were pushed by Atlantic winds over the beaches of Kitty Hawk, North Carolina. Roosevelt's policy to "speak softly and carry a big stick" specifically envisioned an oceangoing navy as the ultimate big stick. The massive 100,000-ton nuclear-powered aircraft carrier named after him, USS *Theodore Roosevelt*, today sails proudly with the fleet nickname "The Big Stick." Fair enough.

After the collapse of the complex structure of European alliances in the late summer of 1914, "the lights went out in Europe" and the Atlantic again became a field of maritime battle. Both Britain and Germany possessed powerful fleets centered on capital warships, notably the battleship. Indeed, the construction of the German fleet had been one element that raised British suspicions and concerns—logical enough if the long history of British maritime strategy is considered. Most of the German ships had fairly limited cruising ranges, which further convinced the British that they were designed to attack England and cover an invading force.

As the two massive battle fleets of Great Britain and Imperial Germany each sought to bring a "decisive fleet action" off in their respective favor (geopolitical-speak for destroying an opponent's ability to effectively wage war at sea), the scene of potential battle became the North Sea between the two countries. Given that the British home islands are athwart the exit from the North Sea, the German Imperial fleet was effectively held prisoner throughout the war. The two countries fought a series of inconclusive engagements, including at Dogger Bank in 1915, in the center of the North Sea, and at the more important Battle of Jutland in spring of 1916. Several Atlantic battles also took place in the far South Atlantic off the coast of South America, including the Battle of the Falkland Islands. Despite the actions at sea, the land armies quickly bogged down across the center of Europe and the war turned into a slugging match of attrition on land. This led the Allies, especially the British (who were being bled white ashore), to seek alternatives: they seized on the idea of a maritime campaign in the Mediterranean, the "soft underbelly of Europe." With the urging of Winston Churchill, then a very young first lord of the Admiralty, the British launched the Dardanelles/Gallipoli campaign, as he said, "*totus porcus*," or whole hog. It was a fiasco, described more fully in the upcoming chapter on the Mediterranean. Its tragic human consequences are well depicted in the film *Gallipoli*.

Nevertheless, these actions—fought on the periphery of the central theater of the North Atlantic—were of less strategic importance than the war against shipping waged by both sides. The Germans responded to a British blockade with their own U-boat campaign. They began by attacking British blockading vessels with their U-boats, and seeing the strategic effect, added surface cruisers to the mix of ships conducting attacks. By 1915, the U-boat campaigns had increased in strategic importance, and in May 1916 they sank the merchant liner *Lusitania*, a story sharply told in Erik Larson's *Dead Wake*. The killing of 128 Americans helped pull the United States into the war, although not immediately. The declaration of unrestricted U-boat warfare at the end of 1916 both accelerated the British response and forced the Allies to institute a system of convoys.

The United States' increased participation in the form of troops sent to Europe turned the tide of the war. Using the groundwork in the U.K. built by Admiral William Sims, the Atlantic became a bridge across which flowed war materials, supporting soldiers and Marines, and perhaps most important, trade and commerce that fueled the Allied efforts. It was during the First World War that the idea of the North Atlantic community of nations evolved in the writing of geopolitical commentators like Walter Lippmann, who referred to "the profound web of interest which joins together the western world." As he put it, "Britain, France, Italy, Spain, Belgium, Holland, the Scandinavian nations, and Pan America are in the main one community in their deepest needs and their deepest purposes. . . . We cannot betray the Atlantic community. . . .

What we must fight for is the common interest of the western world, for the integrity of the Atlantic powers. We must recognize that we are in fact one great community and act as members of it."*

Tragically, the United States essentially rejected the construct of an Atlantic community after the First World War, declined membership in the League of Nations (the forerunner to today's United Nations), and embarked on an ill-conceived course of isolationism. As I listened to the overheated rhetoric of the 2016 election campaign roughly a century later, I heard echoes of those misjudgments in the words of Donald Trump, who would seemingly have us turn our backs on the larger world, rebuild walls of protectionism, construct a physical wall between the United States and Mexico, dissolve NATO, and repudiate our linkages with allies around the world. This reflects a certain strain of isolationist DNA that has run through our nation's psychology for two centuries. And frankly, we've seen that movie before in the interwar years, and the world reaped a predictable and terrible harvest in the form of the Second World War. Furthermore, the "great wall" of its time, the Maginot Line constructed by France to protect itself from a resurgent Germany led by Adolf Hitler, was a complete failure.

In the run-up to the Second World War, despite efforts to limit naval construction by treaties, the major world nations all rebuilt their fleets. Collective security died a premature death along with the League of Nations, and fascism began its rise in Germany, Italy, and Spain. Britain and France desperately wanted to avoid another world war, and looked away as Hitler annexed various territories and nations in Europe. Appeasement failed, as it always does, and Germany invaded Poland in 1939. The United Kingdom and France both declared war on Germany,

---

* Bernard Bailyn, *Atlantic History: Concept and Contours* (Cambridge, Mass.: Harvard University Press, 2005).

and Europe was again plunged into war. On the Atlantic, at least, the British had a significant advantage because Germany had not invested in significant capital ships to the degree that it had invested in land forces. This allowed Britain to maintain its independence even after the fall of France in 1940.

Yet even with a relatively small fleet, the Germans were able to strike at British sea power, including sinking both warships and merchant shipping, with their highly capable and technologically advanced U-boats. Even the reconstruction of a strict convoy regime did not stem the losses across the North Atlantic. In addition to the U-boats, German capital warships were engaged in commerce raiding from the northern reaches of the Atlantic down to the coast of South America. By mid-1941, the situation for Great Britain—alone and defiant, but under real threat of collapse—was dire. The U.S. Navy was conducting essentially an undeclared war in the North Atlantic, with Navy destroyers attacking U-boats and torpedoes fired against U.S. ships in turn. When the United States entered the war in earnest after the attack on Pearl Harbor in December 1941, the Battle of the Atlantic was already well under way. Victory at sea in the Atlantic during World War II would turn on the battle to defeat German submarines, and it would be, as the Duke of Wellington said of Waterloo, a very near-run thing.

As the Germans "flooded the zone" with U-boats, the Allies reached back to World War I tactics, techniques, and procedures. The Germans operated in wolf packs, improved their surveillance and targeting ability, and instituted a system of logistics to resupply the raiders at sea from much larger mother submarines. The Allies reinstituted a complex system of convoys, added significant antisubmarine warfare warships to protect them (destroyers and corvettes), and increased the use of new technologies, including surface radar and sound imaging (sonar) to detect the U-boats while submerged. Newer, bigger, and rocket-thrown depth charges were also added to the arsenal of Allied ships to counter the U-boats. U-boat attacks ranged as far as the coast of the United States and deep into the Caribbean. In the summer and fall of 1940, German tactics sank hundreds of thousands of tons of Allied shipping each month, including more than 350,000 tons in October 1940 alone.

Turning the tide after the U.S. entry into the war required cracking the communications code used by Axis powers to target submarines against specific Allied convoys and shipping. It also hinged on improvements in radar and sonar, and the attrition of U-boats, which were difficult to reconstruct as pressures mounted on the European continent. There were also significant operations in Arctic waters as the Allies sought to resupply Russia through northern convoys along the Arctic Circle to Murmansk.

Despite Allied momentum in the Atlantic, the Germans launched a second surge of U-boat attacks across the Atlantic in the spring of 1942, and in May and June of that year managed to sink more than a million tons of shipping. The effects of the attacks eventually peaked in November 1942 with 700,000 tons going down. At the time, Admiral Karl Dönitz had more than three hundred U-boats at play, which he estimated were enough to effectively starve the English people. While the Allies possessed new technologies to combat U-boats, their operators were not experienced, and the Germans had the upper hand. Additionally, a new cipher had been produced and the Allied ability to track the German submarines was again limited. The Allies responded by instituting new tactics, including picket lines to kill U-boats in transit. They also recracked the cipher, and by early 1943 there was improvement (although in March 1943, nearly 700,000 tons were sunk). Two factors were crucial to the Allies' newfound success: first was the Allied ability to more effectively attack U-boats with better technology and tactics; and second was the U.S. industrial machine's production of overwhelming numbers of convoy escort warships. By late spring of 1943, the worst had passed. Despite German hopes of a technological breakthrough of some kind (a new acoustical torpedo, for example), it was clear that the Allies would gradually kill enough U-boats to break the campaign and permit the safe transfer of sufficient U.S. troops to Europe to win the war (alongside the enormously critical Russian campaigns as well). Despite destroying nearly three thousand Allied ships and well over 20 million tons of shipping, in the end the U-boat campaign was not enough.

As Churchill said, "The Battle of the Atlantic was the dominating factor all through the war. Never for one moment could we forget that everything happening elsewhere, on land, at sea or in the air depended ultimately on its outcome. . . . Many gallant actions and incredible feats of endurance are recorded but the deeds of those who perished will never be known. Our merchant seamen displayed their highest qualities, and the brotherhood of the sea was never more strikingly shown than in their determination to defeat the U-boat."* Given that Great Britain needed more than a million tons of food and material weekly, the greatest strategic chance the Germans had to destroy the United Kingdom was to choke it to death. In the end, the battle turned—as battles always do— on a combination of courage, innovation, and communication. The real keys to defeating the U-boats in the Atlantic were longer-range aircraft, radar mounted to the U-boat-seeking aircraft, improvements in depth charges and sonar, British intelligence and code-breaking skills (like Enigma), tactics of avoidance in regard to convoy deployments, and

---

* Winston S. Churchill, *The Second World War*: vol. 5, *Closing the Ring* (Boston: Houghton Mifflin, 1951), quoted in Martin W. Sandler, *Atlantic Ocean: The Illustrated History of the Ocean That Changed the World* (New York: Sterling, 2008), 439.

optical devices like the Leigh Light (a searchlight used in conjunction with radar to help Allied aircraft hunting submarines at night as they surfaced to recharge their diesel batteries).

After the final defeat of Germany and Japan and the end of the Second World War, the United States crucially decided to remain engaged in the world, as opposed to another abrupt withdrawal à la the post–World War I world. The United Nations and the so-called Bretton Woods institutions (the World Bank, the International Monetary Fund) were designed to help ward off another global war. Despite this good news, the Soviet Union emerged in the post–World War II era as a global threat, requiring significant U.S. response and launching what came to be known as the cold war.

This was also the start of my own military career in the mid-1970s, and for the first fifteen years of my seagoing experience I was a true cold warrior, essentially chasing Soviet ships, submarines, and aircraft or being chased by them. These days, given Russia's recent assertive geopolitical behavior in Ukraine, Georgia, Moldova, and Syria, I am often asked, "Are we headed into a new cold war?" The answer is "probably not." I am certainly old enough to remember the cold war, in which I spent a great deal of time on the broad Atlantic tracking Soviet platforms. The cold war was millions of well-trained troops on both sides facing one another across the Fulda Gap in Central Europe; it was two huge battle fleets playing cat and mouse from the High North and Arctic Circle to the bottom of the world off the coast of South America; it was two huge nuclear arsenals on a hair-trigger alert, twenty thousand warheads ready to utterly destroy the world. We are not remotely in that world today, and that is a very good thing, but we do need to be mindful of the geopolitics of the oceans or we risk stumbling back into that late-twentieth-century world.

What was the cold war like in the Atlantic? First and foremost, it was a battle for control—really complete surveillance and the positioning of strategic and tactical assets—in the Greenland-Iceland–United Kingdom (GIUK) gap. This zone of thousands of miles of empty ocean became critical strategically because whichever side controlled it would be able to monitor and channel all the maritime traffic (including subsurface) into and out of the North Atlantic. It therefore controlled the flow of men and material to Europe in the case of a Soviet attack on western Europe. Unlike the Germans in World War II, the Soviets had a huge and capable seagoing fleet; allowing them to break out of northern ports and flow into the GIUK gap would have ceded control over the supply routes to Europe—the precise thing that Germany strove for so mightily with its U-boat fleets.

Thus in the cold war, there was a constant maneuver between the Soviet Union (and its Warsaw Pact allies) and the NATO forces led by the United States for control of the gap. This required significant deployments of U.S. combat power to Iceland, Canada, Denmark, Norway, and of course the United Kingdom itself. Combat power was also stationed at bases in the Northeast of the United States. The operative maritime forces were long-range P-3 Orion antisubmarine warfare aircraft, formidable hunter-killer machines used to find Soviet submarines; nuclear attack submarines of the United States and our allies; satellite coverage of the deep ocean; and occasional deployments of flotillas of destroyers and cruisers (like mine) with significant sonar, torpedo, and other sensors suitable to pursue submarines. The Soviets deployed their ballistic missile submarines (equipped with long-range missiles tipped with nuclear weapons) as well as flotillas of submarines and surface ships. While not exactly crowded up there, it was a "target rich zone" for antisubmarine forces.

The Atlantic was also increasingly a huge trade path for the expansive economies of western (free) Europe and the United States. As the

Europeans moved gradually toward a better state of economic union, it became increasingly clear that this commercial connection across the Atlantic would be vital for the United States as well.

There was a final bloody spurt of combat in the deep southern reaches of the Atlantic Ocean as the twentieth century moved to a close: the Falklands War. In the spring of 1982, over the course of ten weeks, Great Britain and Argentina fought a short, sharp war that cost a thousand lives, sank sixteen ships, and saw more than a hundred aircraft destroyed. It was fought over the Falkland Islands, which had been (and still are) a British protectorate with a British population but are long claimed as the Malvinas Islands by the Argentines. The classic description of the battle from the British perspective is Admiral Sir Sandy Woodward's *One Hundred Days*, his memoir of leading the British flotilla that wrested the islands back from Argentine invaders after a demanding campaign fought as winter drew on in the southern latitudes. While the two nations still disagree over ownership of the islands, another round of violent conflict appears unlikely. The war has been studied by naval strategists and historians and provides a good example of the vulnerability of surface ships to air attack in the era of cruise missiles. As I progressed through my cold war career in the Navy, I would often open up Sir Sandy's remarkable book to help me think through how best to prepare my various at-sea commands for potential combat around the world. It was the final spasm of international violence in the long history of the Atlantic in the twentieth century and, let us hope, the last.

The Atlantic today is, for essentially the first time in its long history, a zone of cooperation and peace from the Arctic Circle to the shores of the Antarctic in the far South. While there are still a few lingering territorial issues to resolve—some African littoral claims, islands in the Caribbean, and the aforementioned Falkland Islands/Malvinas in the South Atlantic—the ocean itself and almost all of its tributary seas are in a relative state of peace. Only the eastern Mediterranean and to some degree the Black Sea present the potential for serious conflict. This is a remarkable change to a body of water that has long been viewed, correctly, as the canvas of war upon which too many admirals have quite enthusiastically painted in blood.

3.

THE INDIAN OCEAN

THE FUTURE SEA

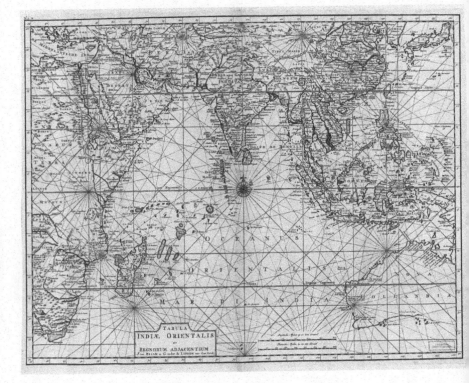

India is the center around which its ocean turns.

Map created by Joannes van Braam, 1726.

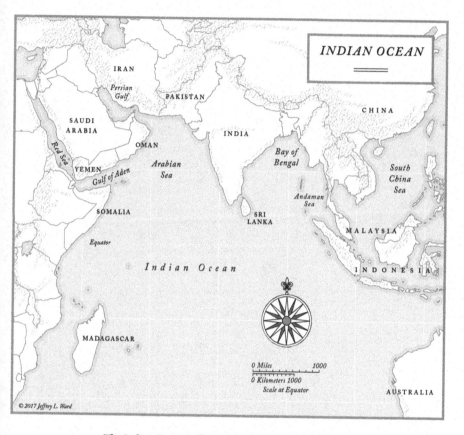

The Indian Ocean will remain a driving economic force
in the world oceans for decades to come.

*T*he Indian Ocean is a vast body of water—20 percent of the world's surface and third in size behind the Atlantic and Pacific oceans. If you were to drop the entire continental United States on top of the Indian Ocean, it would fit quite comfortably within its borders as a sort of very large island. In fact, you could probably squeeze three continental United States into the water space and be able to navigate comfortably around them. Yet with all that space—and a sense of real openness for a sailor—the Indian Ocean itself has relatively less human and geopolitical history than either of the other two major oceans, the Atlantic and Pacific. And it is worth noting that even the tributary seas—the Arabian/Persian Gulf and the Red Sea—have become particularly important in a geopolitical sense only in the post–World War II era with the rise of global shipping and the export of oil from the Gulf region. While that absence of global impact is about to change as India rises in its global ambition and reach, it is still relatively a tabula rasa in geopolitical terms.

I first entered the Indian Ocean from the east, through the Strait of

Malacca, in the mid-1980s. I was operations officer in a brand-new AE-
GIS air defense cruiser, USS *Valley Forge*. AEGIS is a hi-tech, automated
command and control and weapons system that can detect, track, and
shoot down multiple targets simultaneously. Our mission was to head
through the Indian Ocean to the Arabian Gulf at best speed, first taking
on fuel and supplies at Diego Garcia, a small island and British possession in the center of the vast ocean space. As the operations officer, I had
prepared the charts and set the course, and took the first watch as we
drove out between Indonesia and Malaysia and headed toward the Indian Ocean, watching the stars open above us in the unlit sky.

We sped through the long Strait of Malacca after departing Singapore. The night watch was a blur of huge tankers, coastal junks and small
boats, and occasionally other warships flashing their signal lights at us.
Singapore guards the eastern entrance to the Malacca Strait, one of the
busiest in the world, and its multinational character—with Malay, Chinese, Indian, Anglo, and many other residents—makes it a gateway city
in every sense of the word. As you get under way from its busy ports and
take on speed entering the very crowded Strait of Malacca, you have a
sense much like coming through the Strait of Gibraltar into the Mediterranean Sea—yet knowing that unlike the Med, the Indian Ocean is
essentially a vast open seaway.

After that long night watch, I was still on the bridge as the sea and
anchor detail officer of the deck as we came off navigation detail (additional watches set for close-to-land or very dense traffic maneuvering)
and watched the sun rise up as we entered the broad reaches of the Anda-
man Sea off the western coast of Thailand. Suddenly, we were in an
enormous expanse of open water, and we shaped our course for the
southwest and the tiny atoll of Diego Garcia.

Sailing across the Indian Ocean, unlike the Med, a sailor is hit by a
sense of wide-open space, much like the central and western Pacific.

While you occasionally pass other ships, it is a relatively rare moment to be within visual distance of another vessel. As you stand the long, boring watches, you can easily imagine slipping back over the centuries and seeing, across the horizon, not a smokestack rising where the next ship should be, but instead a set of huge sails as one of the great hulls of the British or Dutch East India Company bears down upon you, the classic northeast monsoons and equatorial currents driving it straight at you. Or so it felt to a very young lieutenant who had probably read too many novels set in the nineteenth century by George MacDonald Fraser, C. S. Forester, and Patrick O'Brian.

But actually it *is* apt to think of a trading ship rather than a warship coming over the horizon. For the Indian Ocean's most salient characteristic is that unlike its massive cousins the Atlantic and Pacific, and as particularly distinct from the perpetual battlefield of the Mediterranean, the Indian Ocean has been primarily a zone of trade. Beginning with the earliest Indian civilizations of the Harappans in the Indus Valley nearly three thousand years before Christ, there have been frequent trading ventures along the coast of modern India and Pakistan, across the Red Sea between the Arabian Gulf and Africa, and indeed between the ancient Mediterranean and the early societies of the Indian Ocean littoral. The engine that drove all of this through the long centuries of the age of sail was mother nature: the monsoon winds, the powerful and perpetual wind patterns that drove ships of trade and of war in the days before mechanical propulsion, coupled with the equatorial currents.

In an oddly named document, the *Periplus of the Erythraean Sea*, written by an ancient Greek of Alexandria whose name is lost to the ages, we see evidence of the commercial potential of the Red Sea, the African coast, and the Indian subcontinent as well. This is matched by discoveries from more than two thousand years ago of Greek amphorae, coins, and other physical evidence of trade in the coastal waters of the Indian

Ocean. The ancient sailors knew of and mastered the monsoons, which provided the ability to transit significant distances. These winds are predictable and therefore recordable. In the fall and winter, the northeast monsoon blows down from Asia toward the Indian Ocean, accompanied by currents that can reinforce voyages in that direction. This is reversed in the spring and summer as southwest monsoons blow back from the Indian Ocean toward Asia and the currents reverse themselves. While their appearance is not always guaranteed, it is sufficiently reliable to have powered the ability for trading across the seemingly endless sea relatively early in the course of human development.

Ancient Indian civilizations probably began sailing the waters of the Indian Ocean as early as the fifth century B.C. As the waters of the Tigris and Euphrates rivers emptied into the northern Arabian Gulf, the conflict between the Persian Sassanian Empire and various Indian empires (Harappan, Mauryan, Guptan) flared back and forth. There is little evidence of major sea battles as was the case in the Mediterranean, largely because the geography is so different. The strategic geography of the Indian Ocean is one of vast, open space—essentially one massive littoral, with the exception of the two inland seas, the Arabian Gulf and the Red Sea. While there were sporadic naval engagements across these two areas, most of the major warfare was focused on the land and the holding of territory.

The ancient Egyptians and Greeks traded with the Indian and Persian civilizations, as well as conducting wars. Trade goods included myrrh, incense, ebony, oil, wood, crafts, crops, livestock, and gold and other metals. The brief but impactful life and adventures of Alexander the Great influenced the rise of trade, opening new cities and extending cultural influence, including the founding of the great Egyptian trading city of Alexandria and even ports on the Arabian Gulf. As a young junior officer ashore for the first time in Kuwait, I was fascinated by the ruins of a Greek temple. The Egyptians and the Greeks both traded across the Red Sea, and when Rome conquered Egypt around the time of Christ, Rome became part of the expanding level of trading in the Indian Ocean. Roman Alexandria became a kind of early hub for the trading runs into the Indian Ocean—the goods included textiles from distant China, glass and crafts, and—as was to be a constant driver in Indian Ocean trade—spices, notably black pepper.

At the same time, on the eastern side of the Arabian Gulf, the various Persian empires opened new ports and began both importing and exporting across the Gulf. In addition to the goods above, pearls, carpets, and horses were part of the mix. The strategic value of the Strait of Hormuz, which guards the entrance to the Arabian Gulf, began to emerge. You can drop a plumb line through the more than two millennia since the Persians established forts and seaports to control the narrow choke point to the present day, which continues to occupy the attention of the world.

The Arabian Gulf and its exceedingly narrow opening, the highly strategic Strait of Hormuz: this seemingly perpetual flashpoint of collision between civilizations was much on my mind the first time I sailed through it in 1984. The USS *Valley Forge* was sent to the Arabian Gulf escorting tankers through the dangerous waters of the Gulf. The threat was from missile strikes or even missile boats attacking tankers bound in and out of the Gulf during the long war between Saddam Hussein's Iraq and Iran under the ayatollahs. Our job was an uncomfortable one: to come close aboard to the massive oil tankers—ten times our size by tonnage—and use our highly sophisticated radar and missile systems to defend them from attack.

It was harrowing work, and I stood long, tension-filled watches as a tactical action officer (entrusted with the authority to launch missiles) in the combat information center, the dark heart of the ship, lit only by the glowing radar screens. Every watch had its inevitable call to general quarters, when everyone in the ship was rousted out to battle stations. Our missiles were in the ready-to-fire position, and fortunately we were being backed up by combat aircraft flying from the rolling decks of a U.S. carrier outside the Gulf in the North Arabian Sea. The real threat was from Iran, which was unpredictable in its intent, although somewhat limited in capability. The other problem was the possibility of a mistake or miscalculation by Iraq, which was trying to export oil under the missiles and guns of archenemy Iran. Our job was to keep the sea lanes of communication open by protecting the U.S.-flagged tankers, while also trying to avoid escalating the situation.

Frankly, not much has really changed down through the centuries in the Arabian Gulf. Just as the geography of the Indian Ocean is one of openness and seemingly limitless horizons, the Arabian Gulf is tight, confined, constrained, and shallow—all things a sailor hates. That trade has crossed the Gulf more or less perpetually has not reduced its fundamental danger to those who would fight in its tight spaces.

The Arabian Gulf has its own history, of course. It is intertwined with the larger Indian Ocean, but has been a distinct Islamic sea since that religion emerged on the landmasses around its periphery. From its northern tip, at the Shatt al Arab delta where the waters of the Tigris and Euphrates flow into the Gulf, to the narrow thirty-five-mile Strait of Hormuz at the south, it is just over six hundred miles: the distance from Washington to Boston. Islamic countries surround it, although they are religiously split between Shi'a and Sunni governance. Iran is a Shi'a nation, and Saudi Arabia, Oman, the United Arab Emirates, Bahrain, Qatar, and Kuwait are predominantly Sunni. Iraq, which has only a small aperture on the Gulf through the Shatt al Arab and the port of Basra, is a mix of Sunni and Shi'a, a source of constant turbulence and disturbance.

. . .

As a result of not only religious differences within Islam but also geopolitical rivalry, the Gulf is today a "cold war" lake between the Sunni bloc led by the Kingdom of Saudi Arabia and the Shi'a world led by Iran. Over the past decade, Iranian influence and power in the region have increased, and today Tehran either directly controls or has significant influence in Iraq, Syria, Lebanon, and Yemen. The Gulf itself has become a place of constant cat and mouse between the naval forces of Iran and those of the Sunni Arab states. In the center of it, of course, is the United States and its Fifth Fleet, one of the largest of all the U.S. global fleets. And this Sunni-Shi'a conflict—both geopolitical and religious in character—gives every impression of being capable of leading to outright conflict between the two nations, which face each other, as Arabs and Persians have done for centuries, across the light blue water of the Arabian Gulf.

The Fifth Fleet is based out of Manama, the capital of Bahrain. It is here that the U.S. Navy has a huge command and control structure, headed up by a three-star vice admiral in one of the truly plum jobs today's Navy offers. It is a large command, both ashore, with thousands of sailors and their families living in Bahrain, and at sea, with at least one aircraft carrier and its attendant escorts under operational control at all times. There are also logistic, patrol, and intelligence-gathering ships and aircraft under the command of the admiral's staff.

All of this seems ironic when you consider the history of the Arabian Gulf—a supremely hot, windy, shallow, and resource-poor body of water that slept its way through the millennia until the rise of oil and natural gas. Even as recently as the time of World War II, "cities" like Bahrain, Dubai, and Abu Dhabi were essentially fishing villages. Dhows plied the waters as they had for centuries, doing some listless fishing, pearl diving, and smuggling. All that changed as the world realized that perhaps two thirds of the earth's oil reserves and a third of its natural gas reserves are in the immediate region, both ashore and at sea. The Safaniya offshore oil fields are the largest in the world, and the shallow depth throughout the Gulf (an average depth of only 150 feet) makes it an easy place to work offshore. Today Dubai is one of the first cities of the commercial world, of course, with Abu Dhabi and Doha, the capital of Qatar, not far behind in sophistication and elegance.

The military technology that resulted from the geography and the political competition reflected more than anything the prevailing conditions of wind and current. Ships within the Gulf were typically dhow-like, with lateen (triangular) sails rigged fore to aft. The term "dhow" covers a multitude of vessels, by the way—African, Arab, Persian, and Indo-Pakistani. They can be very small and coastal—much like the classic dhows that ply the Gulf today—or rather large. A key feature is that they were built "carvel style," which is to say the boards were not nailed or bolted together but rather sewn with rope and then caulked. They almost always have a large square stern.

Because of the nature of the dhows, the use of mounted guns came very late, and the idea of using marines—soldiers specialized in maritime warfare—did not emerge. In the broader Indian Ocean, the winds gave impetus to the rise of sailing over rowing very early on in the developmental process and also spurred the building of more square-rigged sailing ships. Overall, the ships of the Indian Ocean were optimized for sailing and trading, not for fighting—although they were certainly used for all three over time.

My own history in the Arabian Gulf is extensive, as is the case for most U.S. Navy sailors of my generation, officer and enlisted. I went there first in the mid-1980s on the tanker escort operation described above. Shortly after my ship departed following a successful series of escorts, our relief—the ill-fated cruiser *Vincennes*—inadvertently shot down an Iranian commercial airliner, killing 290 innocent civilians in what many in the Navy regard as the worst chapter in our cold war history. It was a terrible mistake caused by the high state of tension in the region, the confusion and fog of war, and a belief on the part of the *Vincennes* crew that the aircraft they saw on radar was an Iranian F-14 carrying either bombs or missiles. If there is any incident that illustrates the danger and confusion of the Arabian Gulf, it is the shooting down of Iran Air Flight 688—which to this day is the number the Iranians always use for the same flight (Tehran to Dubai) as a memorial to the victims.

I have pulled into virtually every open port in the Gulf (obviously not into Iran), and each has its own culture and relationship with the U.S. Navy that shapes the visit. The most open and overtly welcoming is Bahrain, where the Fifth Fleet maintains its headquarters. Here our sailors can enjoy not only first-class hotels and the chance for a cold beer, but also the support of a fully operational U.S. military base with medical, dental, Navy exchange stores, recreation, and all other amenities. Liberty in the United Arab Emirates is a different experience and has evolved over time. Initially, the vast majority of ships were confined to a restricted area in a huge port called Jebel Ali, located in between Dubai and Abu Dhabi. But over time the restrictions have been eased, and today our sailors enjoy themselves in both metropolitan areas.

For me, one of the strange enjoyments of the Gulf is being out at sea, even on the hottest of summer days, when the temperatures can rise to more than 120 degrees and the steel decks nearly glow with latent heat. I always enjoyed going for a (brief) run around the decks, almost like running in a sauna, and the normally flat calm of the turquoise waters is beautiful and quiet. But the operational tempo is the hardest of any spot in the Indian Ocean because of the complexity. At all times, the watch stander is thinking and worrying about Iranian naval ships and aircraft, with which we have a tense relationship (although generally professional). Since the signing of the nuclear arms agreement with the Iranians, there have been some untoward incidents that may be a sign of hard-liners in Tehran trying to ratchet up pressure and perhaps even sink the agreement. Too soon to tell, but it seems clear that the Arabian/Persian Gulf will continue to be a fault line in international geopolitics, and a source of tension that bleeds into the larger Indian Ocean.

All of which brings us to the earliest and darkest forms of trading and commerce along the Indian Ocean and its tributary seas: slavery and piracy. The movement of slaves was a brisk trade throughout the recorded history of the region, persisting to the present day. The transport of slaves from various conquests was part of the shipping routes of the region, including slaves taken by capturing ships at sea in acts of piracy. While slavery and piracy have diminished somewhat, both still exist in parts of the Indian Ocean, albeit with modern tools and sophistication, something I learned a great deal about as the NATO commander charged with eliminating piracy along the eastern coast of Africa, which I will discuss in depth below.

It is worth noting that Indian Ocean trade in the sixth and seventh centuries A.D. dropped dramatically as several of the key trading empires declined in power and influence. Both the Sassanian Persians and the Guptans of India—who had attempted to control trade along with Chinese and Malay entities—shrank significantly in population. This may have been partly due to a global epidemic (paralleled by the bubonic plague in Europe), sometimes called the Plague of Justinian, a disease carried by fleas and rats and well known on ships.

But the energy from the east and west of the Indian Ocean would again reignite the trading regime with vigor. Both from Arabia and from China, the pressure for trading began to put life back into the commerce across the broad ocean. Both gold and ivory were important, as well as the hard woods of Africa; but the rising trade in African slaves was a powerful driver as the religion of Islam appeared, the Arabian caliphate expanded, and much of the Indian Ocean littoral, particularly in the west, became part of the Islamic world. Trade between Arabs, Persians, and the Chinese of the Tang and Song dynasties expanded and drove the trading patterns through the thirteenth century. These included formal trading arrangements, embassies, protected ports, and many advanced mechanisms to expand relations. It also included the expansion of Islam to the littoral of the region, albeit much more slowly in Southeast Asia and much of what is today India. Ports like Calicut and Khambhat became global centers. All of this progressed without significant warfare, at least at sea. But looming from the west was the coming force of Europe as it entered the Age of Discovery and exercised its appetite for trade as well.

Vasco da Gama was a stocky and emotional man of middle-class origin, born around 1460 in southwestern Portugal. He undertook perhaps the most epic and impactful voyage of exploration in world history in 1497–98 when he led four Portuguese ships down the Atlantic coast of Africa (building on decades of exploration led by Prince Henry the Navigator). He then continued into uncharted waters of the South Atlantic, sailed around the Cape of Good Hope at the bottom of Africa, between the island of Madagascar and Mozambique on the east African coast, up the east coast of Africa to an Indian Ocean port called Malindi, and on to the southwestern tip of India, landing at Calicut in the spring of 1498.

The entire length of the voyage was at the time the longest conducted out of sight of land, and was longer than sailing around the earth at the equator. Da Gama returned to Portugal in 1499 to much acclaim, although overall his record is sullied by a variety of massacres attributed to him in India (including burning alive a boatload of hundreds of Muslim pilgrims, among them women and children, who were begging for mercy and posed no threat to his expedition). He returned to India on another expedition several years later, where he was still unable to fulfill his fundamental mission of obtaining a treaty for trade. He eventually died during a third and final voyage to India in 1524.

What began as a spice trade, initially based on pepper and cinnamon, soon expanded as the Portuguese consolidated their head start to India, with England, France, and the Netherlands not far behind. The key for the Portuguese was finding an independent path to the spices, one not dependent on crossing the dangerous Mediterranean and going overland to the Red Sea. This seagoing route was perfect for a small, seafaring nation like Portugal, and allowed it to break the monopoly over the spice trade heretofore held by Venetian, Arabian, and Persian traders. Although there were frequent diplomatic missteps (including by da Gama himself) based on simple ignorance of the cultural mores of the Indian trading culture, gradually the Portuguese were able to insinuate themselves into the trading patterns of the western Indian Ocean.

The nation that soon followed up as more nautical knowledge became available and ships' capabilities improved were the Ottomans, seeking to create a Muslim protectorate over large portions of the Indian Ocean littoral. This was facilitated by the Ottoman conquest of Egypt in the early 1500s, which gave them convenient access to the length of the Red Sea. Soon the Portuguese and the Ottomans were in full competition, each seeking exclusive trading treaties, bases for logistic support, and engaging in combat where they could bring maritime forces to bear. This was difficult for the Ottomans as their sea power was optimized for the more restricted coastal waters of the Mediterranean. In the mid-1500s, the Ottomans launched a fairly large fleet of more than fifty vessels to attack Portuguese positions around the Indian Ocean with a particular focus on Hormuz at the entrance to the Arabian Gulf, sailing this time from bases in present-day Iraq at the northern end of the Gulf. They were crushingly defeated, but the rivalry continued for another century until finally the Ottomans essentially withdrew and the Portuguese turned to face new rivals.

Their legacy at this point included introduction of a kind of patois of Portuguese and local dialects that was used for commerce (often referred to as Portuguese Creole), adapting their ships to long ocean voyages through new sailing technologies, and fusing the power of the state to the commercial interest of quasi-private companies in fairly creative ways. The latter model—of commercial and state interests blending—was raised to its highest level over the next several centuries in the Indian Ocean.

We see this first with the British East India Company in 1600, followed very shortly by the Dutch East India Company. Both used the model developed by the Portuguese as their basis, and both companies existed to create commercial trading opportunities that led to state power. The Dutch began to focus on the eastern parts of the Indian Ocean, including what is today Sri Lanka and parts of Indonesia. They also established a foothold at Cape Town at the southern tip of Africa. Their initial product offerings were traditional spices (pepper, cloves, mace, cinnamon, nutmeg) and, increasingly, coffee. The British, on the other hand, began with a focus on gaining control of as much of the Indian landmass as they could. They built forts and created a string of bases around the periphery of the country in the 1600s and on into the early 1700s.

Despite the increasing level of imperial competition between the Portuguese, Dutch, and British, the fundamental trade routes remained largely in local hands. The Chinese, who had no appetite for colonization and no significant deepwater military capability, were nonetheless involved in all aspects of the trade as well—often providing loans, cooperative arrangements, chandlery, and posted both in China and other parts of Southeast Asia along the trading routes. Each of the imperial competitors created its own string of bases—the Dutch, for example, centered their operations in Batavia (now Jakarta), but with robust capability in Cape Town and present-day Sri Lanka.

While there were occasional indigenous challenges, for example from the Yaarubi regime in Oman, the power of the two increasingly dominant imperial powers—Britain and the Netherlands—gradually consolidated. The big winner as the eighteenth century ended, of course, was Great Britain. Having essentially seized control of Oman, Kenya, and India, the British went on to create a British lake in the center of the Indian Ocean. Neither Portugal nor the Netherlands was strong enough to face imperial Britain, and the defeat of Napoleon in the early 1800s ultimately limited France's ability to play a global role. As a result, much of the maritime history of the nineteenth century in the Indian Ocean is Britain's, upon whose empire the sun never set "because God cannot trust an Englishman in the dark."

While it is certainly fair to say the Indian Ocean became a sort of British lake, it is also quite true that the gaze of the British was ashore, not at sea, once they had established dominance over their imperial and local rivals. There was wide realization on the part of the British that they needed to control the sea lanes to control India, and every English viceroy sent to India reiterated to the crown his need for sea power to ensure dominance. The challenges were from France early in the 1800s, and to some degree from the Dutch, as well as concerns over piracy and slave trading. Each was overcome through a combination of ruthless conquering of needed bases, intricate systems of alliances and commercial trading agreements with littoral states and local rulers, and new technologies—especially the switch from sail to steam power and the completion of the Suez Canal by 1869.

. . .

THE SUEZ CANAL is an interesting place for history buffs. There were ancient attempts by both the Egyptians and the Persians to construct small waterways through the Sinai desert and connect the two ancient waters of the Mediterranean and Red seas. It is possible the Persians successfully did so under Darius, but it is difficult to say with certainty. Napoleon expressed a high degree of interest in such a project before his hopes of global empire were thwarted. It was the French who took on the canal as a commercial venture in cooperation with the Egyptian government, interestingly originally vociferously opposed by the British. But by the time it was complete, the British understood its value and eventually took it over as a "protectorate" for decades. In an interesting bit of nautical showmanship, when the canal was to be first opened to traffic, the French empress Eugénie was scheduled to lead a host of international ships down the Canal with the French ship at the lead. But to the horror of the Egyptians and the outrage of the French, a British warship managed to steal a sail on everyone by maneuvering its way through the assembled fleet in the course of the night without lights and managed to be the first ship through the canal—thus presaging the eventual British takeover. The captain was officially reprimanded and unofficially commended.

My first trip of the many I have done both north and south through the canal was in the mid-1990s. I was a relatively inexperienced captain and just thirty-eight years old in command of a 9,000-ton Navy destroyer with a crew of three hundred. I did all the reading I could on the protocols of the canal, and knew that we would have to depend a great deal on the "professional" pilots (former Egyptian naval officers) who would guide us through using their local knowledge. I was told to be prepared to offer some baksheesh, a sort of cross between a gift and a bribe. The usual thing was to offer up multiple cartons of cigarettes. Foolishly, I decided to spare us the expense of a hundred dollars in smokes and offered the pilot instead the "highly coveted" baseball cap of my ship and a hearty handshake. He went immediately into a huge pout, unfolded a canvas stool, and sat passively on the bridge. We were on our own.

Fortunately, my navigator was a brilliant young officer, Lieutenant Robb Chadwick, and he had a crack team of quartermasters who had spent a month learning everything there was to know about the canal and devouring the various charts and descriptions of it, called "Sailing Directions." They managed to get us to the midpoint at the Great Bitter Lake, where the north- and southbound traffic divides up to allow passage, as the canal can handle only one stream of ships at a time. As we maneuvered to our anchorage, the Egyptian pilot finally roused himself and began insisting that we come hard to starboard to a completely different anchorage from the one we had been assigned. Thinking he must know what he was talking about, I started to bring the ship in that direction. Lieutenant Chadwick literally threw himself between me and the pilot and said, "Captain, if we keep heading there we are going to go aground." My choice: follow the advice of the local pilot and fifty-year-old expert, or that of my twenty-six-year-old Annapolis grad on his first voyage through the Canal? I ordered all stop, swung the rudder to port, and headed to where Robb indicated and dropped the hook. The pilot lost his temper and stormed off the bridge. In the ensuing calm, Robb showed me precisely on the chart where we would have gone aground under the direction of the pilot.

Had we gone aground, I would have been a retired Navy commander and probably doing something very different with my life. It was one of those pivot points in life that flashes across the screen when a single decision establishes a very different trajectory depending on the choice we make. So many of our lives and careers depend on others, and very often they are the people who work for us and whom we are mentoring. As an aside, in a cosmic way I returned the favor on 9/11, when I invited then-commander Robb Chadwick to pay an office call on me in the Pentagon. He stepped away from his desk in the Navy Intelligence Center to spend time with me, and thus was out of his office when the plane crashed more or less directly into it. All of his office mates were killed, several of them good friends to us both. Robb and I have had a close relationship since.

It strikes me that the Suez Canal is above all a symbol of the power of connections—between ancient seas, civilizations, rivals, and friends. It became in the nineteenth century a vital interest of Britain's and continued to be so essentially through the late 1960s when the British withdrew their forces from "east of Aden" after Indian independence. With the speed and mobility that the canal provided the mid-nineteenth-century Royal Navy and the East India Company, the British were able to increase their domination over the Indian Ocean.

Indeed, throughout the nineteenth century, the British avoided the kind of major set-piece battles that we see in places like the Mediterranean, but were kept quite busy controlling their rivals, suppressing individual revolts and uprisings (the so-called small wars, although no war feels small when you are in it), weeding out the slave trade, and trying to stop piracy. The heart of nineteenth-century piracy was in the waters between the South China Sea and the Bay of Bengal—essentially in and around the Strait of Malacca. Here again we see the strategic importance of geography, which allowed pirates the ability to build safe havens (much as we will see in the Caribbean) from which to operate beyond the reach of deeper-hulled warships. By 1824, the British and Dutch had reached an accommodation that included a stated intent to work together to reduce piracy and eliminate slavery.

This proved to be no easy task, as many of the pirate regimes were backed by city-states and countenanced by local rulers who would take a cut of the profits. Some operated from fairly large vessels that, when gathered together, could threaten any commercial ship and even some small warships. Some of the pirate fleets boasted hundreds of vessels of varying sizes and required real application of shipboard firepower to suppress. Hence these sea routes continued to be very dangerous throughout the region.

During this period, the British and the Dutch consolidated their colonial control of huge swaths of population and land. All of this had an extraordinary effect on the colonized populations, a phenomenon that is best understood on the British side—the rise of the culture of British India is still part of the DNA of modern India. Reading the superb novels of George MacDonald Fraser, four of which are set in and around India during this period, is not only entertaining but also reasonably historically accurate. Centered on a British officer named Flashman, they show the dark side of colonization in vivid anecdote. The first of the series, *Flashman*, is set in India and today's Pakistan/Afghanistan region as Flashman is an appointed official with the East India Company in 1839. Over the next twenty years, he goes to sea to rescue his wife from pirates (*Flashman's Lady*) and survives the Sepoy Mutiny (*Flashman in the Great Game*), among other adventures. I have read them all over the years, and for a view of how disturbing the colonization of the Indian Ocean littoral must have been for the indigenous populations, they are hard to beat.

The strategic motif of trade as the central focus continued throughout the nineteenth century, with coffee and spices continuing but with the additional inclusion of sugar, cotton, tea, and rubber feeding back to the Industrial Revolution in Europe. The critical ports and territories gradually accrued to the British: Kenya, Somaliland, Sudan, Egypt, Oman, Bahrain, Qatar, Kuwait, Iraq, Mauritius, India, and of course Singapore guarding the gates to the east. France had hung on to a scattering of islands including Madagascar, Réunion, and the Comoros, while Portugal still held Mozambique, East Timor, and the trading port of Goa on the Indian mainland. The Dutch held what is today Indonesia, styled as the Dutch East Indies. Even Italy found its way into the colonial scramble around the Indian Ocean with the acquisition of Eritrea and Somalia.

Throughout the nineteenth century, the advent of new technologies—notably the steam engine—coupled with the opening of the Suez Canal to vastly increase the movement of humans around the Indian Ocean. Indians and Chinese moved back and forth between their regions, and smaller groups of Malays, Indonesians, and Filipinos were moved as low-cost labor: slaves by another name, living under brutal conditions of indenture. Such workers were used on plantations under conditions of complete penury to the benefit of colonial businesses.

In addition to the movement of indentured laborers, another dark side of the trade routes across the Indian Ocean during the nineteenth century was the movement of opium. It was produced in India and Java to feed the markets of China, a trade encouraged by the colonizing powers. This led to the 1839 First Opium War between Great Britain and the Qing dynasty of China. Both Singapore and Hong Kong were central to the highly profitable opium trade.

As the century concluded and the European world headed toward the "dimming of the lights" with the coming of World War I, the changes across the entire Indian littoral were immense. Most important were the movement of workers and the entrenchment of significant colonial regimes throughout the region. Surprisingly, there had not been an outbreak of major great-power combat, and World War I would have little lasting effect on the Indian Ocean—it would be as distant thunder. But of course what lay ahead for the region was the Second World War and its attendant effects—violence, especially on the northeast corner of the

Indian Ocean in Burma and down the Malay Peninsula—but above all the end of colonization.

As World War II loomed on the horizon, British planners understood the vulnerability of the Indian Ocean to Japanese attack, either overland or via the sea. But they thought Singapore would hold, preventing easy maritime access, and the huge distances and the need for Japan to subdue and hold China seemed to mitigate the overall threat. It is easy to understand why the British thought Singapore—the "Lion City"—would hold out against the Japanese onslaught. It has strong geography that ought to favor a determined defender (it lies on an island, for example), and at that point in the conflict, the British still believed that their military simply had better discipline, skills, and technology than the Japanese. They were terribly wrong, and the city fell into Japanese hands on February 15, 1942. It was held until the surrender of Japan in 1945.

I first sailed into Singapore in the mid-1980s, and even then it was a clean, technologically advanced, multicultural city, which used a combination of strong social networking, enlightened racial and educational policies, strict policing, economic incentives, and political control to build a powerhouse city-state out of virtually nothing but raw geography and human capital. Under an inspired leader, Lee Kuan Yew, Singapore has emerged as a showcase city, easily ranking at the top of all social and economic indices in Asia and in the top ten in the world. As I walked around the city looking for a place to play squash (and found one at the "American Club"), I was struck by the incredible contrast with every other major Asian city at that time. It was scrupulously clean, full of public gardens, signed in English (the lingua franca of this most multicultural city-state), and very, very law abiding. Like most tourists of that time, I went to Raffles Bar (named for Sir Stamford Raffles, the founder of the trading post which evolved into modern Singapore) and had a too sweet Singapore sling, a sappy cocktail.

But what is really striking about the city is its geopolitical position. Sitting astride the most important shipping strait in the world, defended by water on all sides, blessed with a fine dockyard and a now-powerful military, Singapore is a good country to have on your side. The United States has a very close relationship with the highly professional Singapore military, and my work with them in the Arabian Gulf on the maritime side over the years left a deep impression on me as to the seriousness with which they take their defense. Given their enviable position, they need a strong military and strong friends as well.

Since that first visit, I have returned to Singapore many times. The most illuminating visit was in the mid-2000s when I served as the senior military assistant to Secretary of Defense Donald Rumsfeld. We went to see the former prime minister, Lee Kuan Yew. It is hard to describe how he is viewed there—sort of George Washington and Abraham Lincoln together, with a little Franklin Delano Roosevelt thrown in. At that point in time he was in his eighties and Secretary Rumsfeld was in his seventies. A former prime minister and nation founder meeting with a two-time secretary of defense, White House chief of staff, and ambassador and having a long cordial conversation. To see these two lions in winter, in the City of Lions, spar about the world was extraordinary. What they agreed upon was that it takes discipline, vision, and some tough decisions to build something lasting. Hard to argue with that, and the nation of Singapore is a pretty accurate reflection of that approach. And the food was a lot better than on my first trip.

All of that modernization came long after the fall of Singapore to the Japanese in 1942, which opened up the broader Indian Ocean to the Japanese war machine. Their naval planners were beginning to think about campaigns—both overland and at sea—that would cut India itself off from the British Empire. Meanwhile, both Italy and Germany mounted maritime campaigns throughout the northern Indian Ocean.

While the Italian forces, operating mainly off the coast of East Africa, were soon neutralized, the Germans continued significant U-boat operations throughout the war. In addition to the German submarines, Nazi surface ships—including the pocket battleship *Graf Spee*—conducted commerce raiding. The strategic theory was to cut off the sea lanes of communication between Britain and its colonies; destroy the general commerce in the region, which benefited not only the United Kingdom but also France and the Netherlands; prepare for further land operations; and conduct harassment against Australia. There were much fewer significant fleet-wide actions in the Indian Ocean than there were in the central and western Pacific, which was the main theater of war, but there were literally hundreds of single-ship and small-group combat operations throughout the region. Overall, operations were a draw, with both the Axis and the Allies having ships "at sea and operational" throughout the conflict.

FOLLOWING WORLD WAR II, the key geopolitical change in the Indian Ocean was the essential departure of the United Kingdom. The Indian Ocean had been largely a British protectorate for more than two hundred years as a result of the "jewel in the crown" of empire, the Imperial Raj of India. The ocean had been ringed by British colonies in East Africa, South Asia, and the western side of Southeast Asia. In today's world it is hard to imagine the power and scope of the British Empire globally in the Victorian era through the end of World War II. By 1968, Britain—which had never truly recovered as an imperial power after the war—made a strategic decision to withdraw "east of Aden" on the southwestern tip of the Arabian Peninsula. In practical terms this meant that a strategic vacuum would be created, just as the cold war began to truly unfold.

Nature abhors a vacuum, and when the British left the waters of the

Indian Ocean, the fleets of the United States and the Soviet Union arrived. Both nations decided to increase the levels of their patrols throughout the region, although their objectives differed. The United States wanted to maintain stability in a vast and now relatively ungoverned part of the global maritime commons; protect the flow of tankers providing needed oil to and from the Arabian Gulf; and ensure a ready, maritime-based supply of strategic minerals and materials—chromium, rare earths, cobalt, manganese, copper. For Russia (which had its own supply of oil from its huge reserves), the objective was first simply to compete with the United States for political influence among the nations of the region and to maintain a strategic partnership with India, which it saw as a potential counterbalance to NATO.

Although today we think instinctively of the Arabian Gulf in terms of the supply of oil globally, it is important to remember that all of those nations did not become major producers until the mid-twentieth century. As other sources of oil ran down, the percentage of oil held in the Gulf region, Iran, and Iraq soared (all this before the advent of a great deal of offshore oil and the use of fracking, of course). This made the region of extreme importance strategically, with tankers departing the Gulf many times an hour and the nations of the region developing OPEC to control the price and quantity of oil on the market. All of this contributed to the strategic importance of the region and in a maritime context to the vital protection of the Gulf region. American war planners were concerned that the Soviet Union might make a play to drive south or at a minimum to achieve warm-water ports on the Indian Ocean—something that history has not shown persuasively to be the case, although it was a commonly held view at the time.

Of note, by the early 1970s neither the United States nor the Soviets had any actual naval bases in the region. The Soviets had a treaty with Iraq that gave them access at Basra, and the United States maintained a very small naval force in Bahrain (only three warships and a generally unhappy two-star admiral, pondering the reasons for his exile). As the importance of the flow of oil increased, the nations in the region began to think about how to improve their geographic and strategic positions. And both nations sought to marginalize China, which for two millennia had been an important player in the Indian Ocean but which neither the United States nor the Soviet Union wanted to see in the region then.

The United States throughout this period cooperated closely with Saudi Arabia and Pakistan (as it does today, of course) as well as with Iran under the shah. Both nations received billions of dollars of training and equipment from the United States (paying for almost all of it from their oil revenues). The United States also exploited the British-owned island in the center of the Indian Ocean, Diego Garcia, where U.S. engineers in the early 1970s built a huge airstrip, massive fuel tanks, significant docks, housing, communications, and intelligence-gathering facilities.

In the mid-1980s, about a decade later, I sailed into the lagoon at Diego Garcia, not quite sure what to expect. A standing joke in the Navy among junior officers was that if you screwed up badly enough, you'd be sent to either Adak, Alaska, or Diego Garcia in the Indian Ocean. From what I had heard, I would have requested Adak. But when we arrived ashore, I found an intriguing and not uncomfortable environment: nice barracks ashore, primitive but acceptable golf and tennis facilities, a small but decent officers' club, and a place of incredible natural beauty. That it was the strategic hub of the Indian Ocean didn't dawn on me, but I sure enjoyed hitting some tennis balls after a few long and boring weeks at sea sailing from Singapore.

The Soviets, on the other hand, worked to conduct frequent "show the flag" cruises throughout the region—to Sri Lanka, Iraq, Iran, Yemen, Pakistan, and of course to India. Over time, the Soviets were able to develop cooperation agreements with India, Yemen, and—on the east coast of Africa—Somalia. As a result, they had access to ports for their warships, with supplies and logistics as well. All of this in accordance with the Mahanian doctrine of sea power both nations followed.

Both nations competed for influence and control over two perceived "treasure houses," as Soviet leader Leonid Brezhnev called them: the energy and oil of the Gulf and the strategic minerals of sub-Saharan Africa. The breakdown for the United States was the collapse of the shah's regime in Iran and the rise of the Ayatollah Khomeini's government, which truly, madly, deeply, hated the United States. This effectively closed off one side of the Arabian Gulf (this was the time we switched to calling it "Arabian Gulf" instead of what we had historically called it, the "Persian Gulf"). It also put a bitter enemy in effective control of the entrance to the Gulf, the Strait of Hormuz.

The Soviets had several successes in this period as well. The Soviet adventures in southern Africa, both in Angola and Mozambique, were initially successful (especially with Cuban troops fighting alongside the Soviets in Angola) and two new client states emerged. And when Somalia and Ethiopia went to war in 1977, the Soviets shifted sides and pocketed a strong relationship with Ethiopia (more than 30 million people) at the cost of betraying the smaller nation of Somalia. Yemen also became a Marxist state. Suddenly, the only major client of the United States was Saudi Arabia, and the Soviets were picking up relationships, bases, and political support around the rest of the Indian Ocean littoral. As a theater of political cold war, the Indian Ocean looked very much like a Soviet win.

In the complex geopolitics of today's world, perhaps the two most dangerous state-on-state confrontations exist around the littoral of the Indian Ocean and the Arabian Gulf. We discussed the Arabian Gulf "twilight war" between Saudi Arabia and Iran earlier in this chapter, but the most dangerous of all—because of the availability of nuclear weapons—is the cold war between Indian and Pakistan. The British departure from the South Asian subcontinent after World War II eventually led to the division of that vast region into three nations: Pakistan, the second most populous Muslim nation in the world; India, which will soon overtake China as the world's most populous state (and possessor of the third largest Muslim population, by the way); and Bangladesh. The Indian-Pakistani hatreds are deep-seated and are partly religious, partly cultural, and partly geographic (with the flash point of the disputed Kashmir region at their tactical heart).

While the divisions between India and Pakistan seem insurmountable at the moment, there is at least a ray of hope in the conversations between Nawaz Sharif of Pakistan and Narendra Modi of India. The United States has a vital interest (as does the entire world) in avoiding a nuclear confrontation between these two states. While their disputes do not typically unfold at sea, it is entirely possible that an incident could cause a flare-up at any point. This is the most dangerous aspect of the Indian Ocean, which has been generally a commercial and not a warfighting body of water.

One tragic incident that illustrates that not all problems are man-made was the devastating tsunami that struck much of the Indian Ocean littoral in 2004 on the day after Christmas. A 9.0 undersea earthquake off the west coast of Indonesia caused it, and the resulting tidal waves almost instantly killed well over 200,000 people. Some estimates of total deaths rise to nearly 300,000, concentrated in Indonesia, Sri Lanka, India, and Thailand. The waves were as high as one hundred feet in places as they crested across densely populated portions of those nations. I had only recently assumed duties as the senior military assistant to the secretary of defense, and we quickly assembled a crisis action team in the Pentagon to see what the Department of Defense could do.

We put a superb U.S. Marine general, Lieutenant General Rusty Blackman, in charge of the response, and he swiftly marshaled the huge logistic, humanitarian, and medical capability of the department. Conducting daily video-teleconferences with the secretary, he was able to get U.S. hospital ships, big-deck amphibious vessels, and aircraft on scene and dispensing aid and assistance to the various devastated populations. As I watched night after night in the command center in the Pentagon the videos of our sailors, Marines, airmen, and soldiers wading into water to rescue people, moving huge bags of relief supplies, and caring for the wounded and the sick, I was deeply moved. We spend a great deal of time in the military conducting lethal combat operations—that is who we are. But we also can deploy soft power in massive ways that can make a real difference in the world. And the result—a changed view of our nation—is so often the way we can create real security over the long haul. In some ways, the deployment of our massive, 60,000-ton hospital ships, *Mercy* and *Comfort*, can do more for our security than the combat cruises of our nuclear aircraft carriers. Both have a role, and our ability to balance both hard power (combat) and soft power (disaster relief, medical assistance, diplomacy) has been called "smart power." An apt term, and it came home to me in the Indian Ocean during those terrible weeks after a quarter of a million people died on the television screens before our eyes.

Piracy was part of the mission set I inherited in 2009 when I became the Supreme Allied Commander for NATO. The twenty-eight nations of NATO had collectively voted to join the effort to stop the worst of the piracy that was emanating from the largely ungoverned space of what had once been Somalia. Fueled by khat, a soporific drug they would chew, Somali ex-fishermen would mount skiffs and set out to take down large container ships by scaling the sides, overpowering the crew, and then sailing the ships into Somali anchorages and demanding ransoms of millions of dollars. As I took over the mission, there were nearly twenty ships and more than two hundred mariners held hostage, and the number of assaults was rising.

The international community cannot agree on much, but on the view of piracy as an ancient scourge that is punishable by any sovereign nation there is universal agreement. Therefore, my task was to gain additional resources and warships from a broader coalition than just the twenty-eight NATO nations. We cast a wide net, including some traditionally non-NATO-aligned countries: Russia, China, India, Pakistan, and Iran all responded in a positive way—either sending ships, participating with intelligence, or at a minimum providing logistic and refueling support. This was quite unprecedented: a grand nautical coalition that included the United States and Canada from North America, more than thirty European nations, and five aforementioned countries that do not wake up in the morning looking for ways to cooperate with NATO.

Thus we saw in the Indian Ocean a good example of a strategic approach that provides a means to cobble together nations that are normally at one another's throats. That we could in the process significantly knock down piracy was equally good. By 2013, as I was departing NATO, we had just a couple of ships and a small handful of mariners still being held. The bottom had been knocked out of the piracy business, and many of the pirates had been apprehended and remanded to justice. Not a single ship has been pirated at sea off the coast of East Africa in the past couple of years. Partly, this is because of progress ashore as well, fueled by the good work of the European Union. But in terms of reducing piracy in a region of the world that has seen it often, this is a rare good story of coordination at sea, and full of lessons for seeking other zones of cooperation on the world's oceans.

. . .

To summarize: Throughout this book and in our world, discussions about maritime issues tend to focus on the Atlantic Ocean, with its attached Mediterranean Sea; and the Pacific Ocean, with the South China Sea. There are endless discussions about the emerging conflicts, the flow of refugees, and competition over vital hydrocarbons, as well as the geopolitical impact of the two "major oceans." Yet the twenty-first century will be more about the Indian Ocean than either of the other two—and the sooner we fully realize that in the United States, the better.

We cannot forget the facts of the case: The Indian Ocean, while admittedly smaller than the Atlantic or the Pacific, consists of nearly a quarter of the waters on the globe, especially when one counts its major subordinate seas, the Red Sea and the Arabian Gulf. Across its vast expanse move 50 percent of all shipping and containers and 70 percent of all oil, making it quite literally the crossroads of globalization. Nearly forty nations border it, with more than a third of the world's population. And it is the beating heart of the Islamic world, with Pakistan, Indonesia, Bangladesh, Iran, Saudi Arabia, Egypt, and the Gulf States all having coastal access to the Indian Ocean. More than 90 percent of the world's Islamic population is in this massive catchment basin.

And it is highly militarized and constantly in a high state of tension. The highest potential nuclear conflict in the world today is between Pakistan and India—two huge, capable, professional, and nuclear-capable militaries. Iran is an adventurist state with an innovative and battle-trained military force. Many of the other nations along the littoral have internal conflicts and significant chaos along their borders, particularly in East Africa. Piracy, while reduced over the past several years, remains a threat both along the coast of East Africa and in the Strait of Malacca connecting the Indian Ocean with the Pacific.

The history of the Indian Ocean certainly does not inspire confidence in the potential for peaceful governance in the twenty-first century. As we have seen, throughout the centuries its trade routes have inspired competition and conflict since East met West with the arrival of Vasco da Gama in 1497. The British conquest of India and the commercial muscle of the British East India Company dominated the region for a time in the nineteenth century, but the breakup of the Ottoman Empire and great-power maneuvering during World War II led into the long twilight of the cold war when American, Soviet, Pakistani, and Indian vessels played cat and mouse.

There are other flashpoints centered in the Indian Ocean beyond India and Pakistan. There is no love lost between China and India in the region, particularly as China continues to expand its commercial influence and basing throughout the Indian Ocean littoral. There is piratical activity along the East African littoral and throughout the western Indonesian archipelago. In the Arabian/Persian Gulf, the Sunni-Shi'a conflict continues to play out at sea as it does ashore. Yemen is on fire in a manifestation of Sunni-Shi'a conflict as Houthi rebels seek dominance of the poverty-stricken nation. Much of this is well documented in Robert Kaplan's superb treatment of the region, *Monsoon: The Indian Ocean and the Future of American Power.*

The salient question for the United States is simple: What is our role? How can we help create U.S. security and stability in the global oceanic commons upon which we depend for so much of our international trade?

First, we must recognize the vital importance of the Indian Ocean itself. On our maps and globes, it tends to be depicted as split (in order to give primacy to "our" oceans, the Atlantic and Pacific). Our strategic and geopolitical mental map reflects this, and in all of our thinking—from the Pentagon to our Fortune 500 companies to our academic and humanitarian institutions—we should consciously consider the importance of this vast body of water and its littoral nations.

Second, we must consider India. It will soon overtake China as the world's most populous nation, it is led by a dynamic and globally oriented leader in Prime Minister Modi, its lingua franca is English, and—above all—it is a vibrant, legitimate democracy with whom we share fundamental values. Too often in the international conferences I attend all over the world we end up discussing China, the United States, and the European Union—important to be sure—but never even mention India. In this century, the rise of India may be the most important single geopolitical driver, and its engagement in the Indian Ocean will be an enormous part of that.

Third, we must deploy and operate in the region with all of our forces. This most obviously requires a strong and deployable Navy and Air Force, but the Army and Marines have work to do as well. The Department of Defense should be building more exercises in the region like the Exercise Malabar, which brought U.S., Indian, and Japanese forces together in naval exercises.

Fourth, we should continue the global counterpiracy campaign, which has shown real success off the coast of East Africa. When we can bring together not only NATO, European, and Asian allies but also Russia, China, India, Pakistan, and Iran, there are few things we cannot successfully do. Within the turbulence of the Indian Ocean, counterpiracy operations are something almost everyone can agree upon—we can help lead that effort.

Fifth, one enormous key to unlocking the potential of the region is solving two difficult challenges: the Indian-Pakistani conflict, centered on the disputed Kashmir but in reality the result of religious, cultural, and historical differences; and the Shi'a-Sunni divide, which continues to make the Arabian Gulf volatile. These are long-term challenges, but whatever U.S. diplomacy can do to reduce tensions and avoid open confrontation will be helpful.

Sixth, the Arabian Gulf will not simply be a "lesser but included" subset of the Indian Ocean. Because of its particular place as the fault line between the Sunni and Shi'a worlds, it will demand a significant level of U.S. involvement in order to fulfill our objectives there: freedom of the high seas and an open sea lane of communication through the Strait of Hormuz, particularly for oil; capable allies in the Sunni Arab world, led by Saudi Arabia; a functioning modus vivendi with Iran; and an environmentally safe region given the high potential for ecological disasters.

In 2016, we saw several incidents of U.S. warships involved in disturbing scenarios in and around both the Arabian Gulf and the Indian Ocean. There is today a particularly high general state of tension with Iran at sea, in spite of the negotiated nuclear arms agreement. Since the agreement and the lifting of sanctions, Iranian naval forces—and particularly the Revolutionary Guard—have become emboldened. In January 2016, they came upon two U.S. Navy riverine craft operating innocently in their waters (one had broken down, the other was helping, and both had poor navigation and communication equipment readiness). In a violation of international law and seafaring custom, the U.S. Navy sailors were not assisted but instead were disarmed, put into humiliating stress positions, and taken into port. The Iranians used video of the sailors to further humiliate them, in direct contravention of international norms.

Late in 2016, U.S. Navy destroyers operating in international waters off the coast of Yemen were attacked by cruise missiles fired by Houthi rebels, who probably had Iranian training, targeting, and concurrence, considering the staunch Iranian support for the Houthis. Both incidents are harbingers of much more tension to come, particularly in the Arabian Gulf, but also in the northern Indian Ocean.

Above all, we simply need to factor the huge Indian Ocean and the smaller but vital Arabian Gulf fully into our thinking—they must not be forgotten as we sail into the twenty-first century. There will clearly be greater impact from this heretofore less noticed but still enormous body of water, and sailors will find the Indian Ocean far less domesticated than its twin cousins, the Atlantic and Pacific. How the geopolitics of the Indian Ocean unfolds will be a crucial vector for the overall trends of twenty-first-century geopolitics.

4.

THE MEDITERRANEAN

WHERE WAR AT SEA BEGAN

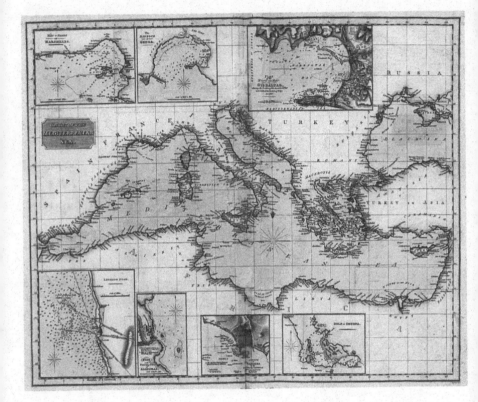

The Mediterranean was the source of the Western world's best sailors for millennia. *Map created by Samuel John Neele, 1817.*

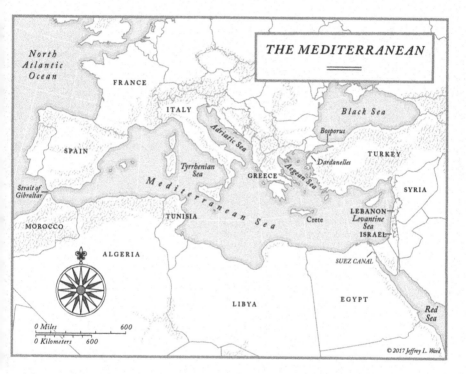

With frictions over natural resources and migration resurfacing, the
recent peaceful history of the Mediterranean is under threat.

*M*ankind's geopolitical journey upon the seas began in earnest on the waters of the Mediterranean. Through the centuries of man's sailing across the ocean's waves, it was in the Mediterranean Sea that sailors created and then perfected the idea of war at sea. As a result, no other body of water can lay claim to such a central place in early global history—at least when it comes to war. If the remains of long-dead mariners were suddenly to float unencumbered to the surface, you could easily walk the length of the Mediterranean over the bones of warriors who died at sea.

The Med is close to a million square miles in area, more than 2,400 miles from east to west, and is spread out along 23,000 long miles of coastline. Yet the opening strait, the only part that links the Med to the vast Atlantic Ocean, is less than ten miles wide at the highly strategic Strait of Gibraltar—which was known to the Greeks and Romans as the Pillars of Hercules.

Another way to think about the size of the Mediterranean would be to imagine the Med superimposed over a map of the United States. The

Strait of Gibraltar would be roughly where San Diego is located on the West Coast. The Suez Canal and the approaches to the Red Sea would be on the northeast coast of Florida, near Jacksonville. The top of the Adriatic Sea would be almost to the Canadian border, just west of the Great Lakes; and the Libyan Gulf of Sidra would touch the Gulf of Mexico. Highway 66, stretching all across the United States, would fit from east to west. This is a big body of water, to state the obvious.

And most important, it has a series of fateful geographic features that appear again and again in the long throw of Mediterranean history: the narrowness of the opening in the west, of course, but also the enormous central importance of the largest island, Sicily—a prize over which nations have fought for more than three thousand years. Likewise, the dagger of Italy thrusting toward Africa and effectively bifurcating the Med is a geographic feature that will continue to make itself known. Its length and central position, with excellent ports both east and west, gave rise to Roman trade and enabled its sea power through the long Pax Romana. And to the south of Sicily, its smaller but almost equally strategic cousin Malta will appear repeatedly in the strategic drama of the Med.

Continuing east, the rocky island terrain of the Aegean has been a maritime battleground that echoes today as Greek and Turkish warships and aircraft conduct a delicate dance of confrontation that seems to belie their common NATO alliance membership and reminds us of Christian and Muslim hatreds from a thousand years ago that drove events through the eastern Med. Here the key islands are Cyprus, dominating the approaches to the Levant, and Crete, long and bulky, guarding the entrances to the Aegean.

To the north of course is the Black Sea, truly deserving of its own place in the books of history, but forever serving as a sort of "Med in miniature" through the millennia, with many of the same conflicts playing out north of the strategic passage of the Bosporus. And to the south, the flat terrain of the North African desert, the rich delta of the Nile, and the harsh land crossing the Suez all play a continuing part in the history, politics, and culture of the Med.

The name of the sea itself derives from the Latin word *mediterraneus*, which can be translated as "inland" or as the "middle place between the land." The Romans thought of it, appropriately, as the mare nostrum, "our sea." From the beginning of recorded Western history, it functioned as a sort of global commons in a relatively confined space, providing a path for trade, an accessible source of protein, a field of transport, a ready battlefield, and a natural barrier.

And it supplied much to the imagination of man as well. As the geography of the Mediterranean gradually revealed itself through the centuries, the legends grew of what lay beyond the Strait of Gibraltar. Dragons, sea monsters, the gates to Hades, the lost city of Atlantis—all occupied a place in popular imagination and culture. Rowing their graceful and reasonably reliable triremes, ancient sailors seldom chose to venture beyond the Strait of Gibraltar, where fear of the unknown held sway.

The Med has also played a central role in both the development of war-fighting technology and the creation of maritime strategy. As the ancients gazed on the Med, they quickly developed seagoing means to do what they already did ashore: fight. The Med gave war the battering rams and multilayered oars of the triremes; the use of marines—essentially specially trained soldiers bred to fight on the waves; accurate cannons and early fire control systems; new means of propulsion, as sailing became vastly more sophisticated; and the application of steam, combustion engines, and eventually nuclear power. Each of the advances in combat at sea was tested, refined, and put to brutal use in the Med.

For a modern Navy sailor, the first sense you feel passing through the

Strait of Gibraltar coming into the Med is one of entering an ancient arena of battle. You feel hemmed in and closed off, something a sailor hates. When sailors part, in addition to wishing each other the common "fair winds and following seas," they will sometimes say, "Godspeed and open water." In the Med, you feel surrounded by history and somehow enfolded by the past, with not much obvious open water around—not a good feeling.

I remember the first time I sailed a warship into the Mediterranean as a junior officer in the early 1980s—on the massive American aircraft carrier USS *Forrestal* (CV-59). Named for the first secretary of defense of the United States, James Forrestal, the ship was a floating city full of planes and bombs. It probably carried as much combat power in the high-performance aircraft on its decks as the entire Roman Empire could bring to bear.

My job as an engineer kept me belowdecks much of the time, but when I ventured up to the hangar deck and then to the bridge as we sailed through the Strait of Gibraltar, I was struck by the small scale of the waterway with land close at hand on both sides. We passed through late on a summer's evening, and the sea was beautiful, flat and calm. The Med is famously fickle in its weather, and it is a wise sailor who remembers the long voyage home by Odysseus to his home island of Ithaca from the Trojan War: a mix of beautiful sailing punctuated by terrible storms and disasters every time he and his crew ventured ashore.

Wherever we went in the Med that summer, we had gorgeous weather; but as the fall descended, the days shortened and the weather chilled. The mistrals of winter—the great storms of the Med—were coming, and you could feel it not only in the surface of the sea and the great clouds above, but in the attitudes of the people in the ancient port cities we visited in the course of that long cruise. The French say a good mistral will blow the ears off a donkey—it will certainly make a ship rock and roll across the Med. The sense of history in every port—Athens, Istanbul, Tel Aviv, Alexandria, Syracuse, Naples, Cartagena, Tunis, and on and on—was palpable. The cold war, in full bloom in those long ago days, seemed a logical enough backdrop to our warship's voyage.

It also reinforced for me the various strategic geographical divisions in the Med. In the 1980s, at the height of the cold war, the United States tried to keep two carrier battle groups on call in the Mediterranean. One was typically in the western Med, with access to allied ports, easier logistics, and the ancient Roman ports on the coasts of Spain and Italy. A series of bases kept U.S. warships well supplied. In the eastern Med, it was another story. There was a great deal of Russian influence in Libya and Syria, and we often passed close aboard Russian flotillas. Our smaller ships would make their way up into the Black Sea, that miniature battle zone, knowing that if hostilities broke out, our strikes against the USSR and its Warsaw Pact allies would make the Black Sea a death trap for U.S. warships. While thankfully we never went to war with the USSR, it was clear that operations in the Med were going to be a very dangerous proposition. We were a long way from home, facing a powerful local opponent—much as the Venetians must have felt as they sailed under Ottoman guns centuries earlier.

The real question that kept occurring to me was simple: Why was the Mediterranean such an early crucible of war and conquest?

First is its location as a watery crossroads between competing civilizations.

Maritime geopolitics was born on the Mediterranean in the early battles between the Greeks and Persians, the Phoenicians and the Romans. As mankind started to ply the waters of the Med, vastly different civilizations came into contact—Europe, Africa, and Asia—and along with the exchange of trade, language, people, and other sources of wealth came conflict. The Med was simply an enabler of it all.

Consider the geography of the Med, sitting as it does in a central position among competing societies and nations. Like spokes on a wheel, the key sea lanes of communication across the Med provided access to invading fleets. As early civilizations found their way to the Med, it was easy for adventurous kings and queens and emperors and pharaohs to envision using the water as a means to transport conquering fleets, ships bristling with soldiers, empty holds aching to be filled with treasure and slaves. And the natural geographic divisions—Italy most of all—create smaller individual zones in which to fight.

Second, the Med is dotted with highly strategic islands. Sicily, Sardinia, Malta, Crete, the Aegean littoral islands—all provide convenient stepping-stones. As various empires consolidated and rose in importance, the battle for strategic landholdings in the Med rose as well. This created a second wave of conflict and enabled bases from which fleets could operate with impunity.

It is worth remembering that even as both trade and war increased across the Med, there were many natural challenges that the ancients had to overcome. For starters, the weather is not easy. While the Med is generally a relatively benign environment in which to sail, it can be unpredictable and unforgiving to the unwary mariner. Second, the technology of navigating deep ocean sailing, out of sight of land, had to be developed over several centuries. Third, the ability to build strong and capable ships that could reliably sail over days and weeks was created over time through trial and error, and much loss of life. But as mankind honed the ability to go to sea, navigate effectively, and fight, the Mediterranean began to function in earnest as a kind of Thunder Dome or fighting cage, where two warring nations entered and often only one emerged.

. . .

THE FIRST TWO CIVILIZATIONS to make their mark at sea have both largely vanished: the Minoan Empire, centered on the island of Crete, which flourished for nearly a thousand years beginning in 2500 B.C.; and the Phoenician/Carthaginian Empire, which was destroyed by the Romans more than two thousand years ago in the world's first fight to the death between two relatively advanced societies.

The Cretans (roughly 2500 to 1200 B.C.) were forced to turn to the sea by a growing population four and a half millennia ago. They were natural sailors, and found many islands north of Crete over which they soon held sway. The relatively less advanced mainland Greek societies were forced to pay tribute to the Minoan kings, including sending tributes of young men and women to perform with the bulls in the capital of Knossos. Their story is part of the enduring legends of Greece, including the killing by the young prince Theseus of the Minotaur, a mythical creature that was half bull, half man, and to whom the tributes were sacrificed. Much of their society was probably destroyed more than three thousand years ago by an earthquake that has given rise to the legend of the destruction of the lost city of Atlantis.

I remember sitting in a small café on Crete several years ago on a lovely summer's night, enjoying a meal of grilled fish and Greek wine in the modern city of Chania, the second largest on the island. My host was a Greek general who led their armed forces as part of the NATO alliance for which I was serving as Supreme Allied Commander.

We chatted a bit about the Minoans, and he opined that if their society had survived, the Greek world would have expanded and dominated the Med much as the Romans later did. When I offered that the Greek mainland city-states could never have banded together to conquer others, his response was simple: that was exactly what the Cretans could have done—forced them to work together. Perhaps. A different twist of the historical DNA, and a Greco-Cretan empire shimmers in the distance, challenging the Romans, perhaps alongside the Carthaginians. Who knows?

AT THE EASTERN END of the Med, along the present-day Levant, the Phoenician civilization began about 3000 B.C. and lasted some 2,500 years. Principally traders (as opposed to conquerors), the Phoenicians sailed throughout the known world. Their ships carried tin from Britain, amber and precious stones from the Baltic, as well as spices, slaves, and gold from western Africa. Their intrepid traders sailed beyond the Pillars of Hercules and began the first series of connections between the Mediterranean civilizations and India, operating out of their key ports of Tyre and Sidon. Phoenician trading ports began to dot the islands and the mainland of the Med, and one center began to rise in power on the southern rim of the sea in what is today Tunisia: Carthage.

The Carthaginians, descended from Phoenician stock, eventually created an empire that stretched over the key islands of Sardinia, Corsica, and Sicily as well as much of Spain and great stretches of coastal Africa along the Med. A tough-minded, harsh, and capable people, the Carthaginians competed alongside the early Greek traders (who pushed them out of the Black Sea and the Aegean early on) and finally would end up in a climactic series of wars with the Romans centuries later.

PERHAPS THE EARLIEST "clash of civilizations" (to take a phrase from the late contemporary political scientist Samuel Huntington) was likewise across the eastern Mediterranean—between the Greek mainland city-states and the world-dominating empire of Persia. Surprisingly, the

Greeks managed to stop their fractious internal wars long enough to face the Persian onslaught roughly five hundred years before the birth of Christ.

The Persians had at this point in their long history conquered much of the civilized world, and had expanded control from their bases in Mesopotamia to the shores of the Med. The Phoenicians in the Levant immediately capitulated and were able to provide ships and expertise in all things navigational to their new Persian masters. The Greeks, of course, pursued a different course and fought hard.

By 492 b.c., the first Persian expedition arrived in Greece, but luckily for the Greeks, it was struck by a massive and disastrous storm. A second try also failed as an amphibious attack at Marathon ended in a significant defeat for the Persians. But the Persians were persistent and determined, and they regrouped over the next decade to finally return with what they considered overwhelming force.

Persian king Xerxes brought nearly 1,500 fighting ships, almost 200,000 foot soldiers, and more than 100,000 sailors, marines, and rowers around 480 b.c.: a seemingly invincible force. The Greeks at this point were able to muster only around 500 ships, and were significantly outnumbered both at sea and on land. When the death stand of the "three hundred Spartans" at Thermopylae failed to halt the marching hordes, the last chance of the Greeks depended on the Athenian fleet, which would fight in its home waters.

Led by the courageous and charismatic admiral Themistocles, the Greeks used the natural terrain of the craggy waters surrounding Athens to position their fleet to best advantage in Salamis Bay, just off the coast of Athens. Civilization in Greece was at stake.

The key, in the end, was freedom. Each of the Greeks was a free man, fighting for his family and his city-state. Virtually all of the Persians were conscripts or slaves. Themistocles gathered his sailors and marines around him the night before the climactic battle and challenged them.

Based on the description of the speech by the Greek historian Herodotus, we believe that Themistocles exhorted his men to row for their parents, to row for their wives and their children, to row for their city, and above all to row for freedom. They did, and their motivation and bravery—coupled with superior technology in the form of swifter, leaner, lighter galleys—carried the day.

I have told that story many times, to many different audiences, and it never fails to create a sense in the room of the power of today's all-volunteer military. At a dinner in New York City onboard the museum ship *Intrepid* a few years ago, I told it in honor of Navy SEAL Lieutenant Michael Murphy, who died in Afghanistan and was awarded the Medal of Honor for his heroic sacrifices on behalf of his men, his family (who were present at the speech), and ultimately his nation. Today a beautiful Navy destroyer, USS *Michael Murphy* (DDG-112), sails the oceans. I like to think you could drop a plumb line from the ancient free Greeks at Salamis Bay to Michael Murphy's ship—having in common their courage, honor, and commitment.

With the Athenian- and Spartan-led Greek victory, a sort of potential golden age shimmered before the Greeks; but they quickly squandered it by returning to what they did with the greatest gusto—fighting with one another. Thus the Greeks, despite all of their access to the Med and their highly capable militaries, were unable to truly push outward on the seas to create a significant empire (beyond conquering parts of Sicily and some other shoreline areas). It was the Romans who truly created the "inner sea" and ruled its complete periphery with extraordinary effect for centuries.

THE ROMANS ROSE IN POWER as the Greek city-states sought to maintain control of the waters between Sicily and southern Italy and as the young Carthaginian Empire was expanding from the North African shore. Rome faced competition from both, and as they consolidated their power in the third century before Christ, the Romans overwhelmed the Greeks who ruled small colonies ashore on the Italian peninsula. Across the Med, the watchful Carthaginians sensed the confrontation to come, and the island of Sicily became the first point of confrontation in what came to be known as the Punic Wars (named for the Latin word for Carthaginian).

Once again, the Med became a massive battlefield as the previously land-oriented Romans recognized the need to build a fleet. Their coasts were vulnerable to the traditionally seafaring Carthaginians, and their seaborne commerce was a rich source of plunder that was highly vulnerable to their enemy's capable fleets. Turning to the conquered Greeks, the Romans were able to acquire a fleet—but they lacked the knowledge of how to fight at sea. They were experts at raising an army and conducting combat hand to hand, but at first were not able to bring their approach to bear against the nimble Carthaginian fleet tacticians, who were masters of flanking, breaking through an enemy's ship line, and above all ramming and sinking enemy ships through superior ship handling.

As would often be the case in war at sea, the answer was to invent a new tactic, technique, or piece of equipment: in this case the *corvus*. This was a kind of gangplank made of iron that could be pivoted and dropped athwart an enemy's deck. It had a gripping hook on the forward end, and soldiers could then surge across it to the opposing deck. In several major seagoing battles of the second century B.C., the Romans were able to use this crude but effective boarding tactic facilitated by the new equipment of the *corvus* to destroy large numbers of Carthaginian ships.

As the Roman-Carthaginian Punic Wars unfolded, over time it was the Roman mastery of the sea that led to the defeat of the Carthaginians. Despite the brilliance of the Carthaginian general Hannibal ashore, it was the ability of the Roman fleet to send a major army to North Africa that sounded the death knell of the Carthaginians in 146 B.C. In the end, it was mastering the Mediterranean Sea that provided Rome first the massive island of Sicily, then the rich raw materials of the Iberian Peninsula, and finally the shores of North Africa and the breadbasket of modern Tunisia. Along the way, the Roman navy swept the seas free of pirates and vagabond maritime states, gaining a strong seagoing culture, a naval officer corps, and the confidence to rule the inner sea of the Med with authority and creativity.

I will always recall a trip to Tunisia in early 2001 a bit after I was first selected for rear admiral. It was with a group of fellow newly promoted one-star officers, both admirals and generals. As I walked along the bluffs overlooking the southern Mediterranean, I was reminded about the destruction of Carthage and it made me wonder how differently Europe and the Mediterranean world would be today if Carthage had been preserved, balancing the Roman juggernaut and creating a vastly different set of geopolitical outcomes.

We always tend to think of history as somehow predetermined—of course the Romans would win—but so often the great twists of history turn on a few decisions, a single battle, an unexpected invention, a visionary or a fanatic's charisma. Carthage faded from history forever, and the Romans won; but what dreams of empire died with them?

What crystallized the Roman domination of the Med following the defeat of the Carthaginians was a series of civil wars that moved Rome from a republic to an empire headed by Caesar Augustus. A series of complex rivalries, the assassination of Julius Caesar, the departure of the legendary general Mark Antony to Egypt, and the rise of Augustus Caesar, then known as Octavian, collectively set the stage for the climactic battle at sea that would decide the fate of the Roman world in 31 B.C.: Actium, a small port off the coast of western Greece.

These were not the largest fleets assembled, but it is hard to find a more pivotal battle in the history of the Med. Octavian, who was closer to his base in Rome, was able to bring just over 250 ships into play; while Antony, operating from Egypt and with the mesmerizing Cleopatra supporting him, brought around 200 larger ships to battle—unfortunately for him, heavy and weighed down with supplies and land troops. Octavian and his admiral, Agrippa, correctly assessed Antony's forces as sluggish and lacking in the ability to maneuver smoothly and swiftly.

The key would be nimble use of sail and rudder to isolate the enemy ships while avoiding grappling actions. Agrippa also used fire projectiles to good effect, and at a crucial moment in the battle Antony and his Egyptian consort slipped away, leaving the bulk of the fleet to destruction. Hardly a proud example of leadership in action, and one of the few times in history a seagoing admiral has simply sailed away and left his fleet to fight to its death.

This battle created the conditions for the Pax Romana, the Roman Peace. The Med, for the first time in its history, was truly an inland sea, controlled and patrolled by the power of one nation: Rome. While nuisance piracy was an occasional hazard, the Med enjoyed perhaps the most peaceful prolonged period in its history. Roman rule continued through most of the next five centuries until the decline and fall of the western empire unfolded in the fifth century A.D., followed by the Dark Ages in Europe and the rise of Islam as not only a religion but an enormous motivating geopolitical force. Beginning with nomadic Arabs, Islam spread around the periphery of the Med, conquering all of the Middle East, then Egypt and the Levant. Using this as a base, Islam spread to conquer the rest of North Africa, eventually taking southern Spain and many of the islands in the central and eastern Med. Frankly, it is not impossible to imagine a world in which Islam had triumphed through much of southern Europe. Yet the Christian armies stiffened their resistance, and Constantinople and the Byzantine Empire held firm throughout much of this period. Over time, the Holy Roman Empire emerged in the West, and by the eleventh century the Christians were preparing to strike back, across the Med, and undertake the colossal misadventure of the Crusades.

During the Crusades, the Med served as a springboard for the Christian zealots of Europe to push their way into the Holy Land, and the newly (and relatively briefly) established Crusader kingdoms depended on the seas for resupply, logistics, and trade. The Crusades also gave great impetus to the rise of Venice and the Italian commercial cities over the course of the 250 years of various Christian campaigns.

Here we see again the political importance of geography. Venice was particularly well positioned in the northern Adriatic, with easy access to the trade coming from Europe over the Alps and superb, relatively safe access to the Med itself. The Venetians were crisp geopolitical actors indeed—rather than seeking to hold huge swaths of territory (with all the attendant headaches of administration), they sought a series of trading bases. They acquired Crete and Cyprus, two of the most strategically positioned islands of the Med. They also built smaller forts and trading stations around the periphery of the eastern Mediterranean. In a way, their sea power strategy anticipated Rear Admiral Alfred Thayer Mahan by some six centuries in systematically pursuing key commercial and trading stations around their world.

All of this was militarily anchored by the great Arsenal of Venice, which was an early technology assembly line construction facility producing great galleys. The Venetians used seagoing technology cleverly and at one time had a fleet of thousands of ships and tens of thousands of seamen—despite having a core population of only around two hundred thousand souls. Their relationships with other kingdoms and empires were based largely on trade, and they were adept at playing off Christian rulers against one another and manipulating them with the power of the Church and the control offered by the papacy. They seemed destined to dominate the eastern Med, and were growing richer and richer—all due to geopolitical planning, excellent use of geography in the Med, and the application of new technologies in construction, weaponry, and administration.

And of course it was not just Venice that displayed power on the waters of the Mediterranean. The great trading cities of Italy and southern France all participated in the rising level of trade. The Italian city-states—Genoa, Ragusa, Pisa, and others—were essentially small maritime nations that developed new types of ships and sails and fueled their wars (and the Crusades) with wealth from trade linen, dye, spices, perfumes, jewels, drugs, and pearls. From the west came oil, soap, wax, honey, skins, and especially wood and metal. Trade was brisk and enormously impactful to the maritime republics of the central Med.

Yet looming on the horizon was a new power—the rapidly rising Ottoman Turks, who came storming out of Central Asia. By exploiting the constant feuding between Arab potentates, they were able to dominate the Levant by 1400. Consolidating their control of modern-day Turkey, as well as large Arab dominions, they truly took the center stage of the Mediterranean in 1453 by doing what so many had tried and failed to do: conquer Constantinople. The Byzantine Empire had been a haven for culture and Christianity for a thousand years, and it finally fell after constricting and losing its ability to protect itself from the sea, as well as simply failing to produce enough resources (people and wealth) to ward off the Turks.

Whenever I am in Istanbul, I try to visit the superb Naval Museum, which is alongside the ferry terminals for commuters crossing the Bosporus in the Beşiktaş district. It is a quiet place full of the relics of the Ottoman Empire, most notably many of the great barges of state used by the rulers and oared by twenty or thirty oarsmen at a time. There is a nice garden outside with various cannons, as is usually the case at such museums. But the thing that always catches my eye is relatively modest—an anchor chain, of which only a few links exist today. It is black and rough, and appears to be made of iron. The placard proclaims it part of the "great chain" made in the eighth century by one of the Byzantine emperors.

In times of war, the chain was used to protect the city from the approach of enemy vessels by stretching it across the entrance to the Golden Horn. It was used successfully many times and appears for the final time in history in 1453 as the Ottomans were besieging the city. Mehmet the Conqueror could not get through it, but instead moved his war fleet of some seventy vessels overland through sheer dint of manpower. In the end, the chain failed to protect the city, just as the city was unable to protect Western civilization from the energy and dynamism of the Ottomans.

With the fall of Constantinople, the Ottomans were able to push into Europe as far as Vienna, and to increasingly dominate large tracts of strategic seacoasts along the eastern and southern Med. Their practices were brutal even by the standards of the day, and included forced conversions to Islam, slavery, and a particular focus on capturing Christian ships and enslaving their crews. The two civilizations—Christian and Muslim—were on a collision course that would bring great strife throughout the 1500s and 1600s.

As with previous conflicts in the Med, geography played an important role. The Ottomans were able to use their sea bases along the coasts and sought to reach out into the island chains of the Aegean and to the west. The Europeans tried to use the coastal bases of Italy as their strategic bastion, while attempting to dominate the same strategic islands. Technologies—cannons, sail, rowing, marine tactics—were roughly equal, although the Ottomans had a better system of administration and training in that it was relatively uniform throughout their growing empire. The West had a collection of different systems at play, which made it more difficult for them to operate seamlessly when fleets from different national entities came together.

The fall of the strategically important island of Cyprus in the eastern Mediterranean to the Ottomans in 1570 finally alarmed the various competing European nations to the point that Pope Pius V formed what was called "the Holy League," principally backed and manned by the Italians and the Spanish, to counter the Ottomans. The Turks continued to push both on land and at sea, and soon it was clear that a significant sea battle would decide the directions of the maritime campaign, and in many ways determine the fate of Europe. That battle occurred near Lepanto, off the western coast of Greece in the Ionian Sea.

The day of the battle dawned clear and bright: October 7, 1571. The Turks brought more than 250 galleys manned by a total of 75,000 seamen and soldiers, while the allied European fleet, commanded by the Hapsburg prince Don John, was made up of roughly 200 galleys manned by just over 70,000 seamen and rowers. Crucially, the Venetians provided half a dozen galleasses—big, heavy, floating forts with terrible killing power. This would be the first great galley battle since Actium, some sixteen centuries earlier and in roughly the same part of the Med. Notably, the Ottomans came to it with overwhelming confidence, not having lost a significant sea battle in more than a century.

But by the time the battle ended around four P.M., the sea was literally red with blood—almost all of it Ottoman. The Turks lost the vast majority of their ships, escaping with less than fifty vessels at a cost of more than 25,000 skilled seamen and marines. The Christian forces lost only 7,000 men and a dozen ships. It was a day upon which history turned, and it marked the high water level of Ottoman maritime ambitions for the broader Mediterranean. The difference was tactical acumen by the Europeans, especially in the use of the galleasses, which forced the Turks to maneuver around them and sustain heavy losses from their large cannons. Almost all the fighting occurred hand to hand, and the commanders were personally involved, with Don John leading the assault that ended up killing his opposite number.

The battle was incredibly decisive in the moment, preventing the further expansion of Islam into the Christian world; but luckily for the Turks, the lack of follow-up by the Christian powers allowed the moment to pass without loss of territory by the Ottomans. The Christians quickly reverted to form with bickering and argumentation that allowed the Turks to hold Cyprus, and their ships continued to rove the Med in force. Despite the setback of Lepanto, the Turks rebuilt their fleet, worked hard to retrain a sailing force, and continued to be a factor in the eastern Mediterranean, where they skirmished with the forces of the Italian states and Spain for much of the next two centuries; but they never again truly threatened to fully dominate the entire inner sea of the Med, which was at one point a realistic ambition for them.

Their failure at Lepanto meant that the Ottoman Empire, as powerful as it would become and as long as it would last, would be bounded. They would not push by the deserts of Arabia to the south, by the Persians to the east, or by the Europeans at sea and in the Balkans to the west. Perhaps most important, as a result of the Battle of Lepanto, the mortal fear of the "invincible Turks" felt by many southern Europeans was shattered. In that sense, it was a critically important battle.

When I was the NATO commander, I went often to Spain, a country I love for many reasons—from the beauty of the language and culture to the excellence of the cuisine to the deep sense of history on the Iberian Peninsula. It is a place that was once an uneasy part of the Islamic world, and the architecture, language, and culture of parts of southern Spain—think Seville—greatly reflect this.

At one of the military summits we held there in Seville, my Spanish counterpart presented me with a beautifully decorated bottle of Spanish brandy in a hand-painted box. The motif on the box was a representation of the Battle of Lepanto, replete with a bloodred sea and the Spanish and Italian flags flying over the victorious Christian fleets. It is a sea battle that changed history across the Med, from the Aegean and the Adriatic all the way to the Strait of Gibraltar, by shutting the door to further Ottoman expansion into the central and western Med.

WITH CHRISTIAN DOMINANCE ASSURED, it was the turn of the British to begin to move in significant ways into the Mediterranean. They consolidated control over key islands and straits—Gibraltar at the Pillars of Hercules, Malta in the center of the Med, and Cyprus, so large and important to the east. And of course Egypt was a stepping-stone on the routes controlling India. British admirals began to be very familiar with the inland sea—especially Lord Nelson.

Throughout the long summer of 1798, Nelson's and Napoleon's fleets played hide-and-go-seek across the broad expanse of the Med. When, finally, the French dropped anchor off the northeast coast of Alexandria in Aboukir Bay, Nelson closed in for the kill after several unproductive weeks at sea. His direction to his captains was simply to put their ships alongside the enemy. His aggressive and motivated captains destroyed Napoleon's armada while it swung at anchor off the mouth of the Nile, and Nelson (a mere rear admiral at the time) was made a baron and became a hero across Europe. Essentially the entire Mediterranean fleet of France was destroyed or captured, and British naval morale peaked, preparing it well for the victories to come. It was the pivotal maritime battle of the Napoleonic Wars and firmly established once and for all British dominance of the Med throughout the nineteenth century.

In the early 1980s, I sailed into the bay of Alexandria on the carrier

Forrestal, not far at all from the site of the famous battle. We went ashore on small boats, rocking through the surf, mooring at a yacht club and enjoying easy hospitality. It was a far cry from the world war that raged in Alexandria in the early 1800s, and the Egyptians were happy to have our U.S. dollars pumping up their economy.

For Nelson, Egypt was an important way station on the voyage to the destruction of Napoleon at Trafalgar; but the months he had spent crossing the Med to find Bonaparte were the pivot point of an extraordinary career—time well spent indeed. For us on an American carrier at the height of the cold war, it was simply a break for ice cream and beer ashore. For all the wonderful Mediterranean nights he spent in the arms of Emma Hamilton, Nelson's destiny lay outside the Pillars of Hercules, in the Atlantic, at the fateful battle of Trafalgar. The Mediterranean was the proving ground that led him to command and glory and death at the pinnacle of British sea power in the early nineteenth century.

Through the nineteenth century, the Med lay more quiet. The height of geopolitical maneuvering shifted ashore to the continent of Europe itself, as successive waves of revolution pushed back against the compromises of the 1815 Congress of Vienna, which had ended the Napoleonic Wars. The "Iron Chancellor," of Germany, Otto von Bismarck, managed to dominate European politics and ensure that other than the battle for Crimea and later the 1870 conflict between Germany and France there was little geopolitical activity happening that involved the Mediterranean. By the time the nineteenth century ended and the twentieth had begun, many major strategic theorists had begun to believe that war between the major powers was impossible given the cultural, familial, and economic ties between them. Sadly, they were wrong, and in 1914, war came again to the Mediterranean Sea as an important part of the First World War, what came to be known as "the Great War."

. . .

THE FIRST WORLD WAR BEGAN not far from the shores of the Mediterranean Sea, in Sarajevo, Bosnia, on the periphery of the Austro-Hungarian Empire. In June 1914, Archduke Franz Ferdinand—at the time heir to the empire's Hapsburg throne—was assassinated by Gavrilo Princip, a Serbian nationalist. This led to the triggering of the complex system of European alliances and ultimately to the global war that had at its heart the maritime rivalry between the German Empire and Great Britain.

At sea, much of the war was carried out by auxiliaries, including submarines and distant commerce raiders. And of course much of the fighting between Great Britain (the "Grand Fleet") and Germany (the "High Seas Fleet") was north of Germany in the waters between the two nations, in the foggy, harsh conditions of the North Sea. But a portion of the war found its way to the Mediterranean as well, beginning in that peripheral body of water that has seen so much of war as well, the Black Sea. There two German cruisers joined decrepit Turkish warships and attacked Russia's ports in the Crimean—actions that echo through to the present-day NATO-Russia conflict in the area, albeit with slightly different alliances.

In early 1915, an audacious scheme was concocted by the young Winston Churchill and grudgingly accepted by the canny and seasoned first sea lord, Admiral Sir Jackie Fisher. They sought to break the deadlock on the trenches of the Franco-German front with an attack on Turkey at Gallipoli in the Dardanelles, at the edge of the Mediterranean in the Aegean Sea where it opens into the Sea of Marmara and then to the Black Sea. The idea was to ultimately take Constantinople, the capital of the increasingly unstable Turkish Ottoman Empire (the so-called Sick

Man of Europe) and knock the Turks out of the war. It would also open
the southern ports to Russia.

The plan was initially under resourced, and the incremental approach
ultimately led to massive losses, especially of British colonial troops,
when the Turkish army unexpectedly stiffened and beat back the British
attacks ashore on the highly strategic peninsula of Gallipoli. Of the half
million Allied troops who began the campaign in February 1915, almost
half were casualties by November. The reputations of both Churchill and
Admiral Fisher were badly damaged, and the war ended up dragging on
for another three years.

I went to Gallipoli—or Çanakkale, as the Turks call it—on a hot summer's day in 2010 as a guest of the Turkish chief of defense, army general
İlker Başbuğ. We walked the battle lines where Aussies and Kiwis had
fought desperate actions against troops under the command of a young
Turkish general, Kemal Atatürk, who went on to drag Turkey into the
modern world after the war. General Başbuğ showed me the monu-
ments, which are extraordinary and generous in their respect for the
fallen Allied troops. One of them has a famous quote from Atatürk,
which is addressed to the mothers of the fallen soldiers: "Those heroes
that shed their blood and lost their lives . . . You are now lying in the soil
of a friendly country. Therefore, rest in peace. There is no difference
between the Johnnies (Anzac troops) and the Mehmets (Turkish troops)
to us where they lie side by side here in this country of ours. . . . You, the
mothers who sent their sons from faraway countries, wipe away your
tears; your sons are now lying in our bosom and are in peace." While
there is some controversy about the authenticity of the quote, it is moving
and I think has been taken to heart by the Turkish military as part of
their culture and history.

Later, we had a glass of good Turkish red wine and a light meal on the battlefield overlooking the strait. I looked out to sea where the ships of the Allied fleet had launched their inconclusive bombardments and tried to supply the troops ashore, and realized that the troops would have looked longingly as well at the ships, wishing they too could have been saved by simply sailing away. There are times when it is good indeed to be a sailor. General Başbuğ and I took note of the difference between the fate of a soldier on the ground and that of a sailor at sea.

In a strange footnote, General Başbuğ—a superb soldier, deeply loyal to his nation—was later falsely charged with undermining civilian control of the military and imprisoned. Fortunately, he was later released and cleared of those trumped-up charges, and today enjoys his retirement. He was a soldier who understood and appreciated sea power, but knew that the men ashore in this battle were the arbiters of the outcome. Our friendship continues to this day.

THE RESULTS OF the First World War were inconclusive. An angry and bitter Germany fell victim to fascism, hyperinflation, and a sense of victimization, and its anger gave rise to Hitler, who dragged his nation into the disaster of World War II. Unlike the First World War—where the pivotal fight ended up being largely ashore in massive trenches on what was essentially the Franco-German border—the Second World War achieved a level of combat in the Mediterranean littoral that rivaled that of the Punic Wars. It is no exaggeration to say that the Med was a heartland battle domain throughout the early years of the Second World War, including the early destruction of French and Italian ships by the British fleet after the fall of France and Italy's declaration of war.

The most important parts of the Med campaigns were in North Africa, where the Allies chose to make their initial attacks against German forces, led by General Erwin Rommel, that were threatening Egypt while seeking to cut Britain off from India, an important source of revenue and resources.

The American-Anglo force landed on the North African shore in 1942 in Operation Torch near Casablanca, and—after initial setbacks—was able to then invade Sicily (Operation Husky) and make its way to Italy (Operation Avalanche). These actions ultimately knocked Italy out of the war and badly distracted Hitler. They were also the making of General Dwight Eisenhower, who emerged from these Med campaigns as the Supreme Allied Commander who would brilliantly lead Operation Overlord and the invasion of northern France a year later.

At sea, as the war began, the Germans and the British launched a series of battles to gain control of the vital shipping routes that would determine victory in the land battles. The fight for Greece went against the Allies, but they were able to ultimately win on the North African coast. Submarine warfare by the Germans was quite effective in these early days, and the situation in North Africa was of deep concern to the British high command. The Med was again an arena of total war at sea.

It was also a period that highlighted the strategic importance of Malta, sitting as it does athwart the key sea lanes of communication in the center of the Med. Operation Torch and the British army campaign under General Bernard Montgomery were able to destroy the North African forces of the Germans, inflicting heavy losses. Rommel barely escaped back to Germany. All of this was enabled by British sea power operating in the central Med and supplying their forces ashore.

Much as during the Punic Wars, the Mediterranean Sea functioned both as battleground—as ships and aircraft sought to destroy one another at sea—and more important as the passage across which moved all the means of war. In all of my voyages through the Med, I was constantly reminded of those long patrols in the Second World War. In C. S.

Forester's riveting novel *The Ship*, he tells the story of war at sea in that arena perfectly, when British ships sailed out of the base at Gibraltar headed to Malta and Alexandria, always seeking to keep open the vital supply lines. As a destroyer captain in the mid-1990s, I sailed those waters often and always felt the hint of danger and the tingling sense of cruising through the scene of those long-ago battles.

THROUGHOUT THE COLD WAR, the U.S. Navy kept two carrier battle groups on patrol in the Med. The idea was to challenge the Russian ability to conduct flanking maneuvers to get behind NATO lines that were dug in along the Fulda Gap in Central Europe. There were constant games of cat and mouse throughout the Med, and Navy ships (especially the massive aircraft carriers) were constantly shadowed by Russian intelligence-gathering vessels. Occasionally, the Navy would send destroyers to shoulder off the Russian AGIs, as they were called (Auxiliary General Intelligence).

The Med served as a sort of venue for training, engagement, and intelligence gathering throughout the cold war. Given its relatively shallow depth (shallow in comparison to the far reaches of the North Atlantic and the even deeper Pacific), the Med was never going to be a venue for a huge fleet action in the age of nuclear submarines, which need to plumb the deep sea for concealment and preparation for attack. In terms of U.S. versus Russian engagement, the Med was not the battlefield it had been for the previous two thousand years, but there was a series of relatively low-intensity conflict incidents alongside the maneuvers of the Soviet and U.S. fleets.

Notable among them in 1985 was the first significant terrorist incident at sea launched against a civilian vessel—a Palestine Liberation Front attack on an Italian cruise liner, the *Achille Lauro*, in which an elderly Jewish-American citizen who was confined to a wheelchair, Leon Klinghoffer, was executed and thrown into the sea. The perpetrators were captured by the United States and turned over to the Italians for prosecution.

Later in the decade there were significant U.S. Freedom of Navigation operations against Libya (resulting in the shoot-down of Libyan fighters whose pilots were trained by the Soviet Union), as well as the strikes against Libya after a terrorist bombing of a German disco killing U.S. servicemen in 1986. Additionally, following the bombing of a Pan American commercial airliner over Lockerbie, Scotland, in 1988, more intense naval operations were undertaken in the Gulf of Sidra. The pendulum of conflict in the Med was swinging from the big-fleet cold war posturing to more complex operations reflecting the fading importance of the cold war ethos.

Throughout this period, I made several deployments to the Med, and on each of them I felt a sense of connection with the many, many sea battles that had gone before. But we never fired a shot in anger, despite many close encounters and provocations. And finally, the dark era of the cold war ended, with all of us thinking we were headed into a brave new world of peace and prosperity with the "end of history" within our grasp. It certainly didn't turn out that way.

AFTER THE INITIAL EXUBERANCE at the "victory" of the cold war, reality set in as it became clear that knocking off the Soviet domination of various parts of the world would release destabilizing forces. Perhaps the signature conflict in that regard involving the Med in the immediate post–cold war period was in the decade of the 1990s, when the Balkans simply exploded as Yugoslavia broke apart.

Long-simmering religious and ethnic tensions between Bosnian Muslims, Catholic Croatians, and Orthodox Serbs created a vicious war centered in Bosnia in the center of the Balkans. Hundreds of thousands were killed and millions pushed across borders. More than eight thousand Muslim men and boys were slaughtered by Serbians in July 1995 near the town of Srebrenica. This was followed by a second conflict when the largely Muslim province of Kosovo broke away from Serbia in 1998. The international community, after much vacillation, finally intervened both in the air and from the sea. The maritime operations included strikes, an arms embargo, and eventually a significant ground force requiring logistic support from sea. The forces ashore totaled more than 100,000 allied troops between the Bosnia and Kosovo campaigns.

When I was a destroyer captain, my ship, USS *Barry*, had a key role in the mid-1990s as part of the arms embargo preventing weapons from reaching the Serbian aggressors. I remember reading Robert Kaplan's insightful meditation on the region, *Balkan Ghosts*, and thinking that the problems were simply intractable, the well of pain too deep.

And yet, over time, the international community has fashioned a kind of rough peace in the Balkans, and the ships at sea played an important part in it. We had long weeks on station chasing down smugglers and pushing them off the coast under the command of an excitable British commodore. I was glad to put the dark shoreline in my wake and head home. After the Balkan wars of the mid-1990s, things settled down in the Med, but anyone who follows the region knows it was a quiet that would not last—and it has not.

TODAY'S MEDITERRANEAN IS AGAIN a sea of conflict. With Russia's resurgence, we are seeing aggressive patterns of maritime behavior dotting the Med, especially in the Black Sea and the eastern Mediterranean. While the Russian fleet is not the equal of the vast Soviet naval armada, it is quite capable of challenging U.S. interests. Additionally, Israel remains at odds with most of its neighbors, and around Cyprus lie rich fields of natural gas and oil on the bottom of the seabed—with attendant territorial disputes among all the nations of the eastern Med. NATO allies Greece and Turkey still squabble over the Aegean and the islands that make up its beautiful archipelago, and the Black Sea—a subordinate vassal of the Med—has disputes between Russia, Georgia, and Ukraine.

Looking first to Russia, it is clear that Vladimir Putin sees his country as a Mediterranean power and the dominant force in the Black Sea. The annexation of Crimea and the domination of the Luhansk and Donetsk regions of Ukraine in the southeast of the country give the Russian Federation a strong foothold on the necessary strategic real estate. Having had a long-standing treaty with Ukraine to keep capital ships in the port of Sevastopol, it has been easy for the Russians to simply build out the infrastructure there.

In 2013, as the NATO Supreme Allied Commander, I went to the Russian and Ukrainian naval base in Crimea and had lunch on a Ukrainian destroyer with their chief of naval operations. I was there to thank the Ukrainians for their participation in the NATO counterpiracy mission, to which they had sent a ship. After a long, long lunch featuring literally countless toasts with Ukrainian (not Russian) vodka, too much smoked fish, and a half dozen courses based on pork, the navy chief and I went up on deck. He pointed to the Russian ships that were tied up just down the piers as part of the Russian agreement to keep their ships in homeport in Crimea.

I mentioned how it must be somewhat frustrating to have Russian ships in a Ukrainian dockyard now that the countries were not as close as they once were, and that these certainly were not Soviet times. The Ukrainian CNO was smoking a cigarette, and after a long puff, he told me that "Russia will never give up Crimea. Never." When Russia invaded and annexed Crimea a couple of years later, I was reminded of his words. The need to dominate the Black Sea is primal for Russia, and Crimea is the fulcrum that allows it to do so. As the Ukrainian admiral told me, the Russians will never give it back.

It is interesting to put the Black Sea into the historical context of the Mediterranean. It began as a kind of region of exploration, dating to the ancient Greeks—legend has it that the Argonauts sailed to what is today Georgia to find the Golden Fleece. For centuries, it was disputed between Russia and Turkey, a relationship that has had many twists and turns over the centuries. It was essentially an Ottoman lake at the height of Turkish power, then fell under domination by Russia. During the cold war, it was essentially a Soviet lake, with only Turkey as a NATO ally guarding the entrances and controlling the southern coast.

But with the end of the cold war, the Black Sea has exploded into a sort of Wild West, with new NATO allies Romania and Bulgaria joining Turkey; Ukraine is in a deeply troubled relationship with neighbor Russia, including the annexation of Crimea; and Georgia, a close NATO partner and friend, has two significant provinces occupied by pro-Russian separatists and Russian forces. In addition, today smugglers and violent extremists routinely use the Black Sea as a preferred route into Europe. Russia will continue to regard it as a vital interest, and the potential for exploiting hydrocarbons will also be a key focus for Russia.

Putin has also expanded Russia's relationship with the Assad regime in Syria. Russia has had naval access and bases along the Syrian Mediterranean coast throughout the cold war and on into the present day, representing at one point the final geostrategic connection between Moscow and the Arab world. Now that Putin has effectively doubled down on Assad—despite the Syrian leader's vicious and illegal actions against his people during the ongoing civil war—it is clear that Russia intends to maintain its ability to operate in the eastern Med into the future.

This collides with the views of the United States and other NATO allies, which are seeking the overthrow of Assad based on his use of chemical weapons, torture, and barrel bombs in the civil war. The eastern Med, as so often in the past, has become an arena of great-power politics. In today's world, it is eerily reminiscent of the Balkans from a hundred years ago, when the powder keg of Bosnia blew apart the Austro-Hungarian Empire and dragged much of the civilized world into a war that essentially lasted until mid-century.

Even more concerning is the rise of the Islamic State. A group of religious fanatics, they are attempting to rebuild the Islamic caliphate across the Levant and North Africa. Capitalizing on the chaos and destruction in Syria and Iraq, they have dug into the seam between those countries. While they have lost most of their territory in the Levant and do not as yet control any coastal regions, their presence is increasingly felt in Libya, which has a long, exposed coast that is less than a hundred miles from Mediterranean islands and represents a path to Italy and Europe beyond. They have also contributed substantially to the departure of more than a million refugees headed to Europe (as well as several million more distributed throughout southern Turkey, Jordan, and Lebanon). All of this washes up from the shores of the Med, as many of the migrants are coming by sea to Greece, Italy, Croatia, and other coastal regions of the European Mediterranean. At the moment, there is an agreement between Turkey and the European Union to try to stem the flow of refugees and keep them in Turkey. But the fragile accord will probably unwind over time, and the imperative for physical safety and economic opportunity will continue to keep the flow of refugees coming to Europe from across the Med.

. . .

Of PARTICULAR CONCERN from a seagoing perspective is the threat from Libya. In 1942, Winston Churchill said that Italy represented the "soft underbelly of Europe," and directed the Allied invasion efforts there. Today, we are seeing the nascent flickers of an Islamic State strategy that may try to achieve a similar effect.

Following the brutal decapitation of twenty-one Egyptian Coptic Christians by radical Islamists professing an allegiance to ISIS in mid-2015, the Italian government began to ramp up its efforts to defend its territory from attacks. How realistic is this threat, and how capable is the Islamic state of reaching across the Mediterranean and striking Italy? And what should Italy do?

First, we should listen to what the Islamic State has to say on the subject: From the cover of its *Dabiq* magazine is a story titled "Reflections on the Final Crusade." The general idea is that ISIS will conquer Rome, and the images include a photo of a black jihadist flag flying over St. Peter's Square. The article said: "We will conquer your Rome, break your crosses, and enslave your women, by the permission of Allah, the Exalted. If we do not reach that time, then our children and grandchildren will reach it, and they will sell your sons as slaves at the slave market. Every Muslim should get out of his house, find a crusader and kill him. . . . And the Islamic State will remain until its banner flies over Rome."

Hyperbolic? Of course. Literally possible? Not in the least. But worth considering the sentiment as Europe thinks about the increasing possibility of attacks in its homeland coming across the Mediterranean? You bet.

As Graeme Wood points out in his intellectually smart and historically grounded piece in *The Atlantic*, "What ISIS Really Wants," there is a certain underlying medieval impetus to the Islamic State's rhetoric and its actions. Beheadings of innocents, burnings of captured prisoners, rumors of crucifixions, enslavement and sale of comely women and children, the literal sacking of cities—all of these connote a strong desire to play on the international stage as though the Crusades were still in progress. Thus we come to the importance of Rome, perhaps the most potent symbol of all the Islamic State hates.

In terms of capability, ISIS is not going to launch a conventional attack or strike. But it has two potential routes into Italy by sea. One is by infiltrating the many boatloads of illegal migrants that sail across the short distances from Libya to the southern coast and islands of Italy. The other is by using small craft, much as smugglers and drug runners do to cross the Adriatic Sea, to cross the southern Mediterranean. Both are feasible and easier than working across Turkey and the Balkans and trying to pass illegally into a European Union nation by land.

If ISIS wants to inflame a religious war, what better place in Europe to attack than Rome? A significant strike at a Christian holy site would fall directly into both ISIS's self-stated strategy and its building narrative. Our Italian allies are well aware of this and are responding by taking all the right initial steps, starting with putting portions of both their military and the capable carabinieri paramilitary forces on higher alert; adding more nautical patrols between Libya and their southern islands; sharing intelligence widely throughout both NATO and EU/Interpol channels; and publicizing their measures to appear a more hardened target. All good steps.

What else can and should be done to protect the soft underbelly of Europe across the Med?

First, get NATO into the maritime game in the Mediterranean. Italy should convene an Article 4 discussion at the North Atlantic Council in Brussels within the NATO headquarters. Article 4 of the NATO treaty permits any nation to bring before the council matters pertaining to its individual security concerns. Such discussions are typically used to raise issues considered particularly concerning, and occasionally lead to common action—a decision taken by consensus of all twenty-eight members—under Article 5 (the famous "an attack on one shall be regarded as an attack on all" clause of the treaty). Italy should specifically ask that a NATO task force be established for surveillance and patrol across the Med.

When Turkey felt threatened by Syrian air activity several years ago, NATO responded by sending Patriot batteries to southern Turkey to defend Turkish sovereign airspace. Those batteries remain in place today. In the case of Italian concerns about Islamic State infiltration, the use of standing NATO maritime task forces would be a very real possibility to support the overloaded Italian coast guard and navy.

Second, amp up the maritime intelligence collection processes across the Med. The Italians need access to the highest levels of intelligence being collected today in Libya. This means not only working through NATO channels, but also approaching the Arab nations in the anti–Islamic State coalition (Egypt, the UAE, and possibly Tunisia) for assistance. There is no substitute for on-the-ground assets, and these are thin for the Italians despite their close commercial ties to Libya—so Italy should work it through not only high-tech USA/NATO/NSA sources, but also the Arab networks. Much of this can be sea based, with intelligence collection assets operating from coastal shipping.

Third, focus on the maritime dimension, using NATO navies in the Med. This means sortieing the Italian fleet and coast guard to patrol and map the patterns of movement across the 100-to-200–nautical mile stretch of the central Mediterranean; using long-range patrol aircraft from Sicilian bases; cooperating fully with neighboring Malta, which sits astride the sea lane; and employing high-endurance unmanned drones to maintain a high-quality, real-time sense of maritime domain awareness.

Fourth and most important, develop a strategy for addressing the problem at its source: in Libya. Given the chaos and increasing anarchy in Libya, it is tempting to simply write it off and hope that the revolution ultimately burns itself out. Indeed, many observers express a certain longing for the "good old days" of stability under Muammar Gaddafi. But eventually, Libya will succeed—it has big oil reserves (especially on a per capita basis), an educated population, and enviable geography close to Europe with a huge seacoast.

Europe—our closest ally in the world—needs a stable Mediterranean. This will mean engaging more directly in the coastal regions of the Levant to diminish the threat from the Islamic State and the flow of illegal migrants and refugees. It will also mean a maritime strategy to help move Libya toward a more stable situation. This means exploring a UN or EU peacekeeping mission, supporting the relatively moderate internationally recognized government centered in Tobruk, and cooperating closely with Egyptian efforts to take on the Islamic State in military terms with targeting, intelligence, destroying their financial base by cutting off access to Arab banks and, potentially, air strikes. Here in the United States, we should support Italy in helping lead a European approach to stabilizing Libya.

Just as Churchill looked at Italy as a relatively easy gateway to Europe, the Islamic State has geographic, political, and symbolic interests in sailing across the Med to Italy and across the Aegean to Greece. It will seek to accelerate its reach across the eastern and central Med. And Russian adventurism will continue in and around the eastern Med and the Black Sea. It is clear the Med will continue to be a fickle and changing geopolitical body of water, and one where more security operations at sea loom ahead on the horizon. That sense of being closed in an inland sea will continue for sailors in the Med.

I think back on the first time I sailed in a warship through the Strait of Gibraltar, a young and inexperienced Navy lieutenant. Much of my later career would be spent sailing through the Mediterranean, although I did not know it at the time. I would sail into Cannes for the Fourth of July, hosting an Independence Day celebration for the glamorous citizens of that lovely city, and head from there to shore up an arms embargo in the Balkans, where massacres and bombings were the order of the day.

In port calls to Egypt and Athens and Istanbul I would see the most ancient capitals and what their modern civilizations had become. I dropped into the Iberian ports of the Costa del Sol and saw the mélange of Arab and Spanish culture in the south of Spain. Over time, I would sail by and visit every country in the Med, marveling at the diversity and history, the culture and the beauty. But the overriding impression that stays with me to this day is of the battles fought, the lives lost, the collision of empires, and the throaty shout of war.

ULTIMATELY, THE STORY of the Mediterranean geopolitically turns on the rise of technology in response to the wars of the times; the distinctive geography that allows for miniature arenas of combat while still allowing overall passage throughout the inland sea; and the collision of civilizations fighting over trade, slaves, wealth, and land. Each of those has a part to play in the story of the Mediterranean, but in the end it is the maritime character of the sea itself that has driven so many of these battles.

We sometimes think of the Med as a cradle of civilizations, where nations were born and took to the center of the stage in all their terrible power and ultimate glory—and it certainly was all that—but it was also an unforgiving arena of war at sea, which shaped the course of history down through the centuries as well.

As we look to the future, the security challenges represented by the Mediterranean Sea will continue to be part of the landscape of human history. Sailors on modern warships will continue to ply their trade alongside the tankers, container ships, and gleaming cruise liners. Old ghosts of distant battles rattle still around the Med, and any Navy sailor, walking the decks of his warship at sunset of a winter evening, can feel their haunting presence in the sweep of the deep, uncaring waves.

5.

THE SOUTH CHINA SEA

A LIKELY ZONE OF CONFLICT

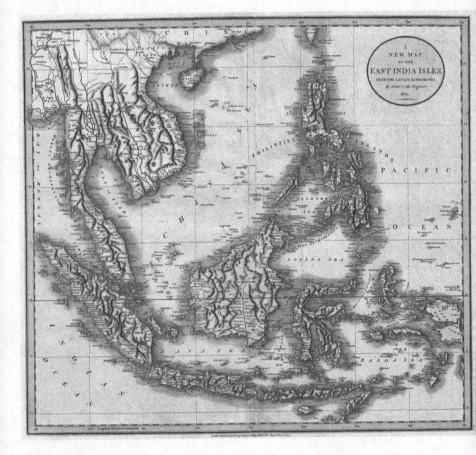

John Cary's chart gives little indication as to how crucial this region,
only known as the East India Isles in 1801, is to our modern world.

SOUTH CHINA SEA

*A*t the heart of the teeming South China Sea is Hong Kong, perhaps the finest natural harbor in the world. The first time I pulled into it was in 1977, as an ensign assigned as the anti-submarine warfare officer on a brand-new *Spruance*-class destroyer named USS *Hewitt* (DD-966). The captain, Fritz Gaylord, foolishly let me drive the ship as the junior officer of the deck for the sea and anchor detail. It was a complex mooring to a buoy, a huge floating concrete hulk anchored to the bottom of the harbor. The idea was to nuzzle the pointed nose of the 9,000-ton warship up to the buoy, hold it steady with the engines and rudder, and allow enough time for a handful of stalwart boatswain mates to jump from a small boat and affix our ship's anchor chain to a kind of connection link on the buoy.

This was a situation that required great ship handling skills which I did not possess, at least not at that early moment in my career. I was dazzled by Hong Kong itself, a spectacular harbor dividing two beautiful landmasses, with thousands of lights glittering on the steep side of Victoria's Peak in the early evening and the bustle of what was then a British crown colony in full bloom. Between my inexperience and distraction, I did a truly lousy job, banging the sensitive underbelly of the ship (where the expensive and somewhat delicate sonar dome resides) against the buoy. Fortunately, the captain *was* a great ship handler, and he took us back off the buoy and coached me through a better landing, despite the brisk wind and steady current.

When it was over, he lit an unfiltered Lucky Strike cigarette (smoking was allowed in those days on Navy ships), smiled somewhat thinly at me, and said, "I hope you're better at finding submarines. Welcome to Hong Kong." It was the beginning of a long and warm association for me with the South China Sea, and the myriad cities, nations, and cultures that surround it.

THE SOUTH CHINA SEA is big—the size of the greater Caribbean—and surrounded by huge economies: China, Vietnam, Malaysia, Indonesia, the Philippines, and others. Through the South China Sea in any given year pass about half of the world's maritime trade, half of its liquefied natural gas, and perhaps a third of its seaborne crude oil. There is evidence of human habitation stretching back thousands of years. Many theories exist as to the origins of the flow of people, goods, and languages across its waters: whatever the truth, we know that an early maritime network quickly became well developed and expansive. It is a sea rich in fish and having plenty of rain, with the access to fresh water facilitating long early journeys of perhaps weeks at a time. There is even scattered evidence of trade between the ancient Mediterranean civilizations and the people of the South China Sea Rim. More recently, in the first centuries A.D., the trade between India and Southeast Asia enriched the people of the South China Sea.

As in the Indian Ocean, the discovery of how to harness the power of the monsoons provided a significant impetus to early trading. Settlements in southern China and the Mekong Delta of the Funan Empire were among the first trading stations in the region. Over time in the first millennium A.D., the rivalry between what are today China and Vietnam first manifested itself as the cultures came into conflict. Also during this period, the South China Sea emerged as the seam between the two great civilizations in India and China, both of which would be impacted deeply by European exploration starting about 1500. Additionally, a trade between China and the Arab world emerged toward the end of the first millennium A.D. Globalization, which we think of as a modern phenomenon, has been alive and well for a very long time.

Across the centuries, various Chinese dynasties dominated the western side of the South China Sea, notably the Tang and Song dynasties, which controlled much of the littoral a thousand years ago. They pressed trade and controlled the ability of individual cities and regions to participate in the lucrative routes. By the time the Ming dynasty ascended in 1368, the DNA of trading, commerce, and seafaring exchanges was embedded in the South China Sea. Even as the Ming leaders looked inward to the land, the sea continued to be a vital part of the region's economy. Illustrating this well are the voyages of the so-called Eunuch Admirals (a term that provides me with a certain amount of personal discomfort to contemplate, I must admit). These were big expeditions, one hundred to two hundred ships, with thousands of sailors and troops. There is a fair amount of controversy about their purpose, but most historians seem to think they were to intimidate, discipline, enforce commercial codes and taxes, and create a sense of awe toward the dominant Chinese. Of note, these voyages were an anomaly; they were discontinued after several decades, and the ships were left to rot. China focused internally for the next five hundred years.

One interesting commodity that flowed across the wide South China

Sea was silver. With Manila as a trading crossroads giving the Spanish Empire in the Americas a toehold in Asia in the Philippines, the Spanish were able to provide much-needed metal currency to the Chinese. While silver also came south from Japan, it was the Portuguese and the Spanish who were largely able to fill China's need for hard currency. This led to the Chinese southern and eastern coasts being integrated into the global economy through access to the South China Sea. What emerged in this period was a trading competition, often verging into open conflict among primarily the English, the Dutch, and the Portuguese. Despite arguments by the Portuguese that they deserved full authority due to their discovery of the sea routes, international law of this period provided the latitude for the intrusion of other trading partners, most particularly the Dutch and British. In the early 1600s, the tiny Dutch state possessed thousands of ships with tens of thousands of well-trained and motivated sailors, and largely dominated global trade with an axis between European Amsterdam and Batavia (Jakarta in present-day Indonesia).

But by the late 1700s the British in the form of the East India Company were coming into their own. This led to the acquisition of Singapore in 1819 and Hong Kong in 1842. The Opium Wars of 1839–42 and 1856–60 were a result of a weak Chinese state colliding with the growing colonial powers. Meanwhile, both the French in Indochina and the Germans on the south Chinese coast were establishing colonial footholds. By the late 1800s, even the United States, traditionally averse to colonial holdings, was seduced into the view of naval strategist Alfred Thayer Mahan that colonies (really "coaling stations" or geostrategic forward bases) provided the foundation of sea power and thus world influence. Mahan's seminal 1890 work, *The Influence of Sea Power upon History*, was taken up enthusiastically by the young American president Theodore Roosevelt at the turn of the century, and the resultant echoes in the South China Sea were profound. And of course increasing in influence and capability, moving along like a shark under the smooth surface of the water, was Japan. The eventual collision of the Second World War was inevitable and enormous, but it began with a relatively mild series of disagreements in the South China Sea.

The key event for the United States in the region was the Spanish-American War, which was precipitated by the sinking of the cruiser USS *Maine* in Havana harbor, in the Spanish colony of Cuba. On a winter day in early 1898, the ship suddenly exploded while swinging peacefully at anchor. Led by William Randolph Hearst's newspaper chain, Spain was blamed for the sinking, the cry of "Remember the *Maine*" swept the country, and the United States declared war on the disintegrating Spanish Empire, leading to the annexation of Cuba as a U.S. territory after the war.

As an aside, I have long kept a painting of the USS *Maine* just before the explosion in my various offices—one hangs today in my Massachusetts office on the quiet New England academic quad of Tufts University, where I am the dean of the Fletcher School of Law and Diplomacy. People often ask me why I keep a painting of a doomed ship on the wall. Why not a valiant and heroic U.S. Navy ship, perhaps the carrier *Enterprise* or the destroyer *Barry*, both of which passed under my command?

The answer is twofold—first, and most important, the painting reminds me that your ship can blow up underneath you at any moment, so you better have a Plan B and, metaphorically speaking, know where the life rafts are located. The second reason is perhaps a bit obscure, but important to me. After the *Maine* was sunk, the Navy salvaged the ship nearly fifty years later, and virtually all of the evidence points to the conclusion that she was not sunk by Spanish saboteurs after all. It appears the explosion was internal, most probably from a boiler or an ammunition storage area. The charge to war was predicated, it would seem, on false evidence. So the second reason I keep a painting of the *Maine* around is to remind me not to jump to conclusions in the heat of the moment. Stop, consider, and above all, question the fact pattern being presented to you—a pretty good reminder.

The reverberations from the explosion of the *Maine*, and the U.S. charge into war, were felt thousands of miles away in the South China Sea. In Manila harbor, the aging Spanish fleet was bottled up and attacked by the superior U.S. fleet under Admiral George Dewey. He pushed his ships into the harbor in a surprise move and caught the Spanish fleet at their moorings. This was on the cusp between the age of sail and the age of steam, and Dewey took full advantage of the maneuverability conferred by his steam engines, passing up and down the Spanish line and hitting them with effective fire that destroyed the Spanish ability to fight. It marked the end of effective Spanish colonization in the Philippines, ending centuries of domination; it also marked the beginning of the engagement of the United States as a colonizing power, something that did not turn out well.

During this period at the tail end of the nineteenth century, the Japanese also were moving south into the South China Sea region. Although they were initially focused on Korea, they also took Taiwan from the ineffectual Qing dynasty in China. This was followed by the Boxer Rebellion, an indigenous uprising that roiled China and affected the colonizing European powers, ultimately causing thousands of deaths. The weakness of the Qing dynasty was an aberration in the long history of Chinese domination of the South China Sea—as Deng Xiaoping was said to have told Henry Kissinger in so many words, China is a great civilization that has had a couple of bad centuries. That weakness, so apparent in the twentieth century in particular, is outside the norm, and current events in the South China Sea show that the pendulum is swinging back strongly toward a policy of strong Chinese activity throughout the region.

By the 1930s, the outlines of conflict were clear. A rising Japanese power needed natural resources and tried to negotiate agreements with a distracted United States just emerging from its own internal economic catastrophe. With Japan rising and increasingly dominating the littoral of the South China Sea—from taking chunks of China itself to Taiwan to moving south into Vietnam—the United States was relatively impotent. The South China Sea, for the first time in a thousand years, was turned into essentially the territorial sea of a single power: Japan. It took four years of war to release it again.

FROM THE VERY START of the U.S. entry into World War II, the South China Sea became a key objective of our strategy. Why? Because it was the highway over which Japanese logistic support was flowing to their forward forces, which were rapidly overrunning large swaths of the western Pacific Ocean and the East Asian mainland.

As discussed earlier in the chapter on the Pacific, the first blows of the Japanese that landed effectively against U.S. forces after the Pearl Harbor attack in December 1941 were struck against the U.S. garrison in the Philippines on the cusp of the South China Sea. On the island of Luzon, the U.S. commander, General Douglas MacArthur, was forced to abandon his headquarters in Manila and head to the Bataan Peninsula, which could be more easily defended. MacArthur also held the nearby Corregidor Island. The South China Sea was clearly going to be a central objective of both sides, controlling as it does the sea lanes of communication that run athwart East Asia and the routes to the oil and rubber of the south. So the garrison at Corregidor grimly settled in for a siege, with little hope of anything beyond a delaying action and the faint hope of relief in place.

But by early March 1942, it was clear that the position was indefensible and would fall, and President Roosevelt ordered MacArthur to

escape; the thought of the most senior general in the U.S. Army falling
into the hands of the Japanese, especially after the Japanese success in
attacking Pearl Harbor, was inconceivable. Nonetheless, MacArthur
tried to stall: after all, he had been a general officer since 1918 and had
held four-star command throughout the 1930s. He was a proud and in-
domitable spirit. But eventually he realized that discretion would be the
better course than valor at that point. His departure proclamation is often quoted today: "The President of the United States ordered me to
break through the Japanese lines and proceed from Corregidor to Australia for the purpose, as I understand it, of organizing the offensive
against Japan, a primary object of which is the relief of the Philippines. I
came through and I shall return."

As a young officer in the 1980s, I met the famous retired vice admiral
John D. Bulkeley, who as a young lieutenant was given the mission of
getting General MacArthur out of the Philippines. He was awarded the
Medal of Honor for his command of the torpedo boat squadron throughout the Corregidor campaign and for the safe passage of General Mac-
Arthur. By the time I met him, he was an intimidating figure, a crusty
seadog who had been recalled to active duty to lead the Navy's Board of
Inspection and Survey. His charge was to make sure that our ships were
combat ready, and he was a good choice for the job.

At the time, I was a young and untested department head on a "fancy
new cruiser," as he styled it, the AEGIS-equipped *Valley Forge*. Bulkeley came down to the waterfront to pick apart our damage control capability, and to stand in front of him explaining why we had failed to correctly
align the firefighting water system on the ship was extraordinarily embarrassing. As he quite artfully chewed me out, I kept looking at the single
ribbon on his uniform, the Medal of Honor, knowing that he also held
the Navy Cross and a slew of other combat awards. I remember thinking
that he represented a direct line from the World War II Navy, and his

combat runs across the South China Sea dodging Japanese gunfire remain legendary. Would I ever be able to muster the same level of courage and honor and commitment, I wondered?

At virtually the same time MacArthur fled Corregidor, the unchallenged Japanese fleet was moving to dominate the entire South China Sea, headed down the coast of Borneo and building forward operating stations for air and ground troops on the littoral of the sea. The only force between them and domination of the South China Sea was the ABDA fleet of light cruisers and destroyers, which stood for American (our small Asiatic fleet), British, Dutch, and Australian. This handful of ships was truly the "Fleet the Gods Forgot," and it was under the command of a Dutch two-star admiral, Karel Doorman. It was destroyed in February 1942, leading to the surrender of Java and the fall of the entire Dutch East Indies. This provided the Japanese with oil (from the oil wells in Borneo, Java, and Sumatra) as well as rubber, quinine, tin, and other strategic necessities. The South China Sea provided a wealth of riches to Japan's so-called Greater East Asia Co-Prosperity Sphere.

But inexorably, the Allied net began to close. From this point forward, the action shifted to the broader reaches of the Pacific outside the South China Sea. The Japanese, bounded by their limited population base, had taken on an unsustainable task, and the blow at Pearl Harbor made any agreement with the United States impossible. The dual thrust of the U.S. and Allied forces began to hammer back, and by the end of 1943, U.S. forces were headed toward the Philippines again.

The bloody battles of 1943, the island-hopping campaign, and a relentless submarine campaign enabled MacArthur to position his forces by March 1944 to head toward the Philippines and the South China Sea. The most important sea battle—while not fully decisive—was in the Philippine Sea in mid-June 1944. Here Admiral Marc Mitscher was able to take the pressure off MacArthur, who then carried the fight back into the heart of the South China Sea. In October 1944, early in the after-noon, MacArthur climbed down from the cruiser *Nashville* into a land-ing craft and went ashore onto the Philippine island of Leyte, taking long strides through the knee-deep water after the coxswain dropped the ramp. As promised, he had returned, and the South China Sea became an American lake later that month, after the decisive sea battle of Leyte Gulf, which shattered the heart of the Japanese fleet. The full liberation of the Philippine Islands followed in short order, and not long afterward—deprived of the resources flowing across the South China Sea and faced with a nuclear armed America—the Japanese surrendered.

In the course of my career, I spent a great deal of time in and around the Philippines, which in many ways are the seam between the broader Pacific and Asia proper. They endured centuries of Spanish colonization, experienced the half-hearted attempt of the United States to be a colonial power in the first part of the twentieth century, and finally, as indepen-dence appeared assured, fell into the center of a brutal world war. Their nation is also like the Caribbean in that it so often resembles a bull's-eye for the various tsunamis that reoccur again and again in that part of the world. Yet despite so much bad luck and poor governance, the people of the Philippines have a lightness of soul that shines through, a kind of good-humored ability to deal with adversity, and a deep spirituality.

I first encountered the Philippines in the mid-1970s as a young en-sign on a destroyer headed into the beautiful natural harbor of Subic Bay, where the U.S. Navy had historically had a large sea and air base. It was a bustling tropical setting, with beautiful beaches, cold San Miguel beer, and very friendly hostesses working across the "shit river" that led to the town and the countless bars, strip clubs, and houses of ill repute.

In fact, as a division officer, I had my hands full trying (and fre-quently failing) to keep my sailors from falling in love with and marrying the beautiful young local women. We had a "cooling off" period that a commanding officer could impose to prevent premature nuptials, but persistence often found young sailors falling into true love. Many of those marriages, by the way, turned out very well when the young brides made their way back to our home port of San Diego, where they more often than not turned out to be thrifty, sensible Navy spouses. Over the course of my career, I have met many a "deployment bride" from the Philippine Islands, and I would say they fared pretty well.

The strategic value of the Philippine Islands is obvious from a glance at a map, and the U.S. bases there—both the huge naval and air complex at Subic Bay and the even larger air base at Clark Airfield near Manila— were mainstays of U.S. naval and geopolitical strategy in the region throughout the cold war. With "an anchor to windward" in the South China Sea, the United States was able to maintain a strong presence in these waters throughout this period.

While there were numerous skirmishes between the United States and China, especially over the protection of Taiwan, the major set-piece battle of the cold war in the South China Sea was, of course, the war in Vietnam. At the outset of the cold war, with former NATO Supreme Allied Commander Dwight Eisenhower in the White House, there was significant reluctance to get more deeply involved in the region, even given the dangerous and seductive idea of what would eventually be called the "domino theory." This was the idea that if the United States did not prevent individual local regimes from becoming Communist states aligned with either Moscow or Beijing or both, they would fall together, like dominoes, and the United States would have to face a significant Communist bloc in the region. There are many problems with this theory, and President Eisenhower, who had seen so much of war, worked hard to avoid entangling the United States in any sort of land war in the region. While he acknowledged the theory, he managed to avoid a significant ground force engagement in Asia.

Even when our World War II allies, the French, found themselves on the losing end of a vicious insurgency in French Indochina—today's Vietnam, Cambodia, and Laos—Eisenhower refused to either send troops or threaten the use of nuclear weapons. The French were defeated by the insurgent Viet Minh, led by Ho Chi Minh, and expelled from Vietnam after a huge loss at the Battle of Dien Bien Phu in 1954. The United States was deeply worried about this, and many here used the domino theory to begin arguing for more U.S. involvement in Vietnam, which of course came to fruition not on Eisenhower's watch, but on that of his successor, John F. Kennedy.

As the 1960s unfolded, the South China Sea became a principal maritime focus of the United States. While the cold war raged globally, requiring the efforts of the U.S. Navy from the Arctic to the Mediterranean to the Baltic to the deep Atlantic, there was considerable naval activity in the South China Sea. This was because of the increasing tempo of U.S. operations on behalf of South Vietnam as it fought against both the North Vietnamese Army (supported by China) and the insurgency of the Viet Minh and Viet Cong within South Vietnam itself. This required increasing the level of U.S. troops ashore throughout the early-to-mid-1960s under both presidents Kennedy and Johnson.

At the peak, the United States supported more than half a million Army and Marine combat troops ashore, with the Navy fleet in constant support. Maritime activity included complex aircraft carrier strikes ashore against targets in both North and South Vietnam; coastal and riverine operations in direct support of the soldiers and Marines ashore; logistic supply to units ashore and operating at sea for prolonged periods of time; maritime surveillance and intelligence gathering; insertion of SEAL patrols and support of them from the sea; and bombardment with naval guns of targets in the coastal regions. The South China Sea became an American lake throughout much of this period, with hundreds of U.S.

warships in operations throughout. The transit route between Vietnam and the Philippines was a well-trodden path for U.S. sailors indeed.

Throughout the early 1960s, U.S. involvement increased year by year, tripling in 1961 and again in 1962. The relatively young American president, Jack Kennedy, sensed the slippery slope toward the "Americanization" of the war effort. As his date with destiny in Dallas approached, his enthusiasm for the war was diminishing rapidly. After his tragic assassination, Lyndon Johnson felt the need to demonstrate his tough approach toward communism. With a war record that was suspect to begin with, Johnson always seemed intimidated by his Joint Chiefs of Staff and his wunderkind secretary of defense, Robert McNamara.

Perhaps the clinching event that drove further U.S. involvement was the so-called Tonkin Gulf incident of 1964, in which a group of North Vietnamese torpedo boats supposedly attacked two U.S. ships off the coast of Vietnam at the northern end of the South China Sea. The USS *Maddox* and USS *Turner Joy* managed to fire hundreds of rounds of heavy artillery at what most observers have since concluded were "phantom targets" in two highly suspect "attacks." These attacks were used by the Johnson administration to gain congressional approval for direct military action in Vietnam, and the rapid increase of U.S. forces in the country followed, as well as strikes against North Vietnam. Thousands of lives ended and many more were dramatically changed by the events that flowed from the Tonkin Gulf incident.

In terms of maritime operations in the South China Sea, the U.S. Navy was the dominant force. Over the course of the war, nearly two million sailors served in theater. The missions were varied, but on the deep ocean, supply and logistics were critical—more than 95 percent of all the material and personnel that headed in and out of Vietnam sailed at sea on Navy and merchant marine vessels. Two Navy hospital ships were the first destination for many of the wounded.

Additionally, the U.S. Navy spent a great deal of time training the South Vietnamese navy, which, by 1972 when the United States disengaged from active combat, numbered more than eight hundred ships and more than forty thousand men—believe it or not, the fifth-largest navy in the world in that year, albeit mostly composed of tiny riverine and coastal patrol craft. Meanwhile, the U.S. Navy continued a strong effort from the South China Sea. In 1972, it was flying more than 3,800 sorties a month, and Navy destroyers and cruisers fired well over 100,000 long-range shells at shore targets. Mines were used from aircraft to seal off North Vietnamese ports.

As the war ramped up, peaked, and gradually began to falter due to a lack of support in the United States, an aversion to mounting casualties, political disillusionment flowing from Watergate, and bad strategic choices by U.S. military leaders, it was clear that the United States would withdraw. Eventually nearly sixty thousand U.S. troops would die in this war, and perhaps five million Vietnamese. The U.S. Navy continued its operations in support of the South Vietnamese government while it still survived, but when Congress cut off funding in the mid-1970s, the game was over in Saigon. The U.S. embassy was overwhelmed, and the last, sad act of the U.S. Navy was to operate air and sea ferries to save as many U.S. supporters among the Vietnamese along with our embassy and remaining troops. Viet Thanh Nguyen's recent novel *The Sympathizer* is a searing portrait of those final days and the evacuations out of Saigon and captures perfectly the zeitgeist of the moment of failure.

Decades later, in the early part of the twenty-first century, I went to Vietnam for the first time. Not to Saigon (now of course renamed Ho Chi Minh City), but to the north, to Hanoi. I was part of the delegation of Secretary of Defense Don Rumsfeld, who firmly believed that a coherent strategic relationship between the United States and Vietnam was strongly in our interest. We were treated like royalty, and I sensed the deep interest on the part of senior Vietnamese officials in a relationship with us. Why? Because of the economic, political, and military benefits that would allow Vietnam to maintain an independent posture vis-à-vis China.

As our motorcade sortied through the streets of Hanoi, I saw a motorcycle go by with a box of small piglets on the back. In a wire box about the size of a small apartment's refrigerator, they were hurtling precariously through the narrow streets and overtook us before zooming on as we pulled up to the famous prison where Senator (then Navy pilot) John McCain had been held and tortured. The United States and Vietnam had shared a dark chapter, but I hoped the future was brighter for the relationship between the nations than it was for those piglets. It appears that is the case, as the relationship between the United States and Vietnam continues to expand across political, economic, and security dimensions.

So as the United States withdrew once and for all from Vietnam in the mid-1970s, the U.S. focus in the South China Sea continued with our allies in the Philippines and Taiwan, as well as working to improve defense and economic relations farther to the south, with Singapore, Malaysia, and Indonesia. The story of the United States and Taiwan is particularly worth considering for its importance in the region.

IN THE 1950S, the other significant conflict affecting the South China Sea was on the sea itself—between mainland or Communist China, led by Mao Zedong, and the Nationalist Chinese in the Republic of China on the island of Taiwan. Sitting astride the northern entrance to the South China Sea, Taiwan has a long and challenging history of being conquered and colonized over the centuries. Also known as Formosa, the island has been subjected to invading forces numerous times (including Dutch, Spanish, and Chinese), and more recently was a Japanese colony from the end of the nineteenth century to the end of World War II. After the loss of the bloody civil war on mainland China, the republican Chinese, led by Chiang Kai-shek, retreated to Taiwan and for several decades maintained the fiction that they were the "true" government of China. They even held the UN Security Council seat throughout a portion of the post–World War II period until it was turned over to the Communist mainland regime in 1971.

Throughout the cold war, the United States stood with Taiwan, and it continues to provide a great deal of political and military support today. But during the late 1970s, the United States noted a change in Chinese global policy that affected events in the South China Sea—the Chinese shifted their top national security threat from the United States to the Soviet Union. The Chinese began to help the United States diplomatically, and the tension across the Taiwan Strait was visibly reduced. As a result, sadly, the U.S. Navy—which for decades had been visiting Taiwan—stopped pulling into port there.

The two great liberty ports, both cherished by sailors, were Keelung and Kaohsiung. Both were notorious for the beauty of the women, the strength of the liquor, and the inexpensive costs of the clubs ashore—all the things our fearless sailors were looking for on a trip ashore after a month or more at sea. I went out as shore patrol officer on one of the final liberty runs ashore in Keelung, a bustling commercial port at the top of Taiwan. It is a warm and tropical city, with a lot of rainfall, and we had our hands full rounding up sailors who had imbibed a bit too much and returning them to face justice aboard their ship. It was all like an extended scene out of the musical *South Pacific*, and I had a couple of burly petty officers to do the heavy lifting.

But what I remember most vividly the next day was taking a tour of the port and learning about the role of the city during the Opium Wars of the nineteenth century. The British were fighting the weak Qing dynasty and tried three times to capture the city, which was strongly held by the local Chinese admiral. He captured and executed a handful of British sailors, and the city remained a free zone throughout most of the century. It reminded me of how the sweep of history had crossed that island so many times—the Dutch, the Spanish, the British, the mainland Chinese of course, the Japanese, and finally the Chinese republican forces who still held out against the Communist regime ashore.

Like Sicily in the Mediterranean, Taiwan was strategic ground and fought over frequently, with the indigenous people endlessly bearing the brunt of war. As I walked about the port in my Navy uniform, it occurred to me how strategically vital this island remains, plugging like a stopper the great flask of the South China Sea and sitting athwart the sea lanes between Korea, Japan, China, and all the states to the south. Mahan would have advocated planting a flag there and building a coaling station. Those days are gone, but continuing engagement by the United States makes a great deal of sense, it seemed to me on that spring day long ago, and still does today.

The final leitmotif of the South China Sea over the past two decades is the geopolitical contest between an outsize China that is rising inexorably and the handful of small but dynamic nations that share the littoral of the South China Sea with their massive and increasingly assertive neighbor. The history of the waterway is not only about ships passing through it, and the small and great wars on the coasts; it is about the scattered island chains that provide a means for nations to claim chunks of the sea if they can only establish claim. This is the story of the seemingly constant conflict over the Paracel and Spratly islands, for example, as well as over Mischief Reef.

What drives all this, of course, is the presence of hydrocarbons and fish in the South China Sea. While most of the nations would be content with the rules and regulations generated by the United Nations Law of the Sea Treaty, which came largely into force in the 1980s, what is in dispute is access to the region's ample fisheries near the seafood markets of Asia and the seabed hydrocarbons. Some estimates put the total amount of oil and natural gas at levels similar to the Middle East. This is a mother lode of resources, especially for the smaller players along the littoral. So it's no surprise that there has been a constant game of occupying the island chains for nearly fifty years.

What is new is China's strategy to build artificial islands. This has begun in earnest in the past several years, and already the Chinese have built dozens of islands, mostly in the southern and eastern portions of the South China Sea. They are making them large enough to have caught the attention of the U.S. military and political actors in Washington. Admiral Harry Harris, who is Japanese American and the first Asian American four-star officer in the U.S. armed forces, has called the construction of the artificial islands "the great wall of sand." The United States has undertaken a series of Freedom of Navigation missions to challenge China's claims of sovereignty. Admiral Harris has elsewhere called the Chinese claims "preposterous," and most international legal scholars agree. And in mid-2016, the international courts ruled definitively against China, which has thus far simply ignored the ruling and continued to aggressively build artificial islands and conduct its maritime operations as though it owned the South China Sea in its entirety. This situation will grow over the coming decades, and the potential for active combat is not insignificant.

Instead of stone, brick, and wood, this new "great wall" consists of artificial islands strung out across the South China Sea—a region Beijing claims by virtue of historical right. China's claim is encompassed by what it terms the "nine-dash line," a radical demarcation of maritime sovereignty that takes an enormous bite out of the legitimate territorial claims of Vietnam, the Philippines, and other countries ringing the South China Sea.

The crucial context of this behavior is that the South China Sea—Asia's "cauldron," as geostrategist Robert D. Kaplan calls it—is bubbling like the witches' kettle in Shakespeare's *Macbeth*. The South China Sea matters not only because it is contested territory, but because it's hugely important to the smooth operation of the global economy. More than $5 trillion of the world's annual trade passes through the South China Sea, all under the watchful eyes of the (oddly named) People's Liberation Army Navy.

China's aggressive behavior in building these artificial islands tracks with its disregard of other norms of international law. Some of these provocations include lack of clarity on the claim itself—a claim that, again, international lawyers widely regard as preposterous—including an air-defense identification zone over the East China Sea directed at the United States, Japan, and South Korea; the placement of a mobile oil platform in Vietnam's coastal waters; and the widely reported (and massive) cyberthefts of U.S. intellectual property, industrial secrets, and personal data.

The specifics on the construction of these artificial islands are staggering. Thus far—and construction continues—China has created nearly three thousand acres of land out of the ocean. Just consider that the highly touted and massive U.S. aircraft carriers (from which can be launched a wing of more than seventy jets and helicopters) are only about seven acres of flattop. Are these artificial islands similar to hundreds of unsinkable aircraft carriers in the South China Sea? Think that shifts the balance between the two competing militaries? You bet it does.

Besides the obvious geopolitical and military issues, significant ecological damage is also under way, according to many scientists. One expert from the University of Miami, John McManus, called China's building of man-made islands "the most rapid rate of permanent loss of coral reef area in human history."

Add to this the internal tension under which President Xi Jinping's regime is operating: falling real estate prices, an aging population, an imbalance of men (too many) and women (too few), terrible ecological damage requiring significant mitigation, and above all, a sputtering economy that is stunting growth. When authoritarian regimes come under pressure, they tend to look outward to find ways to distract the population. Nationalism emerges. Such is the case in China today. Witness Xi's September 2015 speech at the United Nations—full of barely concealed vitriol directed at the government of Japanese prime minister Shinzo Abe. The tension between Japan and China has been waxing and waning over the past several years. Now it's increasing again.

What is the best approach for the United States? This tense situation is out in the open, and Xi's late September 2015 visit to Washington, and President Trump's trip to Asia in 2017, did not fundamentally change anything.

First, despite provocations, the United States must maintain open communications with China and seek ways to reduce the chances of an inadvertent collision either between the United States and China (unlikely) or between China and one of its immediate neighbors (far more likely). The U.S. relationship with China encompasses economic issues, geopolitical cooperation from Afghanistan to Iran, and global environmental issues—the South China Sea dispute is only one element. Dialogue is crucial. And the agreements on military-to-military contact and cybersecurity that the two presidents discussed during Xi's visit are better than nothing.

Second, the United States needs to strengthen its relationship with existing allies and partners in the region and encourage them to work together better. This applies especially to Japan and South Korea, which, for a host of historical reasons, have long had an uncomfortable relationship. The United States can help build better ties between the two neighbors by promoting military exchanges and exercises, enabling conversations at important events like the Shangri-La Dialogue (an annual gathering of strategic thinkers in Singapore), and encouraging so-called Track II engagement, which is exchanges and dialogue conducted not through government channels (Track I) but instead through academic and research institutions. The Trans-Pacific Partnership, a massive multilateral trade agreement, is a big element: building a network of even stronger trading ties can ensure that America's friends and allies cooperate with one another. And in particular, working more closely with Vietnam makes good sense—and this should include lifting bans on weapons sales.

Third, the fundamental tenets of international law are against China's approach in the South China Sea. The United States should sternly emphasize this in international forums like the United Nations, the G-7, and the Association of Southeast Asian Nations. The intellectual underpinnings of international legal judgments on the South China Sea are very clear: nations cannot simply declare a "historical claim" and take over what other nations regard as international waters. The United States, as a global maritime power, should not miss any opportunity to object. The recent negative ruling against China further buttresses this strategic approach. And frankly, the United States should finally sign the UN Convention on the Law of the Sea, the treaty that governs the world's oceans, to maintain the high ground in these conversations.

Fourth, and finally, the United States should exercise its traditional rights of transit under international legal norms: its Freedom of Navigation operations. That means overflying Chinese territorial claims and sailing U.S. ships through China's claimed water space—the waters within twelve miles of these islands. The United States has a long tradition of countering unjustified historical claims by sailing and flying through international waters and airspace. Now is the time to exercise it in the South China Sea.

None of these strategic prescriptions by themselves will resolve the challenges of the South China Sea. Nor will simply moving U.S. military aircraft and vessels through claimed Chinese air and sea space suffice. Pushing back on Chinese claims in the South China Sea requires a broader strategy that treats this violation of international law in the larger context of both Chinese behavior and Sino-U.S. relations. Above all, it will require U.S. leadership alongside America's many partners and friends throughout East Asia. China's Great Wall was at least partially successful in keeping foreigners out. Its Great Wall of Sand will not be.

Echoes of this argument from five hundred years ago—of the sovereign states' rights in the coastal zone versus the value of mare liberum or the freedom of the high seas—are very much with us today. When I first sailed in the South China Sea in the 1980s, we were only marginally concerned about China. Our ships went pretty much wherever we wanted. But of late, the Chinese—advocating ownership of more or less the entire South China Sea—are vastly more aggressive. Even more disturbing, they are building these artificial islands in a further attempt to solidify their claim to these seas. All of this dates back at least five hundred years, and in many ways a couple of millennia in terms of historical claim to the waters. From the perspective of the United States, acquiescing in these claims will lead to further closure of the high seas, and thus necessitate our Freedom of Navigation operations: short, sharp patrols intruding into claimed territorial seas that we contend are in fact high seas and open to all. To understand this controversy requires looking backward into the long history of the region.

HAVING SPENT MUCH OF A long nautical career in the Pacific, I am hard-pressed to think of another time of greater military competition in the Asian region, at least since the end of the Second World War. In particular, arms expenditures are rising throughout Asia, especially in the bubbling cauldron of the South China Sea.

Unfortunately, we are merely at the start of an entirely predictable and dangerous arms race as nations in the region increasingly respond both to the perception of a rising military power in China that seems more assertive in a strategic sense and to growing evidence of instability on the Korean Peninsula. All of this happens as the American "Pacific pivot" fails to gain traction in the face of crises in Syria, threats from the Islamic State, and ongoing tension with Russia over Ukraine, and the Trump administration's isolationist instincts.

In terms of military spending, China (which has the second-largest national defense budget in the world after the United States) is on track to double its already significant defense spending by 2020, increasing about 7 percent each year. Meanwhile, the U.S. defense budget and those of European nations in particular have been declining. The Chinese are also buying and building large aircraft carriers, having just begun construction on the first one to be built in China. They are also rapidly improving their offensive cyber capability, which will be central to military operations in the future.

The other nations of the region are responding. Japan has not only increased its defense budget but also passed legislation (not without controversy and protests) that will allow for offensive Japanese military action in defense of allies under attack—clearly strengthening its military alignment with the United States. Vietnam, the Philippines, Malaysia, and virtually every other nation in the region are likewise increasing their defense spending. On average, the East Asian nations are spending at least 5 percent a year more on defense than was the case several years ago. And we should remember that the United States and Russia, the first- and third-largest defense spenders in the world (and the two largest arms exporters), are also Pacific powers.

At a recently completed World Economic Forum in Davos, we saw a bit less public strain between Asian leaders than in the past couple of years, which is good. But in 2014 at Davos, Japanese prime minister Shinzo Abe said that he saw the Chinese-Japanese relationship as reminiscent of the antagonism between Great Britain and Imperial Germany a century earlier, on the eve of the First World War—hardly a reassuring thought. Since then, the two leaders—Prime Minister Abe and President Xi—have managed to appear together at several events and there seems to be less overt tension in the air. But in a variety of conversations I have had with senior military and political leaders over the past few months, it is clear that the subtext remains one of significant competition and indeed potential conflict.

Several of the nations involved in territorial disputes with China are moving closer to the United States. These include Japan (already among the closest of allies of the United States in the East Asian region), Australia (basing U.S. Marines ashore on its northern coast), and Vietnam (which continues to operate closely with the United States in both military and commercial spheres). The Philippines presents a more complicated case. Until 2016 they were moving toward a much closer relationship with the United States. However, their highly unpredictable populist president, Rodrigo Duterte, is now distancing himself from the United States, which has criticized him for violating human rights and encouraging the killing of drug offenders and criminals with impunity. In addition to swearing (frequently) at the United States and President Obama, Duterte has indicated a desire to reduce overall military cooperation with the United States and perhaps align himself with China (and possibly Russia). This trend has slowed under President Trump but Duterte's mercurial nature makes it difficult to predict how this will turn out, but it certainly throws another layer of tension and unpredictability into the already turbulent South China Sea.

The completion of the Trans-Pacific Partnership (which does not include China) would have further aligned the signatories with the United States. But with the Trump Administration's withdrawal from the process, the United States now must watch while China and others take the lead in establishing the new trade rules for the region.

IN ADDITION TO increased Chinese defense spending and assertiveness, there is the North Korean problem. With yet another nuclear detonation, and a 2017 test of an intercontinental ballistic missile, Kim Jong-un has definitively claimed the dubious honor of leading the most dangerous nation in the world. The North Koreans are armed with a small arsenal of nuclear weapons; led by an inexperienced, unstable, emotional, and medically challenged dictator (with a truly bad haircut); possessed of technologically advanced ballistic missiles; and in a virtual state of war with their closest neighbor, South Korea. All of this has an additive effect on the already tense relationships in the region, especially for Japan and South Korea, which must factor into their defense spending the presence of North Korea.

Another fascinating dynamic is the unfolding role of India as a global security actor, which will have knock-on effects in East Asia. India has historically stood a bit apart from East Asian politics, reasoning that it has enormous internal challenges and plenty to do in operating along the vast Indian Ocean littoral. But increasingly we are seeing India under dynamic prime minister Narendra Modi reaching out to engage with the United States and Japan in increased military and security cooperation. This began with counterpiracy operations off the Horn of Africa and now includes military exchanges and joint exercises.

The outlook remains very concerning, and it appears unlikely that there will be any significant reduction in tensions or in defense spending over the next decade and beyond. What should the international community and the nations in the region be doing to help create stability?

First, at the tactical level, the nations in the region should at a minimum encourage military-to-military direct contact. This can lead to defined protocols to minimize the chances of accidental ship and aircraft collisions, misunderstandings that escalate into shooting incidents, and even structuring agreements that would prevent cyberattacks on military command and control systems, which are highly destabilizing and particularly dangerous. Such military-to-military contact can be done bilaterally between the military staffs or organized in parallel to regional conferences.

Additionally, when such regional gatherings do occur—for example the Association of Southeast Asian Nations (ASEAN) annual convocation—having a portion of the event that includes high-level and candid political conversations about security is important and can create a higher level of confidence. Alongside such governmental conferences, private sector engagement (in maritime shipping, commercial air traffic control, cyber agreements, and environmental technologies for example) can be an excellent way for views to at least be exchanged in a neutral forum.

Third, finding ways for the militaries in the region to collaborate operationally, especially at sea, is important. This can be in simple maritime exercises that focus on noncombat operations—such as medical diplomacy, disaster relief, and humanitarian operations. It can also include quasi-military training or operations together for events upon which the nations do agree—piracy, for example, or humanitarian evacuations from a disaster zone.

Fourth, the use of international negotiating platforms to resolve territorial disputes could be key. Putting such disagreements before international bodies like the International Court of Justice in The Hague, another mutually agreed-upon United Nations body, a third-party government, or even an agreed-upon binding arbitrator should be considered. Unfortunately, such international legal activities are not binding, and it appears unlikely that China will accept such outside interference in its "backyard."

OVERALL, THE ARMS RACE in East Asia is simply a reflection of the geopolitical tensions that will remain high in the region for the foreseeable future. While there are ways to reduce such tensions, they are unlikely to diminish as the twenty-first century unfolds, so buckle up.

After putting all of this together, what is the right U.S. strategy for the South China Sea? Can it be separated from our thinking about the broader Pacific and the world ocean? What would Mahan tell us about its importance and our approach?

While it is impossible to pull out a single sea from the whole of the oceans and develop a global strategy based upon it, the South China Sea is unique in its geopolitical significance. Here resources, great and powerful maritime states, and critical sea lanes of communication converge in the most populous region of the world. The United States must retain a presence here. There are several ways we can do this.

We should maintain a network of bases and access agreements around the littoral of the South China Sea. The logical places to consider are in the east (hopefully the Philippines, perhaps even a return to Subic Bay), the west (in Vietnam, Cam Ranh Bay is a logical spot), and the south (Singapore, where we already have a robust presence, makes the most sense). In the north, we should continue to explore a strong refueling and resupply arrangement with Taiwan, even if this makes China upset (which it will). With a package of four bases, or at least four significant agreements for access and resupply, we could operate quite freely in the region.

Additionally, we need to have a strong relationship with each of the nations around the littoral. We already have such relationships with Japan and South Korea, just outside the South China Sea; but we need to pursue exercises, military exchanges, and maritime engagement with Vietnam, the Philippines, and Malaysia. Continuing to pursue good maritime relations with Thailand, Indonesia, and even Cambodia would also be helpful.

The big question over time will be how closely to engage China. It is too soon to tell, frankly, whether or not China's intentions in this region will permit recognition of international norms, and maritime and littoral boundaries. If China truly intends to attempt to claim the South China Sea as its territorial waters, the prospects are slim for an accommodation.

Having said all of that, it is crucial that we maintain an open and constructive relationship with China where we can. Despite our frustrations with their piracy of intellectual property, cyberattacks, unsupportable maritime claims, internal human rights violations, lack of democracy or liberty, and other points of disagreement, there are ways we can find some zones of cooperation. In the maritime sphere, for example, the possibility exists to work together on disaster relief, medical diplomacy, counternarcotics, counter–human smuggling, and environmental issues. The key is recognizing that there will be areas of significant disagreement, but that does not totally preclude working together on specific areas.

And there will be flare-ups between the United States and China. Over the past decade, we have suffered several, including an aggressive Chinese confrontation in 2009 with a U.S. surveillance ship, USS *Impeccable*, operating completely legally in international waters (although within the exclusive economic zone of China); and a Chinese fighter jet collision with a Navy electronic P-3 Orion aircraft in 2001, forcing it to land on Chinese territory. Both of these incidents were eventually worked out diplomatically, but are indicative of the cut-and-thrust of both U.S. and Chinese maneuvering in the South China Sea. And in fairness, we should consider our own reactions if Chinese intelligence and surveillance vessels and aircraft were routinely operating in the Gulf of Mexico, close to U.S. installations and within our exclusive economic zone (EEZ).

Those incidents bring up an interesting aspect of international law that pertains both in the South China Sea and elsewhere. The United States failed to sign the massive 1984 United Nations Law of the Sea Treaty (one of only thirty nations worldwide to refuse, sixteen of which are landlocked). In that treaty, the conditions under which nations can transit another nation's exclusive economic zone (two hundred nautical miles) are somewhat ambiguous. The United States chooses to interpret it as permitting us to conduct national surveillance (a euphemism for spying); other nations (China, India, and others) vehemently dispute this. The text is unclear. This disconnect is what has led to incidents like this involving U.S. spy ships and aircraft operating inside the EEZ but outside the territorial sea (twelve nautical miles). More such incidents will follow, especially in the contentious waters of the South China Sea.

Overall, the South China Sea will be a maritime hinge upon which huge geopolitical issues will ultimately swing. The United States must consider it a crucial zone of maritime activity in the twenty-first century. If we cede it to China—something China deeply desires and would consider inevitable—our global strategy will fail. While we should not push ourselves into a cold war with a rising China, we need to be mindful of our values and the importance of international law. As a young officer sailing these waters nearly four decades ago, I was deeply impressed with the history and civilization of China. We need to respect its culture and importance in this region and upon the dark blue waters of the South China Sea, but not surrender our own participation on international high seas and with close friends and allies. It will be a delicate balance to strike, but a crucial one. Much as with the Russian Federation, we should cooperate where we can, but confront where we must.

6.

THE CARIBBEAN

STALLED IN THE PAST

The Caribbean as it appeared to cartographers
Pierre Lapie and Ambroise Tardieu in 1806.

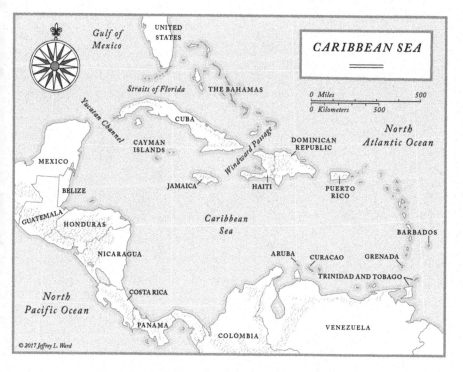

The Caribbean Sea remains the part of America's backyard
about which most citizens know very little.

*A*ny understanding of the modern Caribbean actually begins in Madrid, at the Spanish Naval Museum. I went there first in 2009, on my initial visit as the NATO commander. The chief of defense of Spain, an extremely elegant four-star air force general, put me in the capable hands of his chief of the navy for much of the day, and together we spent a couple of delightful hours wandering through the maritime history of Spain—a good deal of which focused on the Spanish conquest of the Americas, centered upon naval operations in the Caribbean.

In the museum I saw the earliest map of any part of the Americas, the chart of Juan de la Cosa, which despite all of its understandable inaccuracies (it was drawn up in 1500 by an experienced sailor but not a formally trained mapmaker), is quite recognizable to modern eyes. Over the part of the map where Central America ought to be located is an image of St. Christopher, the patron saint of travelers—probably an intended homage to Christopher Columbus.

Columbus, as any pre–politically correct schoolchild of the 1970s will remember, was not Spanish, but Italian. He was born in Genoa in the middle of the fifteenth century, probably around 1450 or so. Known in Spanish as Cristóbal Colón, he has come to us in anglicized form as Christopher Columbus. He probably traveled extensively around the western Mediterranean and down the coast of Africa. This was a period in which the Portuguese were daily discovering new ways to harness current and wind to reliably explore beyond the edges of the known world. Some reports indicate that he traveled north as well, perhaps as far as Ireland.

Genoa in the early years of Columbus was like the bar scene in *Star Wars*, with Marco Polo playing Han Solo. It was full of exaggerated tales of the Far East, the riches of trade, swaggering characters and sea captains, and plenty of shady opportunity. The son of a lower-middle-class weaver, Columbus would have grown up with a sense of horizons opening up, and a dream of making it to the richest lands of all—the China of Marco Polo's tales. By the mid-1470s, he had moved to Portugal and set out to find a sponsor for a voyage to the west, eventually turning to Ferdinand and Isabella of Spain (specifically Aragon and Castile, respectively) for sponsorship.

The year 1492 was important in the consolidation of Spain and the removal of the final vestiges of the Muslim world from the Iberian Peninsula—on January 2, eight hundred years of Islamic rule over some portion of modern-day Spain came to a close through the so-called Reconquista. Given the optimism and enthusiasm over these august events, it was not hard to eventually persuade the royal couple (mainly Isabella, a sea captain's daughter and granddaughter) to finance the expedition to the west, through what was called the Ocean Sea.

Columbus demanded and received excellent terms: the title of admiral, significant control over the disposition of discovered lands, and a large share of the profits. The voyage to the Caribbean was soon financed and the expedition was divided among the three famous ships—the *Niña*, the *Pinta*, and the *Santa Maria*—in August 1492. By early October, the "Admiral of the Ocean Sea" is believed to have arrived in the Caribbean on a small Bahamian island today known as San Salvador, the name first given it by Columbus. Thus did Europeans come to the Americas, at least in the case of the Caribbean Sea.

And what a disappointment for Columbus! Far from the glittering palaces and pleasure domes, the gold and silk, the spice and treasure of Asia, he found instead the traditional culture of the Amerindians, who went about mostly naked, built and produced little beyond bare subsistence, and had little idea about gold. Columbus explored and discovered Cuba and Hispaniola without finding anything of conventional value. He departed at the turn of the year in January 1493, bringing a few pieces of gold (he left nearly forty sailors behind to try to develop a gold mine on Hispaniola), some fruits and birds, and several terrified Indians to show at court.

Despite utterly failing at what he actually set out to do—to find a western sea route to the Far East—Columbus put sufficient spin on the voyage's narrative to intrigue many in Europe. Further voyages quickly followed, and investment flowed. On his next voyage in 1493, Admiral Columbus discovered other important islands—Puerto Rico, the Virgin Islands, Montserrat, Guadeloupe, and Antigua. Small bases and commercial entities were established, and more kept coming. There was a haphazard quality to it all, understandable given the depth of geographic misunderstanding that had led to the discoveries.

When I was first a sea captain myself, in late 1993, my destroyer, the *Barry*, was ordered to the Caribbean to conduct humanitarian work and enforce an arms embargo against Haiti. It was a strange first voyage, as this was just after the end of the cold war and the fall of the Berlin Wall. Frankly, I would rather have sailed my brand-new AEGIS combatant up into the Baltic Sea to chase Soviet submarines, but that ship had sailed, so to speak. So off to apply soft power in the Caribbean I went, with an inexperienced crew and all of us trying to find our sea legs on this, the first significant voyage of the newly commissioned warship.

We sailed right by the island of San Salvador at the entrance to the Caribbean, and I called the crew up on deck and gave a very short description of Columbus's first voyage, calling on my excellent fifth-grade history teacher's pedagogy, concluding with the dramatic words, "Just think, here we are just over five hundred years later—half a millennium—sailing in the same waters as Christopher Columbus, the great explorer, headed to help create security in this part of the world. Columbus's legacy continues." I felt pretty good about my impromptu history lesson.

But when I went down to the wardroom for dinner, a couple of my junior officers (who were nearly two decades younger than me and one of whom was African American) pointed out that Columbus's voyages had led mostly to enslavement and death for the locals. Good point, I thought. We should remember that History, with a capital H, is always a throw of the cosmic dice. It seems to provide both the good and the bad in endless measure, and only God can sort it out in the end, I suppose. One man's vaunted explorer is another man's genocidal conquistador, and how those cosmic dice land on the table is so often a random walk.

Indeed, the "Accidental Sea" could just as easily be the name of the Caribbean Sea given the nature of its discovery; but as my younger and wiser junior officers correctly pointed out, before very long, the deliberate and dark scourge of slavery to fuel the production of sugar and other crops would begin to take root throughout these beautiful and pristine islands. Colonization of the Caribbean was also fueled by the desire to proselytize and convert the indigenous populations to Christianity. The Age of Exploration, setting out on the vast oceans of the world, washed ashore on the quiet Caribbean—with explosive effect felt down to the present day. And on reflection it is hard to deny that the ultimate outcome, sadly, was not so much the product of an accident after all, but of a series of acts of avarice and greed that shape the sensibilities of the islands today.

THE CARIBBEAN IS A BIG SEA—if you include the Gulf of Mexico, which we will do for our purposes, it surpasses the Mediterranean as the world's largest body of water that is not categorized as an ocean (after the Pacific, Atlantic, Indian, and Arctic oceans in that order). It is roughly 1.6 million square miles, about half the size of the continental United States.

It is a sort of massive pot-shaped body of water, and it is easy to picture the Caribbean as the rim of a huge volcano. One side is shaped by the long finger of Florida pointing downward on the western side, dropping like the boot of Italy toward the island of Cuba. Americans don't always appreciate the size of Cuba, by the way—if it were laid out on a map of the United States it would stretch from Washington, D.C., to Chicago. Indeed, when President Kennedy was being briefed on the Bay of Pigs operation in the White House in the early 1960s, the commandant of the Marine Corps, a World War II veteran, overlaid the map of Cuba on one of the United States in that fashion to make the point. He then overlaid on the map of Cuba another map with a single dot at its center—it was tiny Tarawa, where in the Pacific War thousands of Marines had been killed to take that small island. Cuba is a big place.

Cuba runs more or less northwest to southeast, and below it is the large island of Hispaniola, shared by the Spanish-speaking Dominican Republic and the Creole- and French-speaking Haiti, probably the unluckiest and certainly the poorest country in the Caribbean. Below them are the long string of islands forming the western border of the Caribbean, which are a mix of nationalities indeed, representing the constant resetting of imperial European ambitions in the Caribbean: British, French, Dutch, Danish, and Spanish are all represented across the centuries, and the present-day culture of each island is a kind of Euro-mélange.

At the foot of the island chain and just north of South America are the twin islands of Trinidad and Tobago. Richer than most of the rest, and representing a curious blend of English and Spanish culture, T & T in many ways has the best of both worlds: a British language and legal backbone overlaid on the warm Caribbean and Spanish island cultures. Because they are blessed with oil reserves (which has been a mixed blessing at times, in truth), they can afford to provide a higher level of resources for social and structural programs than many of their counterparts nearby. My principal memory of my visits there while I was a combatant commander was the exuberance of the motorcycle escorts that accompanied my convoys from the airport to the capital and the government houses. The tall, elegant police motorcyclists would literally stand on their motorcycles and direct traffic without touching the handlebars, moving at very high speed. I have been in motorcades in more than a hundred countries; this was the most dangerous. I described this to the head of U.S. Special Operations Command, a four-star Army Green Beret who had spent his life in combat and danger, and he said, "Those sound like some troopers with a death wish." Yet it all seemed to fit with the energy and the humor of a nation with a love of public theater and plenty of propensity for risk.

Across the north coast of South America, the Caribbean Sea laps against the three Guyanas: French Guiana, Suriname (the former Dutch Guiana), and Guyana (formerly British Guiana). They are sort of three tin soldiers guarding the southern mouth of the Caribbean, representing the three principal colonizing powers that arrived after Spain. Each has its own character, culture, language, and political situation, but the one that sticks in my mind is Guyana, the former British colony that sits farthest to the west. Known principally to Americans as the site of a bloody cult murder-suicide in 1978 known as the Jonestown Massacre after its megalomaniacal perpetrator, Jim Jones, it gave American English the phrase "to drink the Kool-Aid," as in to believe in the cause despite all evidence to the contrary. It is a physically beautiful and relatively resource-rich nation with a quietly defeated air and a political system straight out of the Borgias.

I went there first in the mid-2000s as the commander of U.S. Southern Command, determined to visit all of the thirty-plus nations of the region in the first couple of months on the job. My staff told me not to bother with the three Guyanas because "nothing ever happens there." But I liked the idea of at least setting foot on each of the countries of the region, and after a brief back-and-forth with my doubting chief of staff, we set up a trip after, of course, visiting the bigger, more important countries: Brazil, Argentina, and Colombia. I arrived and was duly shuttled to see the president (or was it the prime minister?), and in his dusty office with the blinds drawn against the tropical sun, I asked him what the greatest challenge he faced was. Poverty? Drugs? Crime? (All of these were pretty obvious problems.)

He shook his head and sighed, admitting that each of those was indeed a challenge; but he said the biggest problem was emigration. "Everyone who can attain a high school degree leaves as soon as they can. Mostly they want to go north to your country, but they will go anywhere to get out of Guyana." It was a sad comment from a sad man, and made me think how lucky we are in the United States—for all our problems and mistakes and challenges, wherever I go people still want to come to, not leave, our country. We talked a bit more, I promised to be helpful in training and equipping his small and relatively docile military, and on I went. In all of the places I visited on the Caribbean Sea, in many ways Guyana was the saddest.

. . .

COLOMBIA IS THE MOST BEAUTIFUL and troubled country in the Caribbean. It ought to work well given the lush beauty, incredible natural resources (gold, oil, rich farmland, gorgeous harbors), and geopolitical position, both commanding the southwestern Caribbean and possessing a long Pacific coast. It sits at the crossroads of North and South America as well as the Caribbean and Pacific, and would also possess the Panama Canal (and Panama) if the United States had not essentially created an independent Panama in 1905 by financing and guaranteeing a revolution and breakaway there in order to build the Panama Canal ("We stole it fair and square").

I spent a fair amount of time afloat in the Caribbean off the coast of Colombia over the years, especially in the first decade of the twenty-first century while charged with the so-called War on Drugs mission as the U.S. commander based in Miami. I had sailed through the waters earlier in my career, mostly en route to or from the Panama Canal, but as a four-star admiral I was responsible for helping our Colombian friends stop the flow of drugs that departed the Colombian ridge—much of it over water routes through the western Caribbean. The volumes of cocaine are staggering, certainly in the hundreds of tons. At one point early in my tenure, we captured a fully formed submarine built in the jungle of Colombia and launched into the Caribbean Sea with a crew of three, diesel propulsion, an excellent communication suite, and—wait for it—ten tons of cocaine in the hold. Street value north of $150 million: an example of powerful innovation and determination. These were the new pirates of the Caribbean, and their remit was law across much of the western Caribbean.

Just north of Colombia is the beating heart of the American economy

(American in the broad sense, encompassing all of the Americas, North, Central, and South): the Panama Canal. Built on what was once Colombian soil after a U.S.-engineered coup and subsequent "independence," it opened in 1914 after much death and suffering among the workers, most of whom came from all around the Caribbean littoral and were directed by American engineers (after a previously failed attempt in the late 1880s led by Frenchman Ferdinand de Lesseps). This is a story of maritime engineering well told by historian David McCullough in his brilliant book *The Path Between the Seas.*

FOR A MARINER, there is no experience quite like transiting the Panama Canal. It is such a specialized nautical operation that even the United States Navy, which famously believes in full accountability for its commanding officers, relieves a CO of his or her command accountability while in the canal. I went through it first in the mid-1980s as the operations officer on a brand-new *Ticonderoga*-class cruiser, the fourth of the class, USS *Valley Forge.* I loved that ship, which I had helped build at a shipyard in Mississippi. When we sailed away, it very much had a "new car smell," and the paint was pristine on its gray hull. As the operations officer, I had charge of the physical care of the exterior of the 567-foot ship, and my boatswain mates took enormous pride in the sides. When we approached the narrow sliver of the canal, I thought my crusty boatswain mate Chief Petty Officer Gene Jones would have a heart attack worrying about scraping our sides on the tight openings, where ships are literally pulled through the locks by mini-trains on both sides. The Panamanians were experts, and the transit went smoothly with hardly a scrape. But that feeling of coming from the open water of the Caribbean Sea into the tiny, vulnerable locks—of giving over responsibility for navigating your ship to the canal workers and the pilot—was an uncomfortable one. I was happy to break free on the southern side and kick up the speed to a full 30 knots, blasting swiftly into the endless Pacific and leaving the canal behind.

UP THE COAST OF Central America you sail past the most dangerous countries in the world—after Panama comes Costa Rica, Nicaragua, El Salvador, Guatemala, Honduras, Belize, and Mexico. Collectively they have the highest violence rates in the world—more violent deaths per hundred thousand in the population than anywhere else, including Afghanistan and Iraq. Tragically, much of the violence is essentially an export of the United States, driven by the vast demand signal of our market for narcotics, armed by automatic weapons and handguns manufactured in our factories, and led by the gang culture created in southern California and sent south with deportees three decades ago. The Caribbean coast of Central America is a kind of Wild West that in places has changed little from the days of the pirates. It has hidden ports and forts that are no-go zones for law enforcement, places from which the drug runners operate with complete impunity.

I FIRST SAILED to the Caribbean in 1975, while I was in my fourth year, a senior—properly referred to as midshipman first class—at the U.S. Naval Academy. Every summer the entire Brigade of Midshipmen, some four thousand strong, dispersed all around the world on their summer cruises.

These were not experiences like going on a Carnival cruise line and enjoying piña coladas in the sunshine while shopping in the ship's arcade.

Summer cruises for midshipmen at Annapolis consisted of flying to some port of embarkation, slinging a huge sea bag over your shoulder, and trudging up a steel gangplank. The idea was to learn something about "the fleet," which at that point in my seagoing career was merely a distant theory.

In the humid summer of 1975, I was bused down to Norfolk, Virginia, where a dozen classmates and I embarked in the brand-new aircraft carrier *Nimitz*. She was a floating city; more than 100,000 gross tons, the length of three football fields, and from keel to the top of her mast about the height of the Empire State Building. After a quick indoctrination we were under way and headed down the East Coast of the United States into the Caribbean Sea.

After a couple of days, we entered the Caribbean through the Windward Passage, the strait that lies between the islands of Hispaniola (Haiti and the Dominican Republic) and Cuba. The captain came on the ship's announcing system, the 1MC, and said we were passing through the same water as Christopher Columbus centuries earlier, a speech I was to duplicate nearly two decades later as a destroyer captain. As a midshipman on *Nimitz*, however, I was having a cheeseburger in the wardroom and decided to forgo the soft ice cream sundae bar in tribute to the no doubt far more rigorous experiences Columbus and his sailors faced.

Our first port of call was not exactly a tourist destination: Guantánamo Bay, Cuba. In those days, of course, it was not internationally infamous as a prison for terrorists but rather as a backwater training facility for ships getting ready to deploy. The main purpose of Guantánamo Naval Station for most of its history was logistic support—a Mahanian coaling station. Over time, because it was out of the main Atlantic shipping lanes and had a ready logistic base, it became the center of training on the Atlantic coast.

In practice this meant that warships would show up for three weeks of brutal training to prepare for combat. Everything a ship could do was exercised, from gunfire to damage control (fighting shipboard fires and flooding after taking incoming fire) to aviation operations and underway replenishment. It was a tight, twenty-hour-per-day syllabus, designed to put the ship's crew under the maximum amount of stress.

The beauty of doing this off Guantánamo Bay was that it provided an opportunity to get the full attention of the crew—who were a long way away from their families and friends. The bars and tattoo parlors of Norfolk seemed a distant memory to the sailors. But realizing that you cannot get the maximum effect by strictly training the crew at sea, the Navy in its wisdom let the sailors come ashore for a couple of days each week to blow off some steam.

So my first chance to set foot ashore in the Caribbean was as a twenty-year-old midshipman on the athletic fields and tennis courts of the naval station under a full-on summer sun. Along with four thousand of my new best friends, I worked out and drank beer for 35 cents a glass with occasional shots of the high-end 50-cent rum to wash it down. Predictably, by the end of the day, the world was spinning a bit, and I went down to the pristine beach with a couple of my Annapolis classmates to sober up and contemplate the world from the vantage point of the sea.

The Caribbean is a gorgeous body of water at night, and that evening the moon hung full and low over the gently rolling waves. As is the case in most of the Caribbean, the landscape of Cuba is dry and rocky once you get away from the beaches; but the beauty of the trade winds and the luminous turquoise water more than made up for it. As I leaned back and watched the moon rise, I thought of all the ships sailing and steaming by that southern point of the long island of Cuba, centuries of history, much of it bloody, passing by me.

The next day we were back aboard the huge steel decks of the carrier and listening to the endless gong of the general quarters alarm.

IF YOU LOOK BACK at the colonial history of the Caribbean, it is easy to be reminded of Winston Churchill's famous description of the traditions of the Royal Navy: "Rum, buggery, and the lash." Indeed, the sea is named for one of the earlier Amerindian tribes, the Caribs, who were effectively wiped out by the intrusion of guns, germs, and steel, as author Jared Diamond titled his magnificent book on why Europe colonized so much of the world and not vice versa.

Pre-European times in the Caribbean are not well understood or documented. The Europeans gave a variety of names to the indigenous tribes they discovered, all of whom they simply saw as candidates for conversion to Christianity and slavery. Some of the terms from those early days of collision include "Taino" or "Tanyo," meaning a native who was relatively cooperative; or "Carib," meaning a warrior and generally a cannibal; or Arawak, who was somewhere in the middle. Cultural anthropology was not a strong suit of the Spanish conquistadores, and the opportunity to preserve the language, history, and culture of the locals was largely squandered.

What is notable is the lack of seamanship or open sea voyaging on the part of the early inhabitants of the Caribbean. Other than some offshore fishing, there is little evidence or record of serious voyages, the use of sails of any kind, or the construction of vessels capable of containing more than a handful of sailors. Thus the monstrous vessels of the arriving Spaniards, although quite tiny by today's standards, were overwhelmingly impressive to the native populations.

These were not entirely unsophisticated societies. The Caribbean natives had probably come into the broad basin of the Caribbean Sea thousands of years before the arrival of Europeans. The best guess would be that they were searching, not for gold and silk like the Europeans, but for land, freedom from oppressors to the south on the South American continent, food, and fish.

At the time of the European arrival, they lived in villages and settlements, some of which were as large as five thousand souls. The overall population of the Caribbean islands is impossible to estimate, but suffice it to say that the overwhelming majority died in the decades after the European arrival. As Mel Gibson's vibrant movie *Apocalypto* depicts, set on the Caribbean coast of Mexico, the arrival of the Europeans was absolutely an apocalypse to the local inhabitants.

THE NEXT ACT in the drama of the Caribbean actually began when a little-known friar named Martin Luther nailed his views to the door of a cathedral in present-day Germany in 1517. The result ultimately was the creation of a pool of gasoline to which the king of England, Henry VIII, put a match in trying to sort out his marital arrangements. Thus emerged Protestantism and the schism in the Catholic faith, resulting in more than 150 years of significant war and bloodshed, with lingering effects far into the nineteenth century.

Overlaid on all of this, of course, was geopolitics and imperial rivalry. Soon Europe was immersed in political and religious wars between Protestants and Catholics that would continue to burn in one form or another for the next five centuries (and sputter along today still in Ireland and the Balkans to some degree). Inevitably, these huge European wars and disputes ashore began to play havoc with the emerging system of societies in the far Caribbean, especially on the oceans.

The principal combatants were, on one side, the Spanish Catholics who over the next several centuries would do all they could to consolidate a massive empire in the Americas; convert and essentially enslave the indigenous populations; extract great treasures of gold, silver, and precious gems; and conduct monopolistic trade in everything the New World had to offer, notably sugar, and—as time went by—tobacco. On the other side were the hardy Protestant English and Dutch, both of whom launched explorers and raiders from the North Atlantic to the Caribbean Sea itself. Somewhere in the middle, and less effective, were the Catholic French and Portuguese, who carved out holdings on the South American continent. Overall, it was an age of sea empires fighting in a relatively small space in and around the islands of the Caribbean and the littoral coasts of the larger land masses that bound it.

One of the main targets of the Protestant sea raiders was the treasure-laden galleons of the Spanish crown. These would sail every year from Spain, carrying trading goods to the New World. The *flota* (fleet), as it was called, would number dozens of significant ships. Upon arrival in the Americas, they would unburden themselves of goods and load into their creaking hulls the precious spoils of empire—silver from the mines of Potosí in Bolivia, gold and emeralds from Colombia, tobacco and sugar, and even goods from China and the Philippines that came across the Pacific. By the latter part of the sixteenth century, the Spanish had created the first global market, and they took enormous rents and profits from it. Such ships were incredible targets, and both the navies and the authorized commerce raiders from the Protestant states gleefully attacked.

Perhaps the most iconic Protestant sea raider was Sir Francis Drake, who made his name in the Caribbean with a series of daring raids and was the darling of his monarch, Queen Elizabeth, with whom he may or may not have had an affair. In the late 1500s, he conducted raids on Spanish ports in Colombia and Florida, burning and pillaging as he went. After a stint of more honest battle in opposing the Spanish Armada in the Atlantic as it sailed toward England in 1588, Drake returned to his first and best love, pirating. He eventually died of disease in the Caribbean in 1596, having made himself rich.

But Drake was hardly the only pirate. There were hundreds of buccaneers (so called supposedly for their habit of roasting both meat and captives over a slow-burning wood fire on frames, called *boucans* in French) plying the Caribbean during the 1500s and 1600s. The Caribbean was not the scene of large pitched battles, but rather a kind of nautical Wild West. There were certainly naval warships, and as time went on and "civilization" descended, they became the dominant force in the region.

But throughout the first century of the Caribbean's colonization, the maritime dynamic was largely that of commercial trading vessels being attacked by opportunistic pirates—all of this fancifully and farcically brought to life, of course, by the swashbuckling and swishing Captain Jack Sparrow in the blockbuster *Pirates of the Caribbean* films. Many of those incidents are loosely based on the exploits of Sir Henry Morgan, a Welsh-born privateer whose life and career are truly the stuff of legend. After a highly successful (and vicious) career as a buccaneer, he returned to England, was slightly reprimanded (wink, wink), then made the governor general of Jamaica, much to the disgust of the Spanish. He milked that gorgeous island for a great deal of wealth by continuing to make it available to sea rovers, and eventually died there in 1688.

I went to Jamaica for the first time in the late 1970s, a period of considerable turbulence in the island's history. Relatively newly independent, Jamaicans were finding their way through a natural transition from reliance on a British backbone of governance to a system (and a set of political choices) more aligned with their culture, history, and proclivities. Not surprisingly, they turned dramatically left. While as a mid-twenty-something Navy lieutenant this was not entirely clear to me, what came across quite vividly was a sense of dramatic, indeed revolutionary, sensibilities that were sweeping the island. This was not a simple land of Red Stripe beer, jerk chicken, joint-puffing and reggae-playing Rastafarians, and gorgeous tourist vistas. Clearly there was much more afoot.

This became clear to my small liberty party of ship's engineers from the carrier *Forrestal* when we decided to get beyond the tourist zone in Montego Bay and tried to go watch a cricket match being played by two all-black teams. With all black spectators. And no welcoming committee. We weren't exactly threatened so much as aggressively ignored, much like the college students in the movie *Animal House* who try so desperately and pathetically to relate to the band in the all-black roadhouse they invade. Needless to say, we pressed on pretty quickly. After experiencing much the same syndrome in a number of other venues, we decided that prudence was in order and we headed back to the beaches of the north shore.

The following evening, I had the bridge watch as we pulled up the anchor and headed fair out to the clear waters of the Caribbean. The evening winds were pushing us hard, and I was struggling to get the ship on course, despite having four huge propellers and a hundred thousand horsepower at my disposal. Finally, I got us straightened out on course and as the sun was setting we turned east and headed into the winter twilight away from Jamaica. As the watch settled into a routine, I tried to put together the little I knew of Jamaican history with all that I had seen and experienced, and I realized the trip had made a lasting impression on me—especially the sense of the overhang of history, the ghosts that rattle our past and somehow exist just beyond the edge of our vision. Since then the Caribbean has always had that effect on me: of being in an edgy dark dream from which I have just awakened, but incapable of really understanding the land in which I find myself—despite enormous

sympathy and affection for the islands, coastlines, and people of this remarkable region.

THE EUROPEAN LAND WARS of the 1600s inevitably began to bleed
over into conflict at sea. The British came late to the Caribbean, but they
came to see the power, not only of sugar and tobacco, but increasingly of
chocolate, ginger, salt, and indigo. By the latter part of the seventeenth
century, their fleet was sailing for open war in the Caribbean, seeking to
wrest territory away from Spain. After a complex series of battles, the
British ended up with many long-term colonial possessions—Jamaica,
Barbados, Nevis, St. Kitts, and other islands.

The Dutch, not to be left out, took and held several islands more toward the southern Caribbean, as well as Dutch Guiana (now Suriname).
In one of those absolutely delicious and yet tragic historical ironies, the
Dutch traded the colony of New Amsterdam for Dutch Guiana. When
that occurred in the seventeenth century, they were regarded as roughly
equivalent properties. Today, of course, New York City is worth a couple
of trillion dollars, while the capital of Suriname, Paramaribo, is among
the most impoverished capitals in the Americas, a city of less than half a
million people.

And soon the French began to move in, securing smaller islands and
taking a slice of the Caribbean coast of South America, which became
French Guiana (which remains today a department of France). Each of
the colonizing powers merged private and public efforts by creating maritime trading and commercial companies, which functioned as quasi-
official forces to bolster their national claims in the region. These West
Indies companies (by various names among the various nations) were
akin to the East India companies that would ply the Indian Ocean a
century or so later.

. . .

BY THE 1700S, the economic outline of the next two hundred years was set. It consisted of a slave labor–based economic model that brought African labor to the Caribbean to produce sugar and other agricultural products. These were sent to Europe, which provided the muscle to collect the slaves. The triangular flow of ships went from Europe to Africa to collect slaves, then to the Americas with tradable goods and slaves, then back to Europe to bring the treasure of the Caribbean home.

Sugar itself was well known globally before the colonization of the Caribbean, with origins in the Pacific and Indian oceans, and was once planted extensively in the Levant. But those sources faltered, the European sweet tooth grew, and the appetite for sugar began to drive the economy of the region. There were also Indians and indentured whites involved in the extremely labor-intensive process of growing, cutting, crushing, storing, distilling it into molasses and rum, and transporting. Sugar cane has only about 10 percent sugar in it, and the process of extracting it is brutally difficult work.

In addition to the terrible and obvious human misery involved, the triangular trade also contributed to disease and death. This was not only through the exposure of indigenous natives and African slaves to previously unknown microbes; it was also dangerous for the Europeans, who would themselves face diseases rising from the combination of stagnant water and mosquitoes that resulted when land was fully cleared. Yellow fever was a particular scourge that attacked Europeans, but not Africans (who had a reasonable level of immunity, having been exposed to a variant in Africa). This further drove the demand signal for the "adaptable Africans" and away from using white labor of any kind.

All of this shaped the destiny and demographics of the Caribbean through the 1700s and on into the 1800s, until nations finally began to be repulsed by slavery, beginning with Great Britain, which banned the transatlantic slave trade in 1807; the United States, which fought a civil war to end slavery in the 1860s; and finally Brazil, which abolished slavery in 1888. But the damage had been done, the culture of slavery blighted these societies throughout those years, and its effects continue to be felt today. The numbers are extraordinary and utterly tragic—certainly millions were moved across the infamous Middle Passage, perhaps as many as 12 million, with up to 2 million perishing along the way. But we will never actually know the true numbers.

THERE IS ALWAYS a kind of theater about the Monroe Doctrine, which was issued by President James Monroe in the 1820s and largely ignored by the European powers for the next hundred years or so. The idea was that the United States would not permit any further colonization or manipulation of the nations of the Caribbean, and that our nation would be a sort of guarantor of good behavior. It was paternalistic, condescending, and quite unenforceable by a nation with limited armed forces, a small population, and a confused political culture, and an indifferent approach to international relations generally, to say nothing of being a slave-owning country itself. Over the decades, as the strength and power of the United States grew, the Monroe Doctrine began to have more teeth to it, and would be invoked from time to time to push back against European ambitions in the region. Throughout the nineteenth century, it was mentioned but seldom honored, until the United States burst on the colonial scene more or less by accident as a result of the war with Spain.

The principal connection of the Caribbean nations to the wars of the twentieth century was through the soldiers exported to fight for their colonial masters. During World War I, the British West Indies Regiment, formed from the islands, saw combat in Europe, although the black islanders were often relegated to support and logistic duty, to their dismay. French troops likewise participated with their national elements.

The United States confined itself to a series of interventions throughout the early part of the century, principally by the U.S. Marine Corps, to enforce stability, uphold the banking laws, and keep the Europeans more or less out of places like Haiti, the Dominican Republic, and Central America. The United States also purchased the Virgin Islands from the Danes, a pretty good buy at $25 million, even in 1917, when you look at real estate prices there today. I remember taking my destroyer into both St. Thomas and St. Croix in the mid-1990s and thinking what a wonderful stroke of luck the United States had in three national purchases—the Louisiana Purchase, which gave us essentially the western continental United States; Alaska, which gives us our window on the north and vast natural resources; and the Virgin Islands, which afford us strategic reach into the Caribbean alongside Puerto Rico.

THINGS BEGAN TO really heat up in the Caribbean during the cold war. What set the stage, of course, was the rise of caudillos, a Spanish term for military dictators who came to dominate virtually all the nations of Latin America and the Caribbean by the latter part of the twentieth century. These dictators, naturally enough, gave rise to countervailing freedom movements, some of which were associated with communism, and suddenly the cold war arrived in the sunny Caribbean—with ground zero being on the island of Cuba. After the Cuban Revolution, Fidel Castro came and visited the United States, and it looked as though there might be an amicable relationship. But Castro quickly became associated with the Soviet Union, and in the dynamics of the cold war it was "you are either with us or against us" on both sides. The United States did all that it could to undermine the Cuban regime, most notably with the failed invasion at the Bay of Pigs in 1961. This CIA-supported mission ended up with a thousand Cubans dead, a couple of thousand more jailed by Castro, and bitter enmity that endured for decades.

The height of danger, and the moment at which the Caribbean became the epicenter of the world, was over a ten-day period in October 1962 in the Cuban Missile Crisis. This is a story best told by Graham Allison and Philip Zelikow in their masterful book *Essence of Decision*, about the Kennedy administration's successful effort to avoid a nuclear war. The Navy conducted a significant blockade of the island to prevent more Soviet missiles from sailing to Cuba.

Eventually the crisis was defused after some clever diplomatic maneuvering, but it is extraordinary to think how close the world came to a nuclear exchange and a completely changed and diminished world order in those days.

The cold war hovered over the Caribbean throughout the second half of the twentieth century as a sort of ongoing symphony playing in the background, but the real theme was independence. Most of the islands and other small countries finally broke free from their European overseers, virtually all peacefully: Guyana and Barbados (1966), the Bahamas (1973), Grenada (1974), Dominica (1978), St. Lucia and St. Vincent and the Grenadines (1979), Belize (1981), and St. Kitts and Nevis (1983). Each has its own rich culture and history, although in economic terms most remain relatively poor today.

By the 1980s and 1990s, Haiti had become the center of a great deal of violent activity—both from political turbulence and from Mother Nature. In the 1980s, the dictator Jean-Claude "Baby Doc" Duvalier was forced from power and a series of elections and coups ensued. When elected president Jean-Bertrand Aristide was forced out by his military in

1991, the United States put pressure on the coup leaders to turn over power peacefully. My destroyer, USS *Barry*, was dispatched to Haiti as part of an arms embargo (read: show of force) in the mid-1990s, and all I can remember is steaming placidly up and down the coast, boarding a couple of coastal steamers carrying bananas, and holding barbecues on the fantail for a very bored crew. I remember looking at the dark coast of the island and thinking about all the blood spilled there over the years in the slave times, the heroic but doomed slave revolt, the massacres, the earthquakes and hurricanes. There cannot be a less lucky country than Haiti.

I returned to Haiti roughly twenty years later as a four-star commander in the days after one of the seemingly endless hurricanes had knocked down a great deal of the very shaky infrastructure. I visited with the Haitian president René Préval in the beautiful but poorly maintained presidential palace, toured the city, and tried to be helpful by directed delivery of aid and supplies. The country seemed to be on a bit of an upswing, with significant international aid coming in and a real effort at reconstruction getting traction. Over my three years in Southern Command, I always felt Haiti's luck was changing. But I was wrong.

The really big disaster came just after my time, in 2010, when a massive earthquake killed perhaps 300,000 people (these are highly disputed figures) and completely destroyed the capital of Port-au-Prince, including flattening the presidential palace. The epicenter of that quake was just outside the city, and the destruction was essentially complete. Since then, Haiti has had enormous difficulty mustering the kind of support it needs, as the world's attention has moved on to Syria, sub-Saharan Africa, and many other troubled spots.

One other moment of cold war excitement in the Caribbean was on the tiny island of Grenada, which had suffered a left-wing coup in 1979 and then a brutal countercoup that led to the execution of the prime minister, Maurice Bishop. The newly installed government appeared to the Reagan administration as dangerous to the thousand or so U.S. citizens (including, famously, many U.S. medical students). That the government also had Marxist tendencies was an additional problem. The United States invaded Grenada ostensibly to protect U.S. citizens in a scene reminiscent of the many U.S. invasions in the Caribbean in the late nineteenth and early twentieth century—six thousand U.S. Army, Marines, and Navy SEALs came ashore in Operation Urgent Fury in 1983. They easily restored order and turned over power to the governor-general. Ironically, today you can drive by the monument to the U.S. soldiers killed just outside the international airport—named for Maurice Bishop, the left-leaning leader who was overthrown and executed.

Of note, Operation Urgent Fury further exposed the inability of the various branches of the U.S. military to work coherently together, which was first significantly observed following the failed rescue attempt of the Iranian hostages a few years earlier. The problems were in communications, doctrine, logistics, and tactics; the Grenada invasion led to major overhaul and the implementation of a new joint approach for the armed forces. As usual, it is little remembered in U.S. history, but looms as a significant event in the history of this small, beautiful island.

Indeed, that invasion of Grenada is a sort of metaphor for the lack of U.S. interest and engagement that has been the pattern in the Caribbean. Over my years as commander of U.S. Southern Command, based in Miami (some would say the true capital of the Caribbean and Latin America), I came to know the Caribbean very well, visiting every major island over a three-year period. It is a lovely and vibrant part of the world, dominated by a clear and gorgeous body of water, yet despite its preternatural beauty, it is unfortunately also a part of the world that does not live up to its potential, with poverty, poor growth, corruption, and violence acting as the four horsemen of the tropical apocalypse. It is a part of the world that seems perpetually stuck in the past in so many ways. When I contemplate the Caribbean, I am often reminded of one part of the Pirate's Code in the *Pirates of the Caribbean* movies: "Any man who falls behind is left behind." In the Caribbean, it feels like *everyone* somehow fell hopelessly behind the rest of the world, and the region has yet to catch up.

Let's face it: while physically beautiful, the Caribbean is a sea of nations that by and large don't function terribly well. Central America is the most violent region in the world; Colombia fought a virulent insurgency for sixty years; Venezuela is oil rich and politically poor, unable as a result to even stock goods on the shelves; the three Guyanas (British, now simply Guyana; Dutch, now Suriname; and French, still a very poor department of France) are immersed in poverty; almost all of the islands are poor with weak, corrupt governance; Puerto Rico is in economic default; and Cuba, the "Pearl of the Antilles," is shamefully the last dictatorship in the hemisphere. Even the Caribbean coastline of the United States and Mexico, the two wealthiest nations, has some of the poorest internal states and regions along the Caribbean Sea (e.g. Mississippi, the Florida Panhandle, southeast Texas, and much of the Mexican Caribbean.

Why is this? It is the result of a lethal combination of history and geography, including a legacy of racism, slavery, piracy, anarchy, and small wars. Additionally, the region has a pattern of general physical exploitation with little regard to sustainability. What agricultural development has occurred most often has been conducted to the point of exhaustion, using mono-crop agricultural approaches. Finally, natural disasters (hurricanes, earthquakes, fire) are endemic. Just as a nation like Haiti begins to make progress, for example, it seems there is a devastating hurricane or an earthquake or both. There is no other maritime region that has been dealt such a bad hand of cards, both by history and by nature.

Additionally, the region is a significant transit zone for narcotics flowing largely from the Andean Ridge in South America and up into the
United States, the largest drug market in the world. In that regard, by the
way, I would prefer to simply park the moral question of whether people
should or should not use drugs. All of our societies are grappling with
that issue now, and many serious analysts and political leaders are beginning to advocate legalization. My concern here is quite simply about the
money.

The cash that comes out of this huge, multibillion-dollar industry is
unregulated, and much of it goes into corruption and violence, undermining fragile democracies and stifling growth in other sectors. The
idea of a "war on drugs" is limiting and simplistic, and has clearly failed—
we need a strategy to fight corruption and violence, which are the root
problems.

We need to think holistically about the root causes and what we can
do together in the Americas to address them. In terms of causes, it is
tempting to focus on the proximity of the United States itself as the heart
of the problem. The argument goes that the Monroe Doctrine, dating
from the 1820s, made the region into a sort of stifled American lake that
was never allowed to achieve its potential. Mexicans have a saying: "Pity
poor Mexico, so close to the United States, so far from God." There is a
bit of that feeling in the islands as well, where the United States tends to
be blamed for everything from the lackluster economy to bad weather
when it comes. All of that strikes me as a classic H. L. Mencken solution: clear, simple, and wrong. The situation is far more complex.

The great irony, of course, is that the region ought to work very well.
Despite a bloody history early on in the colonial period, there has not
been a major war fought in the region between nations for centuries. The
Caribbean is nestled in the heart of the Americas, the richest zone of
commerce and natural resources in the world. To the north and increas-

ingly to the south are industrialized societies with which the nations of
the Caribbean have strong and important demographic connections—
think of the Dominican Republic, Haiti, Cuba, Puerto Rico, and El Salvador, all with enormous immigrant populations in the United States on
a per capita basis.

While the Caribbean Sea itself can be fickle and bring terrible storms
during the hurricane season, it is a natural "tropical silk road" that links
all the economies and provides a shimmering tourist industry. Despite
the overhang of colonialism, many of the nations in the Caribbean maintain strong links back to advanced nations and economies in Europe,
including the United Kingdom, France, and the Netherlands. There is a
good deal of material to work with in terms of advancing the societies of
the region.

What can the United States do? And perhaps more important, what
are we willing to do?

First, we need to begin with a recognition of our responsibilities to
the region. Despite our frustration with decades of failure to achieve
progress, we have both a moral and a pragmatic set of reasons to expend
resources here in the Americas, and I would argue especially in the Caribbean Sea and basin. Given our historical engagement (including multiple military invasions over the past couple of centuries), as well as our
penchant for claiming responsibility (the Monroe Doctrine), the moral
argument seems fairly clear.

The pragmatic case is equally clear. By building up capable local partners in the region through cooperation—economically, politically, culturally, and in the security dimension—we strengthen our own shared
region. The tired and offensive cliché of "America's backyard" has to go
and be replaced by a Partnership for the Americas, and the Caribbean—
the neediest region of the Americas, encompassing the Central American nations—is a good, practical place to start. If even a tiny fraction of

what has been spent in Afghanistan on development had been deployed in the Caribbean, we might have seen extraordinary results. It is never too late to start.

Second, we need to encourage the nations of the Caribbean to work together. The reality is that they are individually too small to achieve real political throw weight. There are some nascent organizations in the Caribbean, but they have never proven themselves effective in moving the global needle politically. We should provide resources, advice, and training to the Caribbean organizations that focus on collective action, and also revitalize the moribund Caribbean Basin Initiative, which has always been a kind of geopolitical afterthought to NAFTA and CAFTA.

Third, our security cooperation has been limited in its approach and effectiveness. Almost entirely focused on the failed "war on drugs," it has not provided the kind of wide-spectrum engagement that might improve the broader security situation in the region. The local forces need training and resources to improve in rule of law, basic investigative work, advanced anticorruption techniques, surveillance, intelligence, and human rights. U.S. Southern Command is the right conduit for this.

A fourth thought would be to build in a constructive and methodical way to draw on the huge diasporas from the region located in the United States today. The Cuban American community, for example, has resources and deep business experience. Each of the other national groups brings different regional strengths within the United States to bear. Connecting the Caribbean diaspora is crucial.

Fifth, we should do this in cooperation with our partners Mexico and Canada, the other two North American economic powers. We all have a shared interest in a successfully functioning Caribbean.

Sixth, the United States should work to develop a collective Caribbean strategy. We have one for the Arctic—why not one for our southern neighbors clustered around the Caribbean Sea?

Seventh, we should think more aggressively about so-called Track II diplomacy, coupling the private sectors in the United States and the region together. This can be done through educational reforms, programs in the arts, sports diplomacy, and medical exchanges. Given that the languages of the region are overwhelmingly English and Spanish, our two core national languages, we have a huge comparative advantage in doing this in and around the Caribbean Sea. When I was the military commander at U.S. Southern Command, we tried a number of innovative things to connect with the region. One was a series of baseball clinics conducted by U.S. troops (carefully screened semipro-caliber ballplayers) and financed partly through donations from Major League Baseball teams. There are many creative approaches in this vein that would help foster human connections.

Overall, this is a region where a little bit of attention and resources go a very long way. There are humanitarian and pragmatic reasons to overturn the Pirate's Code of "fall behind, left behind"—let's work harder to help our Caribbean neighbors sail ahead.

7.

THE ARCTIC OCEAN

PROMISE AND PERIL

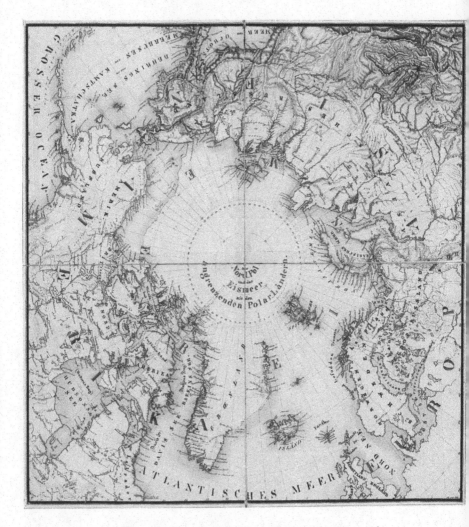

The Arctic Ocean holds a unique place in sailors' lore and explorers' stories. *Map created by Sir John Ross, 1855.*

Despite its rapid opening, the Arctic remains the
world's least-understood ocean.

THE PROMISE OF THE
ARCTIC OCEAN

Almost every one of the world's oceans has been the site of epic battles—some more than others—and there is no well-traveled global body of water that has escaped significant bloodshed. Indeed, it is impossible to estimate how many men and women have died at sea in combat all across the globe down through the centuries that man has sailed the world's oceans. But there is an exception: the Arctic Ocean.

Indeed, with that sole exception, at the bottom of every watery corner of the world lie the rusted weapons of long-dead sailors, their battles ended forever. The last ocean never to have seen any significant level of active combat is the Arctic, existing as it does at the top of the world, far from the reach of mankind. Today it offers the tantalizing chance of becoming a zone of cooperation and peace. But the enormity of its resources represents a prize that will draw increasing attention from many quarters, creating tension and danger.

Today the Arctic world is in a delicate state of tension: between environmentalists who are terrified we will destroy the last pure place on the earth and the developers who want to exploit the enormous natural wealth (albeit responsibly by their lights); between Russia and NATO, which increasingly face off across the Arctic Ocean and are perfectly capable of stumbling backward both metaphorically and literally into another cold war; and between scientists who want to preserve the ocean for science diplomacy and well-intentioned tour operators who want to open a booming ecotourism and educational industry in the last great frontier.

The Arctic Ocean is a place of both promise and peril, as well as mystery.

Above all, as we look at the Arctic, we should consider the place it holds in the collective imagination of the world. The region that even today many in the Scandinavian nations refer to as the "High North" was often thought of as a temperate zone waiting to be discovered. Early maps of the North Pole often showed an area with arable land and a moderate climate at the top of the world, and this misconception persisted for centuries. Early projections by Gerardus Mercator, one of the greatest sixteenth-century cartographers, showed such habitable zones in his 1595 charts. Even as late as the mid-1800s, the theory of mild temperatures and warm climates at the North Pole put forth by serious geographers like the German August Petermann was taken seriously by explorers. And virtually every civilization has a myth or two attached to the Arctic, notably the story of Santa Claus in our own Western canon.

THE SMALLEST OF THE WORLD'S great oceans, the Arctic Ocean (also occasionally called the Northern Ocean) has always been a zone of mystery, shielded from human sight throughout much of recorded history.

Early maps generally depicted it as a huge world of water, replete with gorgeous cartouches on the edges of the charts dominated by dragons and demons; in other cartographic representations it appears with vast oceans but with great hidden temperate land areas in the center of the massive ice fields. Even today, we know more about the moon or Mars, and have mapped them more carefully and fully, than we have the bottom of the Arctic Ocean.

Remarkably, defining the Arctic and the Arctic Ocean remains somewhat difficult, as even the term "Arctic" has varying definitions. It is scientifically and widely accepted to be the portion of the globe north of which there is continuous daylight during the summer solstice—this being 66 degrees, 33 minutes, and 45.9 seconds. Some alternative definitions have to do with temperatures in the region, for example, the portion of the earth with median temperatures of 50 degrees or less in July. Politically, some try to define it as the ocean bordering those countries with Arctic indigenous populations. As always in the human mind, defining a region varies depending on the observer's biases and theories about who should dominate it and how—and the Arctic, despite its shrouded character, is no exception.

It is worth noting in this regard how fundamental the Arctic is to Russia. Fully 20 percent of Russia's GDP and exports come from the Arctic. The Russians, by the way, fully self-identify as an Arctic nation in ways that certainly transcend the feelings of any other sovereign state with the possible exception of Canada. They have just launched the largest and most powerful nuclear icebreaker in the world, the *Arktika*—567 feet long, 33,000 tons, 80,000 shaft horse power, and capable of breaking through up to ten feet of ice. Strangely, for a region that is essentially devoid of human settlement, the Arctic is today the fastest-growing region in the world—each of the Arctic nations is actively pushing for the opening of settlements, increasing military activity, expanding resource exploitations, and generally staking claims with humans in the High North.

In terms of the Arctic *Ocean*, in reality, of course, it is essentially a bounded sea with two major openings, tightly confined at the Pacific end and relatively broadly accessible on the Atlantic side, with long continental shelves along either side. With the warming polar climate, temperatures are higher for both air and water and the permanent ice cover—the central feature to a mariner's cautious and skeptical eye—is eroding year on year. Virtually every reputable scientist looking at the global environment today sees a continuation in this trend, which will provide access for the first time in human history to an enormous trove of treasure in the form of natural resources, geopolitically important terrain, and highly efficient sea lanes of communication.

By 2040 there will be an open passage for essentially twelve months of the year, and another decade later there will no longer be ice over the North Pole. It is ironic that the Western world searched for centuries for the elusive passage to Asia through the Canadian Arctic: the Northwest Passage. Today, with no effort other than pollution and global warming, we have opened it with increasing alacrity. In terms of size, the Arctic is about 5.4 million square miles, covering an area roughly akin to the size of the continent of Antarctica.

This is the promise of the Arctic Ocean: it covers an estimated nearly 15 percent of the world's undiscovered oil (perhaps 100 billion barrels), 30 percent of the similarly estimated gas (some 1,700 trillion cubic feet of natural gas and 44 billion barrels of liquefied natural gas), and possibly a trillion dollars or more of nickel, platinum, cobalt, manganese, gold, zinc, palladium, lead, diamonds, and rare earth metals. In round terms about 25 percent of the proven reserve hydrocarbons (oil and natural gas) are in the Arctic.

It is also a huge incubator for human life–sustaining protein in the form of fish—50 percent of U.S. fish stocks come from the 200-nautical-mile exclusive economic zone off the coast of Alaska, for example. The same is true for many of the other nations that ply these waters, both within their exclusive economic zones and on the high seas (where the competition from non-Arctic nations is robust and rising). All of this takes place in an area that by square mileage is only 2.5 percent of the globe. In terms of geopolitical ownership, it is worth noting that with the full Russian continental shelf claims, nearly 80 percent of the proven reserves of the Arctic will be in Russian hands.

And most important in commercial and geopolitical terms, the fabled Northwest Passage is opening fairly rapidly as the ice cover recedes. Several years ago, over a million tons of cargo transited the Arctic routes and by doing so cut thousands of miles off the traditional sea paths across the lower trade routes. This cargo—which is rising in tonnage each year—falls broadly into three baskets: adventure tourism (the smallest), transarctic shipping (within the port system of the High North itself), and global shipping that has a specific destination around the world but outside of the Arctic itself. There are two key routes that connect Asia and Europe—the Northwest Passage that runs along the North American continent and the Northern Sea Route that runs along Eurasia, essentially along the coast of Russia. Both routes are at present unpredictable and risky, but their use is growing. Obviously, Russia will seek to develop the Eurasian route.

One key sea lane of communication today is the tight Bering Strait off the coast of Alaska, which is the only route between the Arctic Ocean and the vast Pacific Ocean at one end of the Arctic Sea. Taking this as a rude metric of the increase of shipping, the U.S. Coast Guard says that traffic through the Bering Strait increased nearly 120 percent from 2008 to 2012. All of this shipping must move over an area of open sea that is nearly undeveloped in terms of conventional ports, navigational aids, buoy systems, and other supporting maritime systems. For example, Barrow, Alaska—the major U.S. port on the North Slope—is accessible on a reliable basis only by air. Even Russia, which has invested heavily in its portion of the region, has limited coast guard coverage throughout the area.

All of this represents an exciting opportunity for mankind in the form of resources that have heretofore been unattainable given the harsh conditions, ever-present ice, and long distances from global communication centers. The promise of the Arctic Ocean is undeniable, but it sits in the center of a region that presents great peril as well.

THE FIRST TIME I sailed north into the waters of the Arctic Circle, I was in a Navy destroyer in the late 1970s operating in the western Pacific. We were detached from routine patrol around Japan and ordered to head to the west coast of Alaska. Fortunately for us, this was during high summer and while it was not exactly balmy, we were not in unusually uncomfortable seas. The highlight was learning that we would indeed dip our bow inside the Arctic Circle, which would make all of us on the ship "Blue Noses" in Navy parlance. This is usually accompanied by a ceremonial dip in a tub of very cold water on the bow, but because we had no previous Blue Noses in our crew, no one was excited about organizing such a ritual. Thus I earned my Blue Nose certificate without actually taking a dunk in the icy water of the Arctic Ocean.

In geopolitical terms, this was the height of the cold war, and our mission up there was to test the antisubmarine warfare gear on the ship under extreme conditions. We did so without actually stumbling on a Soviet submarine, at least as far as I could tell. As the ship's antisubmarine warfare officer, I was more worried about getting the long towed array cable off the reel on the ship, into the water, and back aboard in one piece than I was about actually finding a submarine. Over the next two decades, there were plenty of interactions between U.S. and Soviet warships in the Arctic, generally under the ice by submarines.

It seems metaphorically sensible that such confrontations were largely conducted in the silent, dark depths of the Arctic, unseen and in many cases unreported. Like those games of cat and mouse, much of what happens in the Arctic, as in Vegas, stays in the Arctic. We dodged a bullet in the cold war and avoided real combat between NATO and the Soviet Union—but looking ahead to the unfolding potential for confrontation around the Arctic Ocean, I often think back on that first voyage and hope that we can again avoid actual sea battles at the top of the world.

THE PERILS OF THE ARCTIC OCEAN

Why do I worry? A variety of perilous conditions will influence the speed with which mankind will be able to exploit fully all of the promise of the Arctic Ocean. Let's examine some of the challenges in the region.

The first and most evident form of peril remains simply the brutal character of the climate. In his extraordinary book (2015) about the doomed U.S. Arctic Expedition of 1879, *In the Kingdom of Ice: The Grand and Terrible Polar Voyage of the USS Jeannette*, Hampton Sides takes the reader deep into the mariners' experiences in the High North. At one point, speaking about the captain of the *Jeannette*, Navy lieutenant George Washington De Long, Hampton says, "He became more and more intrigued by the Arctic, by its lonely grandeur, by its mirages and strange tricks of light, its mock moons and blood-red halos, its thick, misty atmospheres, which altered and magnified sounds, leaving the impression that one was living under a dome." They set sail in April 1879 from San Francisco, and almost all died in the course of their expedition. Today, their bravery in the Arctic is commemorated by a lonely monument in the cemetery at the U.S. Naval Academy in Annapolis. The story is also echoed in Ian McGuire's extraordinary 2016 novel *The North Water*, about a whaling expedition that goes terribly wrong and creates the ultimate confrontation of good and evil—against that most unforgiving environment in the High North.

What makes the harsh conditions even more dangerous, of course, is the lack of facilities for rescue or monitoring of any kind. Taking the U.S. Coast Guard as an example, the closest Coast Guard air station to Barrow—the largest U.S. city on the north shore—is located in Kodiak, about a thousand miles to the south. While there are small commercial airports in some of the northern U.S. cities of Nome, Prudhoe Bay, and a few others, there is very little infrastructure to conduct search and rescue. The Arctic is also famously difficult for the basic transmission of command and control signals. Cellular coverage is virtually nonexistent for obvious reasons, and the general propagation of any form of radio signals is limited. All of this means that if a mariner is in trouble in the Arctic, he or she is in serious trouble.

A second form of peril in the Arctic Ocean today is the confused governance that surrounds the region, especially at sea. Given the confluence of five large key landholders bordering the Arctic Ocean—Russia, Canada, Norway, the United States, and Denmark (by virtue of Greenland)—there are competing national and international regimes at play.

At the international level, there is the United Nations Convention on the Law of the Sea (UNCLOS), which was created in 1982 after more than a decade of negotiation by essentially every nation on earth. It was significantly modified in 1994, and today forms the backbone of the regime of the oceans broadly. Oddly, given its enormous maritime interests, the United States has not signed the convention but instead relies on "customary international law" to gain as many of the benefits of the convention as it can. Most nations believe that the UNCLOS framework is both usable and functional in the Arctic Ocean today, and a 2008 agreement (the Ilulissat Declaration) memorializes that theory.

In addition to the Law of the Sea treaty, there is the Arctic Council, a high-level, consensus-driven forum for the Arctic nations (Russia, Canada, the United States, Norway, and Denmark plus Sweden, Finland, and Iceland). The indigenous people of the region are represented by five nongovernmental organizations that are also permanent participants in the council; they cover the interests of the majority of people living north of the Arctic Circle.

The United Nations has a maritime organization headquartered in London—the International Maritime Organization—that focuses on shipping and its regulation. It has been at work on a so-called Polar Code that would provide agreed-upon guidelines for shipping in the Arctic Ocean. Along with the UN Law of the Sea treaty and the Arctic Council, the International Maritime Organization participates in all the relevant conversations about the Arctic Ocean.

At the national level there are perils as well. Each of the key stakeholder countries has organizations that attempt to provide governance over both its nationals and within sovereign parts of the Arctic Ocean, but that also affect other entities, for example ships in transit.

The third peril of the Arctic is geopolitical competition. It is instructive to look at the alignment of the five key states bordering the Arctic Ocean—four are part of NATO (the United States, Norway, Canada, and Denmark) and one is an uneasy "partner" to NATO: the Russian Federation. As relations continue to deteriorate between NATO and Russia, it is becoming clear that the Arctic Ocean potentially will be more and more a place to revisit the mistakes of the cold war.

Overlaying the geopolitical competition is the warming of the ice, which opens up more and more of the Arctic Ocean for interaction between military forces. The average ice cover in 2012 was 1.3 million square miles below the average of the twenty-year period from 1980 to 2000. In addition, the age of the sea ice is a trend worth noting. Younger ice implies the warming and breaking up of the older caps. The ice caps are both thinning and receding, and the geopolitical impact—opening much more of the open Arctic Ocean—is significant.

There is a growing fear that another environmental danger is not fully appreciated: that the Arctic's permafrost could melt as a result of climate change, releasing massive amounts of methane gas. This would be like dumping enormous amounts of carbon into the world's environment, with potentially catastrophic results. A few numbers to understand this risk: first, the warming trends. Every time the earth's temperature rises one degree, we see the temperature at the North Pole rise about five degrees, largely the result of methane gases.

At the same time, we are globally concerned about the tipping point resulting from carbon emissions, which will occur when around 1,000 gigatons of carbon are dropped into the environment; at the moment, there are roughly 550 gigatons already at play. If we see even a two-degree rise in Arctic temperature, it is possible that 1,700 to 1,800 gigatons of carbon-equivalent methane will be released—immediately overshooting the carbon "budget" that nearly two hundred nations agreed to try to meet at the Paris Climate Summit. While not the result of policy in the Arctic directly, the warming effect on the permafrost there could be the catalytic event that drives global disaster, according to some experts.

Looking at the geopolitical approach of each of the significant Arctic nations is crucial to understanding the complex overlay of relations in the region. While there is nothing inevitable about conflict—or even competition—it appears at the moment that a period of real coordination or cooperation is unlikely. This is the result of the resurgence in aggressive Russian behavior in Europe, which has bled over into relations in the High North. But the view is more complex than a simple "here we are back in the cold war" sigh. Let's look at several of the key Arctic Ocean nations individually.

RUSSIAN FEDERATION

The majority of the vast Russian coastline lies above the Arctic Circle, and the High North is a central pillar of the Russian Federation's worldview. It also has by far the largest Arctic population (around four million) and the best infrastructure. Russia sees the promise of the Arctic with great geopolitical clarity, and will maneuver to be a dominant player. The Arctic is also a part of the world that figures deeply in the Russian mind-set and self-image as a nation of rugged individualists who are capable of surviving in the harshest of conditions. Russia will always care deeply about the Arctic Ocean in ways that other Arctic nations (particularly the United States) do not.

This does not presuppose that we are headed into a new cold war (literally and figuratively) in the Arctic Ocean, a sort of zero-sum Great Game of the High North. It is entirely possible that the Arctic Ocean could become a zone of cooperation, not one of competition or, God forbid, one of actual conflict.

However, it is necessary to be clear-eyed about Russian infrastructure bordering the Arctic Ocean. It will remain as it has been for centuries the home of the North Sea Fleet, and provide the bases for the Russian nuclear ballistic missile submarines, many of which will operate from bastions in the Arctic Ocean. Russia is increasing the number of troops it stations in the Arctic region, as well as expanding its bases dramatically.

All of the Russian Arctic-oriented strategies that we have observed over the past five years—both overtly and through intelligence gathering—view overall national Russian priorities as being centered on the region, featured in documents including *The National Security Strategy of the Russian Federation Through 2020* and the even more specific *Principles of State Policy of the Russian Federation in the Arctic Through 2020 and Beyond.*

Much of the Russian focus will be on developing the Northern Sea Route that runs along its northern landmass. Eventually, this route will save 40 percent off the time between Europe and Asia, which will lower transport costs and connect northern Russia to global markets for Russia's hydrocarbon exports. Use of the route will require shippers to develop vessels that can withstand the harsher conditions, and it will be quite hazardous for many years to come. There are currently very few facilities for refueling, repair, navigation, and search and rescue in the event of calamity. The Northern Sea Route will also create governance challenges given the multiple regulatory regimes that will gradually come into play as this new sea lane comes on line.

Russia will also seek to successfully defend its various territorial claims in the Arctic Ocean, many of which have persisted for more than six decades. Famously, the Russian Federation planted a Russian flag on the Lomonosov Ridge (a huge piece of the continental shelf that is entirely underwater and well beyond the 200-mile limit of the Russian coastline) in 2007, and Russia still has significant border disputes with Norway, the United States, and Canada. With the United States, for example, there is ongoing controversy concerning the maritime boundary in the Bering Sea. With Norway, while some issues have been resolved, there remain disagreements over fishing rights in the Barents Sea. There are claims and counterclaims surrounding extended continental shelf disputes involving Denmark, Norway, Russia and Canada.

While there is a great deal of disagreement and controversy, over time there is reason to hope for cooperation in the High North. In spite of the acrimony and the snippy rhetoric both from and directed at Russia, most of the actions Russia has taken in the Arctic Ocean have been fairly pragmatic. The potential for open conflict, while very low, is not entirely absent—all the more reason that the nations along the maritime borders of the Arctic Ocean should work diplomatically for a zone of cooperation.

CANADA

With more than 1.2 million square miles of Arctic territory and the world's second-largest land area in the High North, staunch NATO ally Canada has always placed a premium on its role as an Arctic protector, in both the idealistic ecological sense *and* in terms of a realistic geopolitical framework. Canada has the longest coastline of any country in the world, and 65 percent of it runs along the Arctic Ocean. Throughout the first decade of the twenty-first century, Canada has consistently spoken and acted with a central focus on the region in general and the Arctic Ocean in particular.

In particular, the Canadian military has expanded its operational surveillance of the Arctic Ocean and the approaches to Canadian territory. Some of its purchases include a new icebreaker, patrol vessels with some "new ice" capability, a deepwater port in Baffin Bay, and a winter "fighting school" for the army. Canadian work in mapping is also noteworthy. The former Canadian chief of defense General Walt Natynczyk was quite focused on the Arctic Ocean. When I asked him slightly tongue in cheek what he would do if the Canadian High North were invaded across the Arctic Ocean, he said, "Well, Jim, I suspect my first duty would be search and rescue to save the invaders"—his point, of course, being that the conditions in and around the Arctic Ocean are hardly conducive to real military operations supporting an invasion.

And this represents the slight Canadian schizophrenia about the Arctic: while they are strategically aware of potential challenges and are willing to play realpolitik to protect "their" parts of the Arctic and the Arctic Ocean, they are also big believers in a balanced and multinational approach to the region. They have been strong supporters of the Arctic Council throughout its history, as well as key participants in international conferences and proponents of focusing on the High North. In the context of NATO operations, the Canadians are the least enthusiastic of all twenty-eight nations in seeing a NATO presence in the waters of the Arctic, preferring an approach that puts the Arctic Council and its military committee in the driver's seat, not NATO. The Canadians, who are otherwise strong NATO players who participate in virtually every operation, are extremely proprietary about the Arctic. They see a significant alliance presence as somehow undermining their stewardship. Additionally, there is a significant pro–indigenous people and antimilitary bias throughout much of Canadian society, cutting across the political spectrum.

All of this is in marked contrast to the Norwegians, who have a more "lean forward" stance seeking a larger NATO presence in the region— largely the result of their centuries of unhappy interaction with the Russians, whom they perceive as particularly aggressive at the moment. In meetings, top Norwegian military personnel often bemoaned to me the "lack of NATO concern" about their part of the Arctic. They have been adapting their command and control systems to make it easier to "plug and play" with NATO systems so that the alliance can at least have situational awareness of what is going on along the longest border of NATO: the High North.

The Canadians also have a handful of territorial disputes at the moment. They are in dispute with the United States on a fairly large portion of the Beaufort Sea (the body of water just north of the eastern Alaskan/western Canadian border). While not of great significance, there is no quick or easy solution to this argument. Likewise, they disagree with the Danes over some of the boundaries of the Lincoln Sea (a tight body of water between the eastern border of Canada and the western border of Greenland) and ownership of a small island—Hans Island. They are also—along with the EU and USA—pursuing an agreement over the disputed Northwest Passage. This dispute is the most significant and quarrelsome. In essence, the Canadians believe that much of the Northwest Passage lies within their "internal waters," while most other nations believe that the passage is an "international strait," which allows greater freedom of movement for all nations. There are significant equities at play, and this argument is unlikely to be resolved anytime soon. The other two disputes are fairly straightforward and are moving toward resolution. None of the three seriously threaten the peace in the High North, but are indicative of the wide variety of disputed elements in and around the Arctic Ocean.

European Arctic Nations: Norway, Denmark, Sweden, Finland, and Iceland

While the northern European nations all have long traditions of engagement in the Arctic, they collectively lack sufficient resources, geopolitical influence, or populations to make a strong case for deep involvement at the level of Russia, Canada, and the United States. They will pursue their individual national agendas through both the European Union (all are members with the notable exception of Norway), in a NATO context (all are members save Finland and Sweden, which are close partners to NATO), and via the offices of the Arctic Council.

Each of the European Arctic nations has a slightly different set of issues in the Arctic, and at the moment they show little sign of cooperating
collectively to establish a European Arctic position on anything.

For Iceland, the Arctic was a zone of danger throughout much of the
cold war, when the relatively small island was in the crosshairs of potential Soviet nuclear strikes to blind the U.S. air and maritime defense
zones. Iceland was also regarded as an "unsinkable aircraft carrier" in the
strategically vital Greenland-Iceland–United Kingdom gap in the North
Atlantic. This was the passage through which many Soviet ballistic missile submarines would have to pass in order to attain launch positions
against the United States. Thus the Icelandic geopolitical status from
those days is as something of a battleground—not a pleasant place to be.

They look askance, therefore, at the deterioration of relations between
the United States/NATO and the Russian Federation. Icelandic diplo-
mats are very hopeful of seeing the High North become a zone of cooperation, not a zone of conflict. The Icelanders, who possess no actual
territory within the Arctic Circle, see themselves as the potential benefi-
ciary of enhanced trade routes, becoming a kind of hub port on the "Cold
Silk Road" across the top of the world. They sponsor an annual confer-
ence that is essentially the Davos World Economic Forum of the Arctic
Ocean, called, sensibly enough, "The Arctic Circle." This provides a
platform for their active approach to peaceful dialogue in the region.
They are also highly interested in potential oil and gas fields within their
exclusive economic zone, as well as their responsibilities for search and
rescue in their "near abroad" in the North Atlantic and Arctic oceans.
The Icelanders will try hard to remain relevant in the core discussions of
the Atlantic Council, trying to stake out a position alongside the big five
(Russia, Canada, USA, Denmark, and Norway).

Denmark is an Arctic nation by virtue of its long possession of Greenland and the Faroe Islands. It has ruled Greenland since 1721, but there

is an ongoing political debate about how this ownership will unfold in the twenty-first century. Greenland and the Greenlanders have been increasingly vocal in demanding greater autonomy, and there are voices increasingly raised in favor of independence altogether. Greenland is huge, and there are many military installations dotting the coastlines to which the Danes grant access to NATO and the United States, including the important Thule U.S. air base in the northwest corner of the island. The uncertainty regarding Greenland's future is exacerbated by the discovery of increasing levels of gas and oil beneath its waters, which provides a realistic level of income and encourages the indigenous Greenlanders to consider independence seriously. Finally, the Danes are pushing for a series of very detailed underwater mapping exercises designed to sustain their extensive claims to great swaths of the Arctic seabed, up to and including the North Pole itself.

Overall, we will see the Danes play a visible and aggressive hand regarding the Arctic Ocean. They will seek to hold on to Greenland and will offer higher and higher degrees of autonomy to the inhabitants there while retaining sovereignty. This will require a higher degree of military engagement in the region, especially from new installations in and around Greenland. Copenhagen will not give up its significant stake in the High North willingly.

Norway, a rich country of vast territory and only five million inhabitants, has the resources but not the population to have significant Arctic impact by itself. The Norwegians, more than any other of the NATO/European Arctic states, keep a weather eye on their Russian neighbors. They have several territorial disputes with Russia, some of which have been solved and others of which linger on with little likelihood of resolution. The Norwegian island of Svalbard, high up in the Arctic Ocean, dominates the Barents Sea and constitutes a significant thorn in the side of Russian ambitions in the region. The Norwegians are concerned not only about hydrocarbons, but about fishery rights as well. There are significant stakes for Norway in the High North, especially as easily tapped oil and natural gas along its more southern coasts are depleted in the years ahead.

Most expect Norway to continue to be the nation most concerned about a potential "resource war," or at least an armed conflict of some sort in the Arctic Ocean. This has led Norway to take an aggressive stance on the role of NATO in the High North, constantly pushing it to be aware and informed operationally as to what is moving in the northern latitudes of the alliance. As the NATO commander from 2009 to 2013, I often conferred with my Norwegian counterparts about their concerns and attempted to assuage them as to NATO's interest and engagement.

Sweden and Finland, the two remaining Arctic nations, are part of the Arctic Council by virtue of a small segment of their land territory that lies within the Arctic Circle, but neither has coastline on the Arctic Ocean itself. Nonetheless, Sweden and Finland—non–NATO members both—watch the Russian Federation with concern over its increasingly expansive operational profile in the Arctic Ocean near both nations. Neither nation is looking for disputes with Russia, and of course both were essentially neutral throughout the cold war. Sweden and Finland have drawn closer to NATO over the past decade, including sending significant forces on deployment to Afghanistan. Swedish Gripen jets also participated with great success in the Libyan operations alongside NATO partners. As Russian behavior in the Arctic and in Ukraine makes these two nations nervous, they can be expected to seek even closer ties to NATO. It is possible they will consider membership in NATO, but that step appears unlikely absent yet another dramatic change in Russian activity. In regard to the Arctic, both will be quietly assertive of their prerogatives as Arctic nations, but both are also well aware that without coastline on the Arctic Ocean, their options for operational activity are limited.

THE UNITED STATES

It is striking to imagine how different the United States' and Russia's geopolitical positions would be if Russia still owned Alaska, which the United States purchased from Russia in 1867 under the vision of Secretary of State William Seward. Derided at the time as "Seward's Folly" or "Seward's Icebox," the acquisition stands second only to the Louisiana Purchase as the best deal this country ever made.

The United States has seldom placed a great deal of emphasis on the Arctic. Throughout our history, the country has placed the most strategic importance first on dominating the vast continental lands, then turned to the Atlantic and Pacific oceans as the highways to the rest of world with expanding trade and geopolitical responsibilities. Until 2009, there was literally no stated U.S. policy articulated concerning the Arctic and the Arctic Ocean. The first such document came out as the Bush administration was leaving early in 2009; titled "Arctic Region Policy," it was issued both as a National Security Presidential Directive and as a Homeland Security Presidential Directive. Frankly, the document is pretty thin reading, with little to encourage the U.S. government to devote resources to the High North.

Throughout much of the cold war, the Arctic Ocean was a busy thoroughfare for U.S. and Russian nuclear submarines playing an elaborate game of cat and mouse, best illuminated in Tom Clancy's unforgettable novel *The Hunt for Red October*. The High North was also an air battlefield minded by the North American Air Defense Command, headquartered in Colorado. Teaming with Canada in air defense, the United States built a system of early warning air defense radars across the Canadian and U.S. coastlines that exist today and are still on watch for long-range forays by Russian strategic bombers and reconnaissance aircraft.

In the post–cold war period, there was at first more amity in the Arctic Ocean region, but as relations between Russia and the United States (and NATO) have deteriorated sharply—especially since the invasion of Ukraine and the annexation of Crimea—the cat and mouse and watchful air defense on both sides have resumed with gusto. There is also the emergence of a more significant Chinese intercontinental strategic missile threat to worry about, and more recently the highly unstable North Korean regime of Kim Jong-un has acquired long-range ballistic missiles to marry up with its small arsenal of nuclear weapons. The North Koreans detonated their fourth nuclear explosion in early 2016. Given that these missiles can find their shortest path from Asia to the continental United States over the Arctic Ocean, it is clear that this Arctic path for ballistic missile launches opens a new strategic front from Asia to the United States itself. All of this places a much higher premium on U.S. strategic focus on the Arctic Ocean than was the case even two or three years ago.

Perhaps even more important to long-range U.S. strategic thinking is the enormous amount of natural resources in, under, and around the periphery of the Arctic Ocean. The Arctic zone possibly holds 30 billion barrels of oil and more than 220 trillion cubic feet of natural gas. Such estimates may only scratch the surface as they are generated in a very conservative way by the U.S. government. Additionally, vast levels of timber, fresh water, coal, copper, gold, silver, zinc, and rare earth elements are present.

Fortunately, given the strategic importance of the region to the United

States, the various governmental organizations are now beginning to spend time and resources conducting coherent strategic planning on the Arctic. The Department of Defense via the Navy laid out a reasonable road map in late 2009 and has updated it along the way. The plan includes budgetary line items for strategic planning, operations and training, investments (including weapons, sensors, and installations), strategic communications, and environmental assessments. More recently, in 2013, the Department of Homeland Security via the U.S. Coast Guard promulgated a similar strategic vision, its "U.S. Coast Guard Arctic Strategy." The Department of State appointed former commandant of the Coast Guard Admiral Bob Papp as a sort of "Arctic czar" and designated him the U.S. representative to the Arctic Council until he stepped down in 2017. Even President Obama has joined in and recently became the first U.S. president to visit the Arctic, in the late summer of 2015. What is lacking, unfortunately, is a sense of a coherent, focused national effort despite the nascent efforts of the disparate interagency organizations.

Much of the U.S. engagement under the Obama administration was focused on working through the Arctic Council. This organization, founded twenty-five years ago, has eight permanent members: Russia, Canada, the United States, Denmark, Norway, Iceland, Finland, and Sweden. It also has twelve permanent observers: France, Germany, the Netherlands, Poland, Spain, the United Kingdom, China, Italy, India, Japan, South Korea, and even Singapore. Obviously, many of these nations do not leap to mind as "Arctic family members." But attaining status as an Arctic observer is tied to international shipping activity and physical presence on other strategic shipping points. More nations will apply and gain observer status in the years ahead. For the United States, the Arctic Council represents the best international forum for raising concerns and questions about the behaviors of other Arctic and non-Arctic states. The council also sponsors dialogue among all of the militaries of its permanent members.

Of note, when looking over a list of the number of operational icebreakers in the inventory of various permanent members of the Arctic Council, the shortcomings of the United States are particularly noteworthy:

Russia: 30-plus icebreakers, of which 7 are nuclear powered, including the new *Arktika*, the pride of the Russian fleet

Finland: 7

Sweden: 7

Denmark: 4

Canada: 6

United States: 3

Norway: 1

China: 3 (although not a permanent member, it has more under construction)

It seems quite clear that the "hidden" days of the Arctic are coming to an end. The High North is an emerging maritime frontier with increasing human activity, rapidly melting ice packs, hugely important hydrocarbon resources, and a competing international agenda.

THERE ARE MANY BROAD CHALLENGES facing the United States as we look north to the Arctic waters. First is the rising geopolitical tension with Russia, which has arisen principally out of events in Syria and Ukraine, but will ultimately have repercussions in the High North. We are seeing increased Russian activity with its highly capable and numerous flotillas of ice-breaking ships (such flotillas are strictly Russian in character, and are clusters of icebreakers that operate together), as well as their stated intent to build military bases in the Arctic region. Second is the environmental and ecological damage brought on by the melting polar ice cap, which is straining the entire delicate ecosystem. Third, associated with the melting ice is the growing commercial sense of an oil and gas rush up north. As the principal Arctic nations explore and exploit hydrocarbons, competition and disputes will rise in number and intensity. Fourth, the United States has no serious culture of engagement in the High North, and as pointed out earlier, today we have only a single truly functioning icebreaker (the other two on the list above are out of service at the moment), compared with dozens operated by Russia. We simply lack the idea of an "Arctic identity" that Russia, Canada, Norway, Iceland, and Denmark (by virtue of Greenland in the latter case) have.

WHAT DOES THE UNITED STATES NEED TO DO?

Ensure that the United States remains a leader in the Arctic Council. All of the nations bordering the Arctic Ocean (the six noted above as well as Finland and Sweden) meet frequently to work on issues in the High North. These include exchanging information about military operations, protecting the environment, creating standards for the exploitation of natural resources, practicing salvage and rescue operations, conducting climate studies and other scientific cooperation, and various other activities in the Arctic zone. The United States needs to put real resources behind our participation, sending top government figures to consultations, appropriating significant funds for the activities committed to by the Arctic Council, and driving policy by shaping coalitions within the council.

Build more icebreakers. If the United States intends to be serious about operating in the Arctic Ocean, we need the ability for both military and commercial ships to get through the ice pack. While many of our submarines are hardened and can break through the ice, if we are going to take advantage of the reduced shipping distances, move our oil and gas offshore structures, and support everything from science diplomacy to responsible tourism, we simply need more icebreakers—this is the path to credibility in the Arctic. At this moment, Russia, Canada, Finland, and Sweden all outpace us, and Denmark and China are building more vessels now. Our weak level of response must be reversed.

A good icebreaker costs money—between $800 million and $1 billion. The reason buying one is hard is because they must compete with other high-cost items like Navy *Arleigh Burke*–class destroyers, advanced fighter aircraft, and sophisticated Army command and control systems. But going forward, the necessity and usefulness of such a vessel seems clear, especially when we have such limited capability in that area.

Take a leadership position within NATO on the Arctic. There are varying views of the role of NATO in the High North, which run from Canada's somewhat laissez-faire philosophy of "High North, Low Tension" in terms of NATO involvement, to Norway's desire to integrate national and NATO surveillance systems to cover the Arctic aggressively and thoroughly from an alliance perspective.

The Norwegians often say the High North is the unguarded flank of the alliance, because they fear Russian territorial aggression and a fight over hydrocarbons. The Canadians lean back and don't want NATO engagement; the Norwegians lean forward and want a great deal of NATO in the High North. The U.S. position tends to lie somewhere in between these two views. We should lead NATO to engage more directly and realistically, with exercises, surveillance, overflight, and training in the Arctic Ocean.

Enhance the dialogue with Russia. The reality is that Russia has the most at stake of any nation in the Arctic, and by working with the Russians we can ensure that the region becomes a zone of cooperation—not of competition or, even worse, actual conflict. Despite our disagreements in other areas, we need to maintain the conversation with Russia about the direction of the High North. Russia is building an operations center focused on the Arctic. We should explore how we could be part of that in some cooperative way, sharing our engagement with our Canadian friends and allies, as well as other NATO allies.

In the dialogue with Russia, much of the conversation will focus on commercial and navigational issues. Of note, some scientists are predicting a truly "blue north"—one that has water, not ice, during much of the year—by 2030. Shipping, oil and gas, tourism, science, and many other commercial interests will dominate the agenda over time. Our Arctic czar should spend time with the private sector to fully understand the issues and find linkages with public sector efforts, which can then be translated into a dialogue with the Russians.

Take an interagency approach. U.S. interests in the High North will cut across cabinet departments—Department of Defense, Department of Homeland Security, Department of State, Coast Guard, Department of the Interior—as well as agencies such as EPA, NOAA, and so on. Working hard to make sure that the entire U.S. government is represented will be important. This concept is of course central to the DNA of a Coast Guard officer, making the choice of a retired four-star admiral and Coast Guard commandant sensible—the "Coasties" work with many other organizations and entities within the big tent of the Department of Homeland Security, such as the DEA, Customs, Fisheries, and so forth, and thus are very comfortable in an interagency environment.

In a metaphorical sense, it is worth thinking about Arctic policy in the same way a United States submarine captain approaches the dangerous navigational task of breaking through the ice with his warship—something our attack submarines do with regularity as they patrol the northern seas. Like our Arctic policy, broaching a submarine through polar ice requires careful navigation, delicate planning, and determination.

Sailing the Arctic Ocean is different from sailing any other body of water in the world, and full of dangerous and unique challenges. Any sea captain planning an Arctic voyage will have spent a great deal of time studying the waters, learning about ice and the damage it can do, and seeking advice and counsel from others about the specific difficulties of the intense cold, the crushing ice, the brilliant lights of summer and the deep dark of the winter nights. Any U.S. Navy sailor who has gone above the Arctic Circle is awarded a certificate as a Blue Nose sailor. But very few even of the limited number of Blue Nose sailors have done the most challenging maneuver of all: breaking through the icepack itself in a submarine and bursting to the surface at the North Pole.

Each U.S. Navy submarine that has performed this feat recognizes the significant danger imposed on the boat by the dangling ice keels, large tongues of ice hanging down from the ice pack itself. Avoiding these is crucial, as is understanding the precise thickness of the ice pack at the proposed point of surfacing.

The entire maneuver is controlled carefully by the submarine's captain himself and uses a detailed checklist with two-man control over each step of the standard operating procedure or SOP. Sonar—a pinging of sound through the water that measures distance by listening to the reverberation back—is used to find a flat spot, and the delicate controls of the submarine are used to maneuver the boat just below the surface of the ice. Throughout most of the cold war, most of our boats had hardened sails (the towerlike structure on the top of the boat) for this operation, but even given the hardening, it remains imperative to lower all masts and antennae while situating the boat below just the right patch of "clean" and hopefully thin ice. To make a cheap pun, finding the thin ice feels like "walking on thin ice" above—you know that a wrong step could be disastrous.

Once the thinnest ice patch is located and the ship is positioned beneath it, air is then blown into the ballast tanks, creating the reserve buoyancy and the essential upward thrusting energy needed to break through the ice. Like most submerged operations, this one is quiet and nearly silent throughout most of the boat. But in the conning space—the underwater part of the submarine where all maneuvering is conducted while the boat is submerged—and of course in sonar control, the crunching sound of the ice on the hull is discernible—a low, grinding, pulsing sound until the final breaking of the ice layer.

Once the boat has broken through, the crew can ascend the tower and carefully open the clamshells on the sail of the submarine and check the full status of the hull of the boat as it hangs just through the ice on the surface. Sailors wearing special cold weather exposure suits are initially tethered to the boat as the hull above the ice is checked for damage. Eventually, the goal is to get every one of the hundred or so sailors over the side to walk on the ice, snap pictures, and safely avoid polar bears— which amble right up to the hull.

There are many places in the world a captain can take his or her ship, but only a submarine can sail through the pure, cold water of the Arctic

Ocean, submerge under ancient ice, and ultimately crash its sail up to the sky at the top of the world.

There is a real danger of militarizing the High North. We cannot afford to stumble back into a new (and colder) cold war. There are essentially three choices for the Arctic: a zone of cooperation (best), a zone of competition (probable), and a zone of real conflict (possible but less likely).

At the moment, with Russian versus U.S. and NATO relations at a post–cold war low, I would bet on a deepening zone of competition. We will see Russia aggressively build out its military presence. In one sense, this is quite natural: as the ice "barrier" that protected that northern coast melts, the natural Russian concern about its borders (the result of many bad experiences over the centuries) kicks in and we will see more military activity. This will quickly become a self-fulfilling prophecy as the United States and the other NATO countries respond. What can break the cycle? As discussed above, it will require a multifaceted approach: international (with the Arctic Council as the primary vehicle), interagency (getting the Department of Homeland Security, which includes the Coast Guard, to work with the departments of Defense and State), and private-public cooperation. We need all three.

A good example of the latter would be building emergency response platforms in the High North. The question is whether the United States can provide international, interagency, and private-public leadership in the Arctic, especially with regard to sustainable infrastructure development in the Arctic Ocean. Given our responsibilities, are we prepared to respond to disasters and fully participate in the High North—with search and rescue capability, environmental disaster mitigation, scientific diplomacy, and other activities?

Unlike centuries past, when sea ice covered the north polar region perennially, today there is navigable open water from the Bering Strait to

the Barents Sea during the summer. This increasing access to rich resources is awakening all flavors of human activities and associated societal responses, not just from the Arctic states but from our entire world.
This leads directly to the hot-button topic of energy exploration, development, and production in the Arctic Ocean.

Oceanic travel across the top of the earth cuts a third off the distance
between Europe and Asia, compared with transits through the Panama
or Suez canals. What are the implications for new trade routes or trading
patterns, which historically have changed the balance of power among
nations? How will we use the Northern Sea Route, Northwest Passage,
or Transpolar Sea Route into the future?

Vast fishery enterprises are seeking to feed a hungry world, preparing to jump into areas of the Arctic high seas where marine living
resources are unregulated beyond sovereign jurisdictions. Can nations
collectively demonstrate shared stewardship and commercial restraint
to ensure the lasting vitality of Arctic marine ecosystems? There is
hope on that front. Nine nations, including the United States, and the
European Union agreed in December 2017 to a sixteen-year ban on fishing in the Arctic. This moratorium should give the international scientific community time to understand Arctic fisheries and how to use them
sustainably.

Wrapped up in charged dialogues about climate, atmospheric temperatures over the Arctic are rising twice as fast as those in the rest of the
earth. Can we turn down the vitriol to appreciate that we are just in our
infancy to address climate and other planetary-scale impacts that require
coordination among all nations?

So as we conclude this look at the Arctic, where does all this leave us
in this vast northern sea? Can we conceive and build sustainable infrastructure in the Arctic Ocean that will resonate with utility and hope,
not just for the region but globally?

In this quest, it is important to recognize that economic prosperity, environmental protection, social equity, and societal welfare are all necessary. We have a responsibility to act in the interests of present generations as well as future generations. Moreover, in the Arctic Ocean as elsewhere on earth, we have a shared struggle to balance national interests and common interests.

The challenge for the United States and the other Arctic states, with the central involvement of the Arctic indigenous peoples and the effective engagement of non-Arctic states, is responding in a balanced manner to the opportunities as well as the risks from the opening of the Arctic Ocean.

MORE THAN A CENTURY AGO, in 1879, the United States was seized with "Arctic fever" tied to the later-disproved notion of a temperate land zone in the center of the North Pole—essentially a "land rush" that never materialized. A U.S. Navy expedition was launched onboard the doomed USS *Jeannette*, which voyaged into the Arctic "carrying 'the aspirations of a young republic burning to become a world power.'" It became icebound and was crushed, stranding the crew as winter approached. As masterfully depicted in Hampton Sides's *In the Kingdom of Ice*, most of the brave sailors died trying to bring the United States into the High North. We have largely stayed on the sidelines since then in this vital geopolitical part of the world. But with the appointment of an Arctic Czar, or what I like to call an "Ice King," and an increased focus on the High North, we must again assert our engagement in a challenging but critical part of the globe.

Broadly speaking, the United States is better positioned to take a significant role in the Arctic Ocean than was the case a decade ago, despite shortfalls in leadership attention, interagency cooperation, icebreakers, and other specialized equipment and appropriate infrastructure and installations. The question is whether in this period of constraining resources for the United States there will be sufficient long-term vision to make the key investments necessary. Will agencies of government invest in training personnel to understand and plan for an Arctic Ocean future for the United States? Will our Defense and Homeland Security departments follow through on the road maps they have generated over the past several years? Will presidential leadership go beyond photo-op travel and renaming mountains in honor of indigenous peoples, and truly grapple with both the promise and the peril of the High North?

William Seward had the vision required to ensure an Arctic future for his nation. It was said of him during his lifetime that he was "one of those spirits who sometimes will go ahead of public opinion instead of tamely following its footprints." Let us hope we can sail into the Arctic with his spirit as a guide.

8.

THE OUTLAW SEA

OCEANS AS
CRIME SCENES

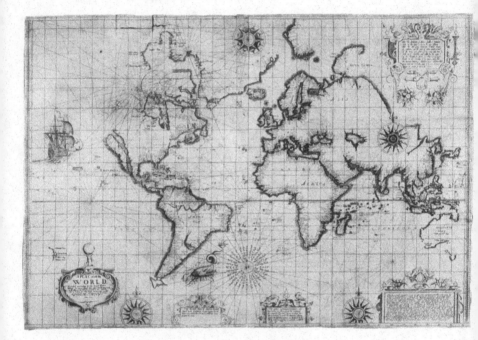

Piracy was a problem in every region from the Americas to Europe and Asia. *Map by Emery Molyneux and Edward Wright, 1599.*

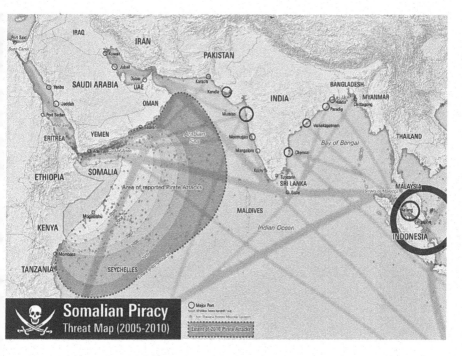

Although the locus of this challenge has shifted to a new region,
piracy is still a scourge in our modern world.

*H*aving looked at each of the world's major bodies of water essentially in isolation, we need as well to examine the entirety of the global ocean system. As I mentioned at the outset, the British Royal Navy, perhaps the first truly worldwide force capable of projecting power anywhere on the face of the earth, put it best: The Sea is One, meaning that no matter how large or small a given body of water is upon the oceans, in the end it is connected and a part of the single system.

And it is a busy system indeed. On any given day, it is impossible to accurately measure the number of surface ships at sea, but we can approximate the number of ships generally. By reading through a variety of sources (including Clarksons, the "bible" of international shipping), it is possible to estimate that there are between fifty and sixty thousand large commercial ships—bulk carriers, cargo ships, tankers, container ships, chemical ships, passenger and roll-on/roll-off ships, and liquefied natural gas tankers active throughout the world. These are the ships that I passed thousands of times in my years as a warship captain. The interactions between the world's warships (perhaps five thousand, including many very small coast guard vessels) are generally quite professional. What I felt over the forty years of my career was the way the oceans became more and more full; by some estimates there are four to six times more ships plying the world's oceans than there were some thirty years ago. If you look at a map of the world from space with the high-density shipping lanes marked in red, orange, and yellow, the strategic highways and choke points are quite clear—red belts through the South China Sea, the Mediterranean, clusters around the Suez and Panama canals, long strips around the bottom of Africa, arrows of red in and out of the Arabian Gulf and through the Strait of Malacca. It is a vast and busy universe in which tens of thousands of vessels of all descriptions are under way at any given moment.

The good news is that over the past three thousand years since man began to explore the world's oceans, we have learned a great deal. Mankind has developed extraordinary technology that allows us to accurately map every body of water, to plunge to the bottom of the sea, to track fish, birds, and mammals that inhabit it, to monitor and navigate the thousands of ships that ply it, and to take highly precise measurements of everything about the waters of the world: temperature, acidity, alkalinity, salinity, and on and on. But despite the fact that we are incredibly informed about the oceans in many ways, there are still vast trenches of the oceans that are unexplored, and there remains much we do not know, especially about how the oceans function as a coherent system. In a certain sense we have incredible *knowledge* of the oceans, but little *wisdom* about them.

Nowhere is this more clearly true than when we look at the broad ocean challenges that exist today. Some have called the oceans "the biggest crime scene in the world," and others have referred to them as "the outlaw sea." Sadly, both of these statements are in many ways quite true;

and worst of all, we do not have real granularity in our knowledge of what transpires on the oceans in two potentially very destructive zones: criminal activity and environmental damage.

IN TERMS OF CRIME COMMITTED on the oceans, there are many sources, but to name a few that are of particular concern: piracy, a scourge that has been part of the oceans since the very beginning of man's intersection with the sea; narcotics smuggling, an enormous business that moves heroin, cocaine, methamphetamines, and other illicit substances on a huge global delivery network with substantial maritime pathways; illegal dumping of toxic substances, which of course bleeds directly into the environmental challenges we will address below; weapons smuggling, which involves moving all manner of lethal equipment from high-end ballistic missiles to small but deadly handguns; illegal fishing, a business that is destroying the world's fish stocks rapidly; and smuggling of contraband, from the level of nuisance shipping of untaxed cigarettes to the movement of big sums of paper money (both counterfeit and valid). Below we will look specifically at piracy as a case study of the criminal activity on the oceans, and examine the ways in which global security forces, the shipping industry, the insurance industry, and international organizations have tried to address the piracy challenge. There are many lessons learned that can be applied to other criminal activities on the outlaw sea. We will also look quite specifically at the world of fishing, where much abuse of the law occurs that thus far has seen relatively little effective mitigation by the international community.

The other significant challenge to the global ocean, of course, is the environment. Here we see extensive damage that has many sources: global warming that is helping melt the polar ice caps and contributing to the rise of the ocean's sea levels; rising acidification in many parts of the oceans, which is highly detrimental to various levels in the global oceanic food chain; warming of the oceans, which changes migratory patterns and again damages fragile ecosystems; construction damage to delicate coral reefs; pollution that is pumped directly into the oceans either deliberately or accidentally from land or sea; hydrocarbon recovery (both oil and natural gas), which has both deliberate and accidental effects on sea life and coastal ecosystems; higher levels of UV and other forms of radiation; mineral recovery, which will be exacerbated over time by the desire to mine the deep seabed for cobalt, copper, nickel, magnesium, and rare earths; and the simple act of humans populating the coastal regions of the world and inserting large urban centers adjacent to the oceans. When these are taken together, the damage to the global maritime environment may be the biggest threat we face as a species.

In terms of impact on the world's oceans, the three biggest topics that completely transcend not only national boundaries, but also the artificial boundaries between various seas and oceans, are piracy, fishing, and the environment. They are intertwined, and each merits a significant look.

PIRACY

I must admit that as I prepared to take up my duties as the NATO commander in 2009, I did not initially put piracy at the top of my list of worries. Afghanistan, the Balkans, Syria, Russia, and Libya looked like the places that would absorb the lion's share of my energy and attention. But as I began to fully comprehend the extent of the piracy challenges in East Africa—centered mostly on the waters off Somalia—it became clear that I would be doing something very traditional for a Navy admiral: chasing pirates.

Certainly piracy has been a part of the maritime landscape for more than three thousand years, with reports of early piracy taking place in the waters of the Mediterranean in the times of the ancient Greeks by the "sea people," as well as parts of the Indian Ocean and the western Pacific. Julius Caesar was captured and held captive briefly by Sicilian pirates. Much of Viking culture was built on the norms of maritime piracy launched both from and on the sea. Over the centuries, pirate cultures have been very entrenched in a variety of locations, notably North Africa under the so-called Barbary pirates in the eighteenth and nineteenth centuries, the Caribbean in the "golden age of piracy" in the seventeenth and eighteenth centuries, and more or less continually in the Strait of Malacca and South China Sea.

While there was a general lull in piracy in the post–World War II period, by the latter part of the twentieth century it had returned in force in a variety of areas around the globe and continues to the present. Notable zones of pirate activity around the world today include the waters of the Indian Ocean and North Arabian Sea off the northeast coast of Africa, the Gulf of Guinea on the central west coast of Africa, the Strait of Malacca between the Pacific and Indian oceans, and to a lesser degree, in the littoral waters of the South China Sea and Caribbean. The acts of piracy range from small-scale attacks on private yachts to major take-overs of massive international tankers, with the objective of holding the ships and crews for ransom. A variety of observers estimate the cost to the global transportation network caused by piratical activity to be between $15 billion and $20 billion. This includes the cost of increased insurance premiums, ransoms, legal fees, embedded security guards on the ships, inefficient routing to avoid highly pirated zones, additional lookouts, technology and equipment added to ships to prevent successful pirate attacks (e.g., concertina wire and other physical barriers, fire-fighting water flushing systems on the sides of the ship), and national expenses in sending warships and operational staffs to oversee global counterpiracy operations.

As I took over the job of Supreme Allied Commander at NATO, I reflected on the slightly delicious irony of the need for the military operational leader at NATO to spend a serious chunk of his time learning about piracy, of all things. Many observers had opined that choosing an *admiral* as the sixteenth Supreme Allied Commander was a mistake—after all, there had been a long, unbroken chain of fifteen prior generals, going back to the first Supreme Allied Commander, General Dwight Eisenhower. The concerns of the alliance had always focused on ground combat and high-tech aviation, with a much smaller level of attention paid to things maritime. Indeed, throughout my own career up to that point, I had not paid a great deal of attention to piracy. But finally, I thought, I am going to have a chance to chase some pirates, a mission near and dear to a seagoing officer's heart.

The reason NATO became interested in the piracy mission off Somalia was simple: money. It was beginning to have a very high impact on European companies and indeed on the cost of goods flowing through the East African and North Arabian Sea waters. Additionally, it was increasingly clear that the local terrorist group, Al Shabaab, was beginning to "tax" the Somali pirates and use the funding to undertake acts of violent extremism not only in Somalia but in neighboring countries as well. And we could see flickers of connection between Al Shabaab and Al Qaeda. Indeed, the African group has now pledged allegiance to the so-called Islamic State. So these international terrorist linkages were of legitimate concern.

The roots of Somali piracy lie in a variety of factors. First is the simple difficulty of making a living in any legitimate fashion in Northeast Africa, which has suffered decades of civil war, strife, and depredation. When young, unemployed men find a relatively lucrative (although very dangerous) way to make a living, they are easily recruited. Second, the traditional source of income for many who turned to piracy had been fishing. Due to overfishing and ecological damage in the immediate waters, the ability to make a living fishing had diminished in the latter part of the twentieth century. An excellent explanation of all of this from the point of view of the Somalis (who have some legitimate grievances against the big shipping and industrial companies) can be found in Jay Bahadur's highly readable book *The Pirates of Somalia*. Third, the local water conditions are conducive to pirate activity. Before the real ramp-up in pirate activity, the normal shipping route was quite close to the coast of Somalia as well-laden commercial ships sailed to and from the Suez Canal. The water conditions are calm enough to permit small-boat assaults on the vastly larger commercial ships. And finally, the shipping companies themselves were largely complacent, not having experienced a high level of attacks in recent decades.

By 2009, the piracy situation was at a level demanding international intervention. As I came into office, the number of attacks was rising dramatically, peaking in 2009–10 at more than three hundred. Nearly twenty major ships were being held hostage and worse, more than a hundred mariners with them. While there was relatively little fatal violence, the insurance rates were rising, innocent sailors were held in execrable conditions (usually confined to a small space in a sweltering hulk of a ship anchored in an inlet on the Somali coast), and the flow of resources to local terrorists was rising. Clearly more needed to be done.

A combined maritime force was increased in the local waters, consisting of warships (typically frigates, destroyers, and light cruisers) from the twenty-eight nations of NATO, the European Union, and a loose coalition of Gulf State navies assembled by the United States. Additionally, a very diverse group of nations decided to pitch in, revulsion of piracy being something virtually every nation can agree upon. This led to the deployment of ships from nations that do not normally cooperate with NATO: Russia, China, India, Pakistan, and—quite surprisingly—even Iran. Indeed, this global maritime coalition became an example of what the international community could accomplish if it chose to work together.

I spent a great deal of time working the diplomatic aspects of the coalition, visiting various capitals. It was relatively easy work given the overarching view that the global commons needed policing against piracy and that it was in everyone's interest to participate. In particular, this became a real zone of cooperation between NATO and Russia that paid dividends in everything from sharing maritime tactics to exchanging communication devices to facilitate connectivity at sea between our forces—hardly something that is the norm in terms of working with Russia pretty much everywhere else.

The effort to overcome piracy in East Africa has been relatively successful: by 2013, as I concluded my service as Supreme Allied Commander, attacks were down significantly and they remain so today. The success is the result of a combination of several key factors.

First, the presence of warships has been vital. A frigate or a destroyer with an embarked helicopter or two can cover thousands of square miles of territory and brings the ability to instantly overcome armed pirates, sink their vessels, apprehend them, and incarcerate them (at least temporarily) at sea. They also clearly represent the international community. Over my four years as NATO commander we typically had three to five NATO vessels on station, matched with a similar number for the European Union. Given that the rest of the informal coalition against international piracy also had three to five ships, this became a substantial force. However, despite the presence of those warships, we were often a step behind the pirates. This was because of the sheer size of the operational area off the coast of Northeast Africa, a space roughly the size of

Europe. When people would question why we couldn't catch all the pirates, I would point out that even fifteen warships would be like fifteen police cars trying to cover all of western Europe.

We also supplemented the ships with long-range maritime patrol aircraft. These heavy, wide-bodied, four-engine aircraft lumbered over vast amounts of territory and could remain airborne for eight to twelve hours, operating from bases in Oman, on islands in the Indian Ocean, or from the Horn of Africa. Used throughout the cold war for antisubmarine patrols, these airplanes have the ability to swoop down to the very surface of the ocean, use radar from higher altitude to scan the ocean surface, and provide command and control to helicopters or ships engaged in searching for the pirates. The United States operated P-3 Orion aircraft and the British the comparable Nimrods, and several other allies had similarly equipped planes. Additionally, for overall command of the operation from the air, NATO had available the massive Airborne Warning and Control System (AWACS) E-3 plane, a flying village with extensive radar, communication, and well-trained personnel. These were under my direct command as the NATO Supreme Commander for global operations, and I deployed them on the counterpiracy mission as well.

Tactically, we decided to use an old-school solution: convoys. Rather than letting each of the fifty thousand tankers and commercial ships that transit the area over the course of a year operate on their own, we insisted that for their own protection they be herded into convoys that could operate together. While we did not have enough ships to provide each convoy with an escort, we were often able to keep a warship sufficiently close to each of the patrols to respond to and ward off the pirates. We also debated whether to go ashore and attack the pirate havens, most of which were well known to us, but we were unable to develop the political consensus for doing so given the chances of collateral damage and the difficulty in absolutely identifying the pirates ashore—because their boats and equipment could look a lot like a typical small fishing skiff or a dhow used for legitimate commerce. There was also the lack of a national government with which we could coordinate such onshore action. So much of our tactical execution was done at sea on international waters, where international law gave every nation the authority to respond to piracy.

The hardest part of the operation was actually what occurred *after* we caught a pirate, which we did with increasing frequency. These were young men, ethnically Somalis, most addicted to a mild narcotic called khat that has been chewed in the area for centuries. They have no papers, don't self-identify with a particular functioning government, and thus we had no one to whom we could turn them over for prosecution. Naturally the minute we closed in on them, they would also throw overboard their scaling ladder and guns, so when we boarded their small vessels we would find "innocent fishermen" and have little evidence of their wrongdoing in many cases (unless we had caught them in the act and filmed them on video camera, of course). Eventually several of the local governments proved willing to take them on for trial and conviction, notably Kenya. The pirates were lucky that we couldn't fall back on the centuries-old punishment for such crimes and string them up from a yardarm. While several of the nations in the coalition might have been actually willing to do so, we followed normal mores of Western judicial process throughout the time I was engaged in the exercise.

In addition to the military instruments, both surface and airborne, the shipping industry itself took on the challenge of dealing with the pirates. Initially, this effort focused on routing and convoying, essentially charging captains to work closely with one another at sea and participate in our convoying mechanisms. They also became much better over time checking into the operational centers we established (in the Arabian

Gulf and other littoral areas) over radio when they entered and exited the area. The ships gradually worked harder at sharing observations of pirate activity, and also exchanged ideas for warding them off. This included using the speed and size of the commercial ships; putting up various reasonable effective barriers on the sides of the ships, including barbed wire; tactics to counter a boarding operation, including use of fire hoses at full blast; nonlethal devices such as sonic blast and shock mechanisms; and simply manning the deck and throwing the ladders back into the sea when the pirates attempted to grapple on.

The problem with all of those measures is that they required the merchant crews to do something for which they were neither trained nor particularly well oriented. Mariners today are used to very small crews, good meals, and creature comforts; the idea of fighting pirates does not come easily. Instead, many of the shipping owners developed plans for the mariners to retreat to a citadel inside the ship and radio from there for help. The film *Captain Phillips* about the taking of the *Maersk Alabama* by Somali pirates and the subsequent rescue of the hostage captain provides a vivid and accurate portrayal of a ship takedown and one way the scenario could play out.

What ultimately changed the dynamic altogether and has largely resulted in the dramatic reduction of piracy on the east coast of Africa was the decision by the shipping companies to put security teams on board. This was a new wrinkle in the millennia-old fight against pirates. Initially, the shipping companies wanted no part of this approach due to liability concerns. They were justifiably concerned that any mercenary team they hired might kill an innocent fisherman or other mariner at sea. This actually happened, by the way, and it was not even mercenaries who made the crucial mistake—a well-meaning Italian marine security team on an Italian-flagged vessel managed to shoot and kill two Indian fishermen in 2012. The case occurred twenty miles off the coast of

Kerala, India—on the high seas but well within India's exclusive economic zone (two hundred nautical miles) and is still in litigation, with potentially a significant prison sentence awaiting the adjudication in an Indian court.

Despite legitimate concerns over the potential for incidents like this, shipping companies have finally turned to mercenary firms for protection. This has led to the embarkation of two to six personnel from private contractors, normally well armed and reasonably well trained (at least in the use of the firearms). The host of problems raised by this include how to provide weapons and ammunition, where to base such groups, how they are trained and certified, and what the rules of engagement are for them. Because their activities occur largely on the high seas beyond the jurisdiction of any one nation, this has become a complicated branch of international law. There is a sort of *Mad Max* quality to these forces, despite the efforts of the contractors to train and certify them. While they are not exactly rogue warriors, their presence can make more traditional military sailors nervous, much as police in a city don't like to see armed bodyguards or armed mall guards for that matter. Nonetheless, the results have been striking: no ship embarking an armed security detail has ever been successfully hijacked. This is because the defending team has such a huge advantage in the height of the big tankers and also because the pirates are very lightly armed, untrained themselves, and quite vulnerable during the actual act of boarding. Knowing all of this, the pirates will normally simply sheer off when confronted with consistent fire from a potential victim.

Finally, in addition to national military action and the good work of the industry, there has been additional work ashore by the international community. Let's face it—we are not going to solve piracy solely out at sea. It will require addressing the conditions ashore that lead young men to take up a dangerous and chaotic life. We also need deterrence in the form of local coast guard and police, and a judicial system with real teeth in it. Much of this hard nation building in Somalia has been undertaken by the European Union, and the results—while mixed—are somewhat encouraging. The nascent governmental structures in Somalia, Somaliland, and Puntland—the three "national entities" on the eastern part of the Horn of Africa—are showing increasing capability to respond to piratical acts from the shore side, receive and try pirates, and incarcerate them.

So the good news is that in the pirate waters off the coast of Somalia, there has been a dramatic reduction in successful piracy. But as is so often the case in fighting transnational threats (terrorism, narcotics, human slavery, smuggling), when the international community is able to address it in a given area, it often pops up in another. So it is with piracy, which is showing a great deal of vitality on the other side of Africa in the Gulf of Guinea.

I remember sailing into the Gulf of Guinea on a short cruise as a splinter off operations in the Mediterranean. It is a huge body of water, with many littoral deltas converging as the rivers originating in West Africa run down into the sea, including most notably the Niger and the Volta. In those days thirty years ago, it was a sleepy part of the world. No more, as it has become one of the largest oil and gas hot spots in the world, with much onshore and offshore production in sight. A long history of outlaw operations has coupled with the rise of an Islamic radical group, Boko Haram (which means literally "the Western way is forbidden"). Together, these twin forces are driving up the incidents of piracy to the degree that a variety of Western nations are looking at "getting the band back together" and mounting a mission on the west coast of Africa similar to the one we did several years ago on the east coast. The good news is that there are more capable coast guards, better police and military ground forces, and at least existent courts and judicial systems, albeit highly corrupt and vulnerable to bribes and outside influencers. It seems likely that the next chapter in suppressing serious piracy will take place in the Gulf of Guinea, which looks and often functions like a throwback to the days of Joseph Conrad's *Heart of Darkness*—chaotic, dangerous, and fully in need of a restoration of order. In the end, this particular problem of the outlaw sea will not be solved on the seas themselves, but will require more stability ashore, honest policing, fair courts, legal incarceration, fused intelligence, and above all the "long game" of jobs and education to keep potential pirates from following Johnny Depp's path.

Globally, the number of piracy incidents is roughly flat over the past couple of years, with the caveat that this has always been a relatively underreported phenomenon, especially on the east and west coasts of Africa. The best overall source of information remains the Regional Cooperation Agreement on Combating Piracy and Armed Robbery Against Ships in Asia (ReCAAP), which is a loosely knit group of nations that work together to fight piracy specifically off the Horn of Africa. The directorate also keeps an eye on global trends, and as the piracy meter creeps up on the African west coast, it is likely we will hear from them. As with the other aspects of crime at sea, the key will be cooperative engagement. Hunting pirates is a team sport indeed.

FISHING

A second major challenge to the legal regimes of the oceans involves fishing. Given the size of the world's oceans, which cover 70 percent of the earth's surface and reach depths of more than seven miles, it stands to reason that there are massive stocks of fish. Innocent of all knowledge of territory or international agreement, they are the subject of enormous global activity, valued at well over $225 billion. Europe, the United States, and Japan all have big and growing appetites for fish, as does China—the largest exporter of fish in the world. It is worth noting that this consumption at the industrial scale is largely centered in the developed world, which imports three quarters of the total value of all fish produced.

There is significant downward pressure on fish stocks through overfishing, much of it in violation of nations' exclusive economic zones, international agreements and conventions, and even customary historical fishing grounds. One recent study hypothesized that more than 60 percent of all fish stocks worldwide require "rebuilding," and the literature is replete with warnings of a global fishing collapse. This is borne out by statistics that show a sharp rise in fish caught "in the wild" (as opposed to obtained from fish farms) from the 1950s to the early 1990s, but essentially no growth since then.

From a nonfishing mariner's perspective, there are parts of the world where it is nearly impossible to sail without becoming encumbered with fishing fleets. In my career, the worst of this could be found in East Asia, where massive Chinese, Vietnamese, and Filipino fishing boats were endlessly plying their craft in the littorals of the South China Sea. As we would approach the Philippine Islands in the 1980s, you could smell the fishing fleets—a mixture of gasoline, wood smoke, and the tang of the fish themselves—from miles out to sea when the wind was right. Often operating with small, dim lights, they were highly vulnerable to our massive, 9,000-ton destroyers and cruisers moving at speed through the waters of the fishing grounds. Since the fishing boats were almost entirely made of wood, they would not "paint" clearly on our surface radars, and we would often station additional lookouts with binoculars on the forecastle to try to pick them out of the hazy horizon.

Fishery management is a big industry unto itself, with many sincere efforts made to regulate this global trade. Since the United Nations Convention on the Law of the Sea was essentially ratified worldwide, nations have worked very hard to control the 200-mile exclusive economic zone that provides the legal authority and the concomitant responsibility to manage fish stocks within those waters by each nation. Beyond the EEZ, fishing is regulated by a series of international treaties—by some counts more than seventy in total. The treaties generally address fish, but also include agreements about turtles, seals, polar bears, dolphins, and other species. Most of the treaties have a designated secretariat (a small administrative organization), but little real means of enforcement. Herein lie the problems, and the perception of an "outlaw sea." Despite well-meaning efforts, most observers believe that nearly 90 percent of all fish stocks are "fully exploited, over-exploited, depleted, or recovering from depletion"* Many are declining rapidly, such as tuna—down 50 percent from peak stocks. Indeed, the "oceans are cleared at twice the rate of forests" on land, a chilling prospect.

There are several discrete problems with fishing that are causing the decline in fish stocks, each worth examining quickly. The first is simply our inability to provide accurate measurement metrics. While we can today track total biomass reasonably well (when it is reported, and let's understand that there is a great deal of underreporting happening on the outlaw sea), we are not able to accurately measure the size and level of reproductive capability of fish that are caught. As Professor Bill Moomaw has said, "the artificial truncation" of portions of the fish population over time destroys the productivity of the populations (Moomaw and Blankenship, 14). It is also worth noting that because nets tend to catch the

---

* William Moomaw and Sara Blankenship, "Charting a New Course for the Oceans," *CIERP Discussion Paper 10*, Center for International Environment and Resource Policy, Fletcher School, Tufts University, April 2014, 14.

biggest fish, the bias of the catch is to remove the larger members of the species, with obviously detrimental effect over decades.

The most blatantly obvious reason for declining fish stocks is simply overfishing. This occurs simply because of greed and economic necessity for poorer fishermen, as well as a lack of concern for the long-term consequences by the big industrial operations. As a seagoing officer, I would often come upon big fishing operations, including the lighter (but still large) long-line fishing platforms, as well as the big net seining operators. There would often be big fish-processing plants located in the same area (Russia and China in particular operate such plants), which were capable of rapidly processing catches and avoiding the probing eyes of inspectors. The key practice contributing to overfishing is destructive fishing practices such as bottom trawling, which not only affects the fish but can be very damaging to the ocean floor as well.

There is also the unfortunate tendency of governments to turn a blind eye to relatively local fishing due to the political impact in the sovereign nation, as well as reluctance to avoid the cost, expense, and inconvenience of an inspection regime (a coast guard) and an attendant court system to rule on charges of overfishing. This tends to go under the header of illegal, unregulated, and unreported fishing, or IUU. Such IUU activities by some measures account for a third of all fish catches, or billions of dollars. Why do we let this happen? As Admiral Hyman Rickover of the U.S. Navy said when asked why he decided to stop naming submarines after fish, breaking a decades-long tradition: "Fish don't vote." Until fish begin voting, unfortunately, it seems unlikely that there will be sufficient political pressure generated to right the ship of overfishing.

Another problem that generates overfishing is one that is quite controllable by governments: the application of subsidies. Governmental monies sometimes directly support the kinds of problems outlined above as national leaders attempt to help local economies. In particular, such subsidies result in the overbuilding of fishing fleets. Some observers believe that nearly $20 billion annually flows to the fishing industry, encouraging the continuation of fishing long after stocks are depleted beyond the point at which such activity remains economically viable.

Shockingly, one out of every four fish (i.e., 25 percent of the world catch) is categorized as "bycatch." This is simply "accidentally" bringing aboard fish and other seagoing species that are not part of the target catch. When vessels use huge, industrial-level trawls—especially when dragged along the seabed—the collateral damage is extreme. The international community has been utterly ineffective in managing this. I think back to my own experience in the Gulf of Mexico watching shrimp boats bring in their big catches with hundreds of sea turtles, ocean fish, and even marine mammals—once you understand the environmentally destructive power of this kind of bycatch, it is hard to watch from the bridge of your warship. Tied to this is a growing trend in using brutally destructive fishing techniques such as explosives and cyanide, which pose a threat not only to the orderly management of fishing but to delicate coral reefs as well. Think of the oceans as a kind of war zone, in which there are daily atrocities, horrifying collateral damage, and no rule of law.

There is an international political component to this, of course: flags of convenience. This is the long-standing practice whereby commercial operators "flag" or register their ships (the way you register a car) in a country that provides, shall we say, a flexible level of enforcement. Not unlike offshore bank accounts, this is merely a means to avoid accountability in the fishing world (and, of course, more broadly in all commercial shipping). In addition to seeking lower standards of enforcement on various practices (fishing, pollution, etc.), shippers also try to find the lowest-priced option. Today somewhere between one thousand and two thousand fishing ships fly a flag of convenience. Many of these are from small Caribbean nations, including Belize (the old British Honduras in Central America), Honduras, and Panama (famous for flags of convenience). The nations profit from the registration fees, and it makes life hard for mariners generally and enforcement personnel (like coast guards) because it is difficult to place effective sanctions on violators—the flag of convenience nation has no real incentive to punish offenders and often has less sophisticated court systems. Indeed, if you look broadly at global shipping, about 55 percent of all ships (fishing, tankers, cargo, passenger, and so on) fly a flag of convenience, and 40 percent are under three nations: Panama, Liberia, and the Marshall Islands. As a naval officer, when I saw those three flags I knew there was going to be a very difficult negotiation if I wanted to send over a boarding party to check for terrorists, drugs, cash, or anything else moving illegally on the high seas.

Taken together, this represents a steady decline in the productivity of the oceans, and the long-range implications for the world's fishing industry are concerning. Unless there is a great deal more regulation and scientific engagement—by private companies, nations, and international organizations—we should fear for the integrity and level of protein we can expect to draw from the sea going forward. After all, in today's world, more than a billion people rely on fish for the protein in their diet, and roughly the same number work on or in the oceans of the world— this despite concerns that fish stocks may have declined as much as 50 percent since the 1970s according to some estimates.

Finally, we should recognize the potential geopolitical tension over fishing that is rising worldwide. Elements of the massive Chinese fishing fleet, for example, consisting of thousands of vessels, have been repeatedly apprehended conducting illegal fishing operations. Indonesia alone has caught and destroyed (by explosion) more than a dozen fishing vessels; Australia has a long record of such apprehensions, as does South Korea. All of this exacerbates the tensions in East Asia and the western Pacific—already one of the most volatile regions of the world.

ENVIRONMENT

Piracy and fishing are sadly very significant sources of illegal activity at sea. But the biggest act of criminal behavior being practiced on the high seas is the willful and preventable damage to the environment that goes on every day. Through the destruction of the maritime world, we are literally watching future generations robbed of their birthright. This is stealing from us all, until and unless we can work coherently together to preserve the riches of the sea for mankind's future. This was a guiding premise in the negotiation of the United Nations Convention on the Law of the Sea three decades ago, but sadly the treaty has not had a sufficient effect on the damage that is unfolding before our eyes.

When I arrived at the Fletcher School of Law and Diplomacy on the campus of Tufts University in Medford, Massachusetts, in the fall of 1981, I was just completing five years at sea on a destroyer and an aircraft carrier. Beginning with my graduation from Annapolis (where we never studied or thought about the environment in any of my classes), I reported to my ships and blithely watched our engineers pump dirty bilgewater, full of black oil, over the side with impunity. We had dumped completely uninspected garbage into the oceans within visual distance of the coasts, and filled the oceans with plastic, toxins, medical waste, slightly radioactive materials, and all manner of utterly unsafe products. I certainly didn't think of myself as a global lawbreaker; everything I just mentioned was "normal underway operations." If I thought about it at all, I would have reflected that the oceans are a huge place, they seem to be able to regenerate themselves, and nothing we were doing was anything other than "the way we always did it."

In my time at the Fletcher School in the mid-1980s, I began to learn about the science, policy, and physical reality of the oceans in ways I never had as a seagoing officer. Sometimes you have to step back from something you love—in this case my seagoing professional life—to really understand it, and especially to be able to judge where it is inflicting harm despite holding no malign intentions. I would have self-identified in those days (as I do today) as someone who "loves and follows the sea." But it took me two years of intensive study and the production of a long dissertation to achieve a PhD in international law with a focus on the Law of the Sea treaty.

Climate change is very real and having increasingly evident effects on the oceans, beginning with the most obvious impact from global warming: sea temperature. As nearly all (more than 90 percent) of the extra heat generated by mankind eventually ends up affecting the oceans, it should be no surprise that temperatures are rising both at the surface and at great depth. There are increases in temperature felt as deep as nearly ten thousand feet, and in parts of the oceans the temperature rise is close to a full degree Fahrenheit. While this does not sound especially significant, it has a gradual but inexorable effect on the existence of life in the sea, and already the migratory patterns of many species are under pressure. There is movement toward the poles, which has knock-on effects, especially on fishing.

Rising temperatures in the oceans also affect ocean currents. There is a complex interplay between salinity, wind, currents, and the resultant upwelling of nutrients from the deep ocean that sustain many of the traditional fishing grounds around the globe. If there is a greater differential between the surface temperature and that of the deeper waters, these upwelling currents are diminished, and it negatively affects ocean life. Additionally, as salinity decreases near melting zones of ice (nearer to the poles), there will be rising levels of acidification and a depletion of ozone—further exacerbating environmental damage.

While such rising temperatures are of concern, it is sea level rise that has potentially the greatest effect on human life over time. The rise in sea level is related to the melting of the polar ice caps and the increase of water volume in the oceans. The numbers are increasingly alarming, and the *rate* of rise is accelerating, with some observers saying that sea levels are rising twice as fast as in the past. This is principally occurring because global warming is causing a melting effect of the glaciers and ice pack at the poles. The potential effects of this are clear: coastal ecosystems are among the most delicate in the world and have important environmental effects such as filtration of water, control of storm waters, and providing nutrients to species in these areas. There would be massive disruption in near-coastal fishing zones and possible knock-on effects in the cycle of global warming. Rising sea levels would also over time claim a great deal of currently arable and habitable land and return it to the sea—meaning coastal living areas would be lost, some small islands would literally become submerged, and current ports would be lost. With nearly three billion people living on coastlines around the earth, all of this will make for difficult adjustments globally.

TWO OTHER CRUCIAL PROBLEMS AFFECTING the oceans are oil pollution and resource exploitation. Both are intertwined, especially in regard to liquid hydrocarbons, and both are having deleterious effects on the oceans, despite improvements over the past decades in awareness, regulation, and enforcement.

Oil spills are the most dramatic and obvious, and they can come from offshore rigs, onshore piping systems, or from oil tankers operating at sea. Perhaps the most obvious visually is the offshore oil rigs. Removing resources from the seabed of the oceans is a very complex and difficult business. Throughout my career at sea, as I approached the coastlines of dozens and dozens of different countries, I would be saddened by the proliferation of big, ugly offshore oil rigs. I have passed through significant oil spills a few times, and the obvious devastation—seabirds coated in oil and struggling on the sea surface, legions of dead fish, a sickly, shiny sheen to the waters—is sadly well known. To sail through such a horrible miasma is a memorable experience. I did so in early 1991 during the first Gulf War, when Saddam Hussein's troops deliberately opened risers into the Arabian Gulf from land-based piping and oil rigs and pumped more than 400 million gallons of oil into the northern Gulf, covering some four thousand square miles with oil. They were trying to reduce the operating efficiency of the coalition forces that were marshaling for the liberation of Kuwait following the Iraqi invasion. It had little effect on our ability to operate in the region, but the resulting damage still plagues parts of the Gulf.

The most iconic and highly publicized example of broad area damage from offshore drilling remains the British Petroleum spill in the Gulf of Mexico in 2010 from the *Deepwater Horizon* rig. The short-term effects are well known, starting with the eleven oil-rig workers—essentially mariners—who died and the more than 200 million gallons of oil that flowed into the waters of the Gulf. Following an explosion on the rig, oil was pumping into the Gulf at well over 2 million gallons a day. Engineers struggled to cap the site for nearly three months, and a wild variety of solutions were put forward, including the use of a tactical nuclear weapon. Nearly six hundred miles of pristine coastland was oiled and ruined, and the livelihood of millions of residents interrupted or lost. An enormous amount of remediation and compensation has been accomplished, as well as significant direct fines levied. Unfortunately, the long-term cost is still difficult to assess, as the damage to so many fish and birds simultaneously may have generational effects; there are reports of defects to the circulatory systems of a variety of species.

Most of the top-ranked oil spills in terms of gallons into the water over the decades have been from tankers. As a mariner, I have passed at sea thousands and thousands of big oil tankers over the years, and the vast majority appear to be well operated and professionally handled. We would often exchange friendly signals, and on one or two occasions provided distress relief or medical support. These enormous tankers, some of them three times the size of the U.S. super aircraft carriers, are operated with a tiny crew—just a dozen or so, as compared with several thousand on a carrier, for example. But when something goes wrong, it goes wrong with a vengeance, and nothing is worse that one of these behemoths discharging oil into the sea. As Americans, we tend to remember the *Exxon Valdez* spill into Prince William Sound in Alaska. This came not from an offshore installation but from a ship that was grossly mishandled, and the spill covered 1,400 miles of coast and killed (by most estimates) millions of living organisms including half a million seabirds. Yet this spill is not even in the top thirty in history and put "only" 11 million gallons into the water as compared with more than 200 million from the BP disaster.

These big incidents from offshore rigs or tankers certainly shock the conscience and are remembered decades later, but they are really dwarfed by the steady amount of oil that enters the world's waters year after year through routine pollution. This comes from illegal dumping in the dark of night, accidental inclusion of oil in garbage dumped at sea, and the flow of oil down to the oceans from freshwater sources, largely rivers, which themselves receive automotive effluents or oil-based pesticides. Some experts believe more than 500 million gallons a year of such steady, insidious oil pollution takes place. While the big incidents like the *Deepwater Horizon*/BP or *Exxon Valdez* disaster can be overwhelming in a given spot and of course receive enormous media attention, it is likely that the long-term, underreported but steady oil pollution into the oceans is actually the bigger threat. This quiet but massive input of oil into the sea deserves much greater study for its potential long-term effects.

While it is easy to focus on oil pollution because the effects are so visible, there is also a high level of concern about chemical pollution. This is most typically from broad industrial activities, which end up producing dangerous chemical substances that then find their way into the oceans. An example would be the flow of contaminated silt, essentially dirt, which rolls into the sea. The silt is carried along by deep river currents and over time can include significant levels of pollutants from industrial and residential activity all along the riverbanks thousands of miles upstream. Man's agricultural activities also contribute greatly to this form of pollution, largely from the use of nonorganic fertilizers. Auto activity, in terms of both exhaust and liquid effluents, also ends up frequently in the oceans. Toxic chemicals such as mercury also find their way into the seas, accumulating in the tissues of big fish species such as swordfish and tuna. And of course there is simple, obvious pollution in many low-regulation nations, where factories pump industrial waste, human excrement and urine, and other liquid substances directly into rivers or the sea.

Another concern that I often witnessed over the years was the dumping of plastics and garbage directly into the sea. Certainly the U.S. Navy's hands are not clean in this regard; I vividly remember all manner of plastic-laced garbage being thrown overboard. I would stand on the fantail of my destroyer in the 1970s and watch hundreds of seagulls come and look over the garbage we tossed carelessly over the side. We have come to understand the damage caused by plastics, and the world's navies and responsible merchant fleets, at least, have modified their behavior accordingly. With apologies to Ian Fleming and his immortal novel *Diamonds Are Forever*, as far as the oceans are concerned it is plastics that are forever.

Even as they degrade into smaller shapes and sizes, they still retain their fundamental composition. As a result, when marine animals—especially birds and turtles—ingest the garbage, they consume plastics, which are increasingly found not just in the seas but in the digestive systems of large segments of marine life. As for other refuse, much of it is biodegradable or can be manufactured so that it will disintegrate without harm to the sea, but some vessels and garbage disposal operations continue to discharge highly toxic materials including contaminated medical waste (needles, tubes, stents, etc.), sewage (close to shore), chemicals, drugs, and other nonbiodegradable items.

Looking to the future, there is both good and bad news. The bad news is that the vast array of activities that damage the oceans will only increase—there will be a higher demand for fish-based protein, and for hydrocarbons, and the increasing world population (probably headed to at least 10 billion by the turn of the next century from the current level of about 7 billion) will cause more pollution, including dumping of garbage, plastics, medical waste, and sewage. All of this will damage the oceans, with particular impact close to shorelines, especially on delicate and important coral reefs. And there will be new activities in the oceans, including a likely increase in the recovery of minerals, probably from the deep seabed where plentiful nodules of copper, cobalt, manganese, nickel, and rare earth minerals lie like so many potatoes waiting to be gathered and hauled to the surface. The good news is that we still have time to react and take measures to protect the oceans, beginning with stronger enforcement of the existing accords, negotiation of new international regimes, and a focus on using the oceans in responsible ways in all of our strategic communications globally. We will never fully tame the vast reaches of the outlaw sea, but we can take proactive steps to reduce risk.

WHAT ARE WE TO DO?

What are we to do about the outlaw sea? As citizens of our individual nations, how do we collectively approach this enormously transnational problem, given that most who follow the sea spend their lives and careers focused on national concerns, as I did? In many ways, this is the most important question that mariners and those who truly love the sea must deal with as we sail further on into the twenty-first century.

At the heart of any approach to the challenges of the outlaw sea is the creation of an enhanced level of international cooperation. Only through a high level of integration among international, interagency, and private entities can there be any hope of addressing the challenges inherent in the vast world of the sea. Unfortunately, to date the results of such efforts have been mixed at best. Certainly the development of the United Nations Convention on the Law of the Sea—an international negotiation concluded in the 1980s—has been largely successful. In the early 1980s, there was enormous enthusiasm for the treaty, a massive negotiating project that created the first truly global regime for ocean management. While it has obviously not solved all the problems of ocean governance, it is hard to imagine the level of chaos on the seas without it—even given that the United States, a huge maritime power, has refused to sign it (in a disagreement over deep seabed mining provisions, a foolish position pushed by U.S. neoconservatives). I remain hopeful that using the Law of the Sea treaty as a base, we will be able to negotiate other international instruments and—even more important—enforce them through a combination of sanctions, judgments in national and international courts, and shaming nations that do not follow the rules. So overall, I am cautiously optimistic about international maritime cooperation.

On the other hand, efforts such as the pledge in 2010 by the world's nations to protect at least 10 percent of the world's oceans as protected reserves by 2020 have foundered—to date only 2 percent of the oceans have been so designated. While there have been some successes (the United Kingdom, for example, has created a reserve area in the South Pacific near Pitcairn Island that is three times the size of Great Britain itself), international efforts are lagging overall. Likewise, the jury is still out on a plethora of well-meaning efforts to address fishing, pollution, and the global environment.

In terms of interagency cooperation, again we see a mixed picture. While the Obama administration moved on creating a U.S. government plan against illegal fishing, there has been a lack of sufficient resources placed against the goals. Neither the Coast Guard nor the U.S. Navy has spare capacity to undertake the kind of sweeping tasks outlined in the plan. The good news is that the interagency spirit is willing, but the flesh, so to speak, is weak. This is typical of how interagency projects fail, both in the United States and in other countries. Unfortunately, there is no consistent voice for the oceans in the vast majority of governments.

Another immensely important zone of cooperation will be the intersection of efforts by the public and private sectors. International shipping companies, for example, are increasingly working together with international organizations (such as the International Maritime Organization of the United Nations) to create norms of behavior on the oceans. These run the gamut from agreements on "pumping and dumping"—discharge of anything from a ship—to levels of qualification of crew members, engineers, deck watch standers, mates, and captains. Many fishing companies are likewise working more closely with governmental and international organizations to bring order out of the largely chaotic world of fisheries. The oil and gas companies are cooperating at a higher level with such authorities as well. Getting past a sense of adversarial politics in all of these ocean areas will be crucial.

In Bill Moomaw's superb report on the oceans, he and his coauthor identify seventy-six "treaties, agreements, protocols, and frameworks that address the management of one or more species, fishing practice, or marine resource at global or regional levels" (Moomaw and Blankenship, 39). This sort of international cooperation demonstrates both the hope and the challenge of such an approach: many were lacking a formal secretariat, scientific body, and enforcement mechanisms. Of the seventy-six, only six had all three. This is the case in other areas of maritime management as well. Clearly, much more work will need to be done in the international space to build not only agreements but the right kind of management and enforcement as well. The best way to do this will be under the overarching umbrella of United Nations organizations (especially the International Maritime Organization) and using the principles that guided nearly two hundred nations through the arduous decade-long negotiation of the United Nations Convention on the Law of the Sea.

We must be more innovative and experiment at sea with new ideas of governance and bring more actors into ocean policy. Creating more protected marine areas will be helpful, as will the idea of establishing sanctuaries at sea for fish, birds, and mammals, much as is done on land. Certification programs that clearly indicate to the public which companies are doing business in ecologically thoughtful ways will matter, and encouraging corporate social responsibility at sea will be crucial. Linkages with aquariums, zoos, environmental advocacy organizations, and think tanks all have applicability as well.

The course we must chart for the oceans involves work between and within governments, and above all within the private sector. But under-lying all of that effort must be a coherent campaign of strategic commu-nications. Unless we can convince the public of all our nations that the oceans are not a vast, invulnerable dumping ground and an endless source of protein, we will not succeed globally in altering the course we are on. We have a long way to sail before we can feel confident that the outlaw sea has been tamed.

9.

AMERICA AND THE OCEANS

A NAVAL STRATEGY FOR
THE TWENTY-FIRST
CENTURY

New environmental challenges will tax the oceans in ways
never seen in human history. This map displays the
world's land and sea elevations.

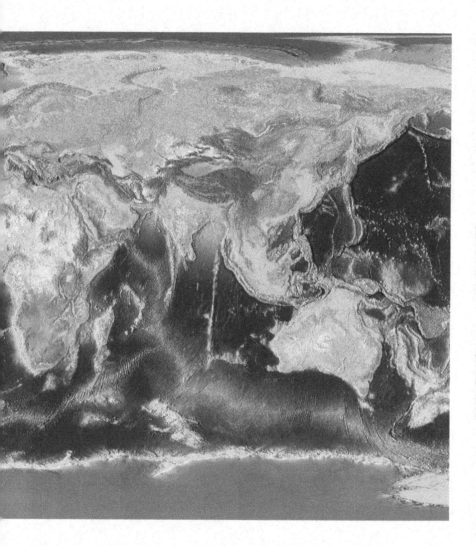

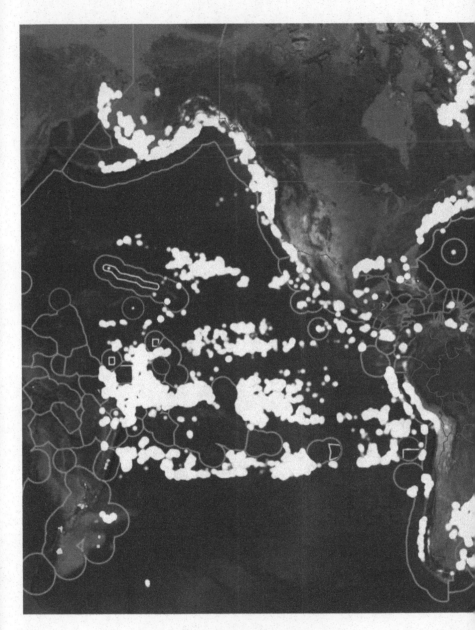

Current global commercial fishing activity.

Courtesy of Global Fishing Watch.

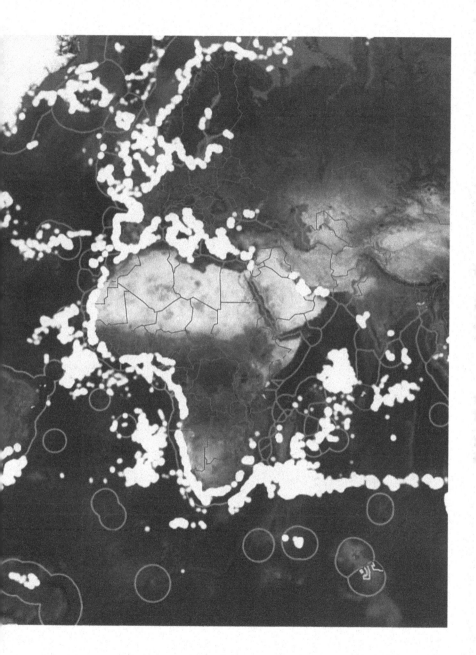

I first heard of Alfred Thayer Mahan when I was seventeen years old and a freshman (a "plebe," as we were not-so-affectionately termed) at the U.S. Naval Academy. Part of the first-year curriculum for the entire thousand-man (and it was all men in those prehistoric days) class was a course titled simply "Sea Power." Some of my wittier classmates dubbed it "Z-Power" to imply that it was boring, but for me it was anything but a sleeper.

The modern version of the course had been created by a venerable historian, E. B. "Ned" Potter, who had also written a classic blue-covered textbook of the same name. Luckily for him, every year he sold a thousand copies of this hardcover text, which no doubt kept him well supplied with the small-batch bourbon of which I am told he was quite fond. I still have my plebe-year copy of the book, a little battered but still very much a text I open from time to time, and of course the title of this work is taken in homage to Potter's course, although the context and approach are entirely different.

The structure of the course was built simply upon the chronological history of man's military journey on the oceans. It began in prehistoric times, moved quite briskly through the age of galleys sailed by the Greeks and Romans, segued into the classic battles like Lepanto in the Mediterranean between the Ottomans and the Hapsburgs, included plenty of material on the American Revolution at sea, followed by a quick nod to the Barbary pirates and the heroics of Stephen Decatur. Then it slowed and began the long sail through nineteenth-century American sea power, with an emphasis on the Civil War, before launching into the real set pieces of World War I and World War II at sea. It was (and remains) unashamedly Western oriented (completing the course, you would have thought that the Chinese didn't build boats). It was unapologetically told from a very American point of view, and was extremely traditional in its outlook. And the high priest of it all was Rear Admiral Alfred Thayer Mahan.

One former secretary of war, Henry Stimson, opined that Mahan manifested "the peculiar psychology of the Navy Department, which frequently seemed to retire from the realm of logic into a dim religious world in which Neptune was God, Mahan his prophet, and the United States Navy the only true church." Mahan was born in 1840 in, of all places, West Point—home of the U.S. Military Academy, where his father was a professor. Mahan's middle name was an homage to the so-called Father of West Point, Sylvanus Thayer. Everything about his early life would have predicted he would become an Army officer, but he set his course early for the Naval Academy and graduated second in his class of 1859.

He was part of the Civil War Union Navy, and over the course of his career spent the requisite time at sea, working his way up to the rank of captain and holding command of a number of ships. Yet he was, by all accounts, an indifferent seaman whose propensity to bump into other ships and navigational buoys was noted by his superiors. But he began writing books early and often, expounding a theory of sea power that would make him perhaps the most influential naval officer of his generation.

Mahan's desire to read, think, write, and publish occasionally landed him in hot water with his superiors, including one famously damning fitness report that said succinctly, "It is not the business of naval officers to write books." (Here I must note that the book you are reading is the seventh I have either written or edited, none at the level of Mahan's classics; but I too found my naval career a bit bumpy at times due to that desire to write. The Navy sometimes retains a level of skepticism toward those who would proffer their views in print, but fortunately I think overall there is a respect for intellectual effort as well as good seamanship in the course of an officer's career.)

Late in his career, Mahan was tapped by Rear Admiral Stephen B. Luce, the intellectual force in the Navy's move from sail to steam in the late nineteenth century, to come to the Naval War College at Newport, Rhode Island, first as a lecturer and later for two terms as the second president of the college, following Admiral Luce. Mahan's lectures, which were deeply admired and absorbed by Theodore Roosevelt among many others, were eventually translated into a series of classic books on sea power and history that are still studied closely today and form the basis for American sea power on into the twenty-first century. He died at the age of seventy-four of congestive heart failure, having finally been advanced to rear admiral (on the retired list) very late in his life and career.

The basic theory of Mahan's body of work is that national power derives from engagement via the world's oceans along three key vectors: production (which leads to the need for international trade and commerce), shipping (both merchant and naval), and colonies and alliances (spread across the globe, forming a network of bases from which to project sea power). All three of these basic concepts still pertain today, although they need a bit of updating as we will discuss in more depth below.

In addition to these three key vectors, Mahan also returns again and again to a handful of principal conditions that affect a nation's ability to develop and wield sea power effectively. The first is the most straightforward and immutable: geography. As he says, "The seaboard of a country is one of its frontiers; and the easier the access offered by the frontier to the region beyond, in this case the sea, the greater will be the tendency of a people toward intercourse with the rest of the world by it." In the case of the United States, our vast coastlines afford immediate access to the Atlantic, Pacific, and Arctic oceans, as well as the Gulf of Mexico and Caribbean Sea to the south. This is an enviable position for developing and exploiting sea power, as we have seen repeatedly in our history. Coupled with enormous natural resources and relatively temperate climate, the geography of the United States features perhaps the best set of circumstances to build the nation into a sea power.

A second factor cited frequently by Mahan that remains important today is the actual size of the seacoasts. Mahan's comments here are quite specific: "As regards the development of sea power, it is not the total number of square miles which a country contains, but the length of its coast-line and the character of its harbors that are to be considered." The United States has 133,000 kilometers of coastline as measured along the tidewater boundaries—an enormous stretch, virtually all of it easily accessible from the land and situated in temperate zones. This is among the largest coastlines in the world (measuring coastlines, by the way, is a tricky business, and the numbers used here are from the World Resources

Institute). Only Canada has a larger coastline by this measure, and much of it, of course, is inaccessible much of the year.

Mahan also cites the importance of the native population in determining a nation's ability to use sea power. As we increasingly see in this century, demography is destiny in many ways for nations. Mahan's view was that it is not only the number of the population, but their fitness to conduct the business of using the oceans—shipbuilding, working on ships, propensity to join the Navy and Coast Guard—that is critical. As he says, "the number following the sea" matters. Closely associated with the number is the "character of the people." In this regard, Mahan (like Theodore Roosevelt as president) believed in an activist philosophy of life, with an aggressive commercial approach to seas—specifically the economic incentive of the people to want to engage in trade globally.

As he said, "The tendency to trade, involving of necessity the production of something to trade with, is the national characteristic most important to the development of sea power." In terms of the characteristic that drives all this, he also said, "It seems scarcely necessary, however, to do more than appeal to a not very distant past to prove that, if legislative hindrances be removed, and more remunerative fields of enterprise filled up, the sea power will not long delay its appearance. The instinct for commerce, bold enterprise in the pursuit of gain, and a keen scent for the trails that lead to it, all exist; and if there be in the future any fields calling for colonization, it cannot be doubted that Americans will carry to them all their inherited aptitude for self-government and independent growth." No shrinking violet, Mahan, but rather an unabashed capitalist (and imperialist, frankly) who also would have been happier to see the United States more aggressively pursuing colonies abroad like our European counterparts.

A final factor upon which Mahan lays emphasis is the "character of the government." Consistently throughout all his writings he calls on the U.S. government to fully understand the importance of sea power—a national imperative in the view of Mahan. He says, "It would seem probable that a government in full accord with the natural bias of its people would most successfully advance its growth in every respect; and, in the matter of sea power, the most significant successes have followed where there has been intelligent direction by a government fully imbued with the spirit of the people and conscious of its true general bent." Mahan— aided by Rear Admiral Luce and truly energized by Teddy Roosevelt— preached this doctrine religiously throughout the senior part of his career. And his ideas caught the attention of policy makers not just in the United States but across the Atlantic as well, including in both England and Germany.

All of these underlying factors are important to his thesis, but at its heart, Mahan's siren call is for a big, muscular fleet: think of the Great White Fleet of Teddy Roosevelt, sailing the globe, refueling at well-selected coaling stations (which we would call forward bases today), and inspiring fear and awe in the nations of the world. This is the relevance of the expression "Speak softly and carry a big stick." The key was being able to overmatch your opponent in terms of fleet fighting capacity— essentially using the inherent mobility of naval forces to concentrate and defeat an enemy at sea in a decisive battle.

But there is a strategic concept behind all of that: the ability of a nation to use sea power to ultimately contain powerful nations that have concentrated their use of forces ashore, ignoring the sea out of lack of interest, or an inability to see the force of the sea power argument, or simply because they lack the geography, character, and political will to exploit the oceans. Let's begin with the ancient Greeks: Athens was a sea power (with a good deal of land force character as well). With both land power and sea power, Athens was initially able to hold off Sparta (an essential land power) in the Peloponnesian Wars. Sparta, with its center of gravity deep inland on the southern peninsula of Greece, was a "heartland" power. Over time, the Spartans realized they needed to create a navy to compete effectively with Athens, learning the lessons of sea power.

Flash forward to the age of Britannic majesty, the British Empire. How did a small island nation, devoid of most natural resources, come to dominate much of the world's land surface? Through the effective use of sea power, building a colonial empire "upon which the sun never set." Mahan seized upon British mastery of sea power to set up the case for the United States to build a similar fleet, and a colonial empire, taking advantage of its coastlines, maritime DNA, and naval approach to have real influence in the world. The British, according to Mahan, were able to challenge continental (heartland) European powers like Germany/Prussia because they were able to dominate the sea lanes of communication around the world.

Many analysts posited this same dynamic in the cold war between the United States and the Soviet Union. The USSR was a classic "heartland power," with huge land-force capability, the advantage of an interior position geopolitically, domination of its near abroad (through the Warsaw Pact), and a mind-set forged in the great land wars against Napoleon, Kaiser Wilhelm, and Nazi Germany. Against the USSR stood the USA, a maritime nation—essentially an island nation—protected by its great oceans and geographic position, underwritten by a strong navy, and perfectly capable of combining with continental allies (via NATO) to ensure that the heartland nation was unable to attain its ultimate desire—to dominate the "world island," as geopolitical analyst Halford Mackinder styled the entire Eurasian continent. As Mackinder said, "Who rules East Europe commands the Heartland; Who rules the Heartland commands the World Island; Who rules the World Island commands the

World." This quote sums up the concern Mahan had about domination by a strong land power, and why sea power was so important as a counterbalance.

The interesting question in the twenty-first century is whether or not shifts in power, international norms, or technology have substantially altered the Mahanian approach. Personally, I believe his message still rings true for the United States. As we seek to craft an international maritime strategy for the nation, Mahan's point of view—adapted somewhat for today's world—still presents a timeless message.

Taking his principles as a starting point, what advice can we imagine Mahan presenting the president today?

First and foremost, he would emphasize the need for the United States to regard itself as a maritime nation. This means supporting a reasonably sized civilian merchant marine; a powerful, capable navy; a robust shipbuilding industry; a competent fishing fleet; efficient ports and infrastructure; ice-breaking capability for the Arctic; and the ability to conduct broad area surveillance of the ocean approaches to our nation.

Mahan would also emphasize to today's president the importance to the United States of defending the concept of an open global commons—the rights of high seas passage and transit, the importance of the UN Law of the Sea treaty (which he would support, as virtually every active-duty admiral in the U.S. Navy does today), and safe passage free from piracy, political interference, or natural barriers. The open flow of free goods on the oceans (95 percent of global trade moves by sea) is crucial to a geopolitical power like the United States. This means challenging attempts to close the global commons by nations such as China, which is building artificial islands and declaring much of the South China Sea a "historic claim."

A third key element in Mahan's prescription would be a strong system of alliances and partnerships around the world. He would have thought in terms of colonies, which are—praise the Lord—things of the past. In their place today, we need strong alliances, with NATO at the top of the list. By working with NATO, the United States has reliable and immediate access to bases and logistic support all around the periphery of Europe and up into the Arctic. Our warships can pull into port in Rota, Spain; Souda Bay, Greece; Portsmouth, England; Toulon, France; Bremen, Germany; and essentially anywhere within the twenty-eight nations of the alliance. Over my time as a Navy commander, I have frequently made port calls, refueled, sent my crew on liberty, conferred with close colleagues from allied navies, and generally found support and sustenance in our alliance. Similarly, in the Pacific, we have formal alliances with Australia, New Zealand, the Philippines, Thailand, Japan, and South Korea—all of equal value in ensuring a global system of operating locations.

In addition to alliances, the United States needs an active network of partners and friends—nations that we are for a variety of reasons not ready to engage with a formal alliance—but with which we have warm relations nonetheless. Nations in this category include Saudi Arabia, Bahrain, Kuwait, Israel, India, Malaysia, Singapore, Finland, Sweden, Colombia, Brazil, Argentina, Chile, and Peru. I have made port visits to each of the nations mentioned above and have found a welcoming committee in each place. These partners and friends are an essential part of our global maritime network as well, and part of our maritime strategy would include embracing them. When you put all the capability of our allies, partners, and friends together, it is a formidable naval force indeed—that approach toward international coalitions must be central to our global maritime strategy.

Fourth, Mahan was keenly aware of the importance of the private sector in ensuring that the United States maintain a robust maritime capability. In his view, the primary key was supporting the maritime industry and the global trading capability. In today's world, both of those are necessary, but they are not sufficient. Another key component of an effective global maritime strategy for the United States must be a high level of private-public operational integration and cooperation. One key example is in the world of sharing intelligence and information on ship movements at sea, both passively through the Global Positioning System and associated beaconing systems, and through active shared reports. This is crucial to ensure an open and free global navigational system, especially in the face of potential piratical activity in places like the Strait of Malacca, the east and west coasts of Africa, and the Caribbean Sea. Another example is specific to piracy, and that is exchanging operational protocols—embarked security teams, convoy operations, distress reporting systems, and countermeasures on individual ships. And all facets of global shipping systems—ships, ports, loading cranes, buoyage systems— are now vulnerable to cyberattack and are therefore a shared responsibility between the U.S. government and the U.S. operators.

Mahan was very focused on the rise of competing sea powers, and in today's world he would signal concern about two: Russia and China. Russia has rebounded from a period of decline in its military capability and is today using a highly targeted program of rebuilding its fleet. While in total ship numbers slightly smaller than the United States, the Russian fleet is very actively focused on the undersea world. While Mahan was not writing about the incredible advancements in submarines, by the end of his life he would have been aware of their growing potential to influence war at sea. The Russians have certainly taken the idea of submarine capability to heart and continue to expand the number, technology, and operational reach of all their submarines—both nuclear and diesel powered, and including both attack and ballistic missile versions. Likewise, the Chinese are improving all aspects of their oceangoing fleet, with an emphasis on technology, undersea capability (both offensive and defensive), long-range surface-to-surface missiles used to attack American aircraft carriers, and long-range land-attack precision cruise missiles. This is in addition to their very capable nuclear-powered ballistic missile submarines. Mahan's advice would be to keep a weather eye on the rising power of both of these potential competitors at sea and maintain the ability to defeat both.

What would Mahan have missed or gotten wrong?

I think the biggest surprise to Mahan would have been the rise of undersea warfare as a critical (some would say dominant) element of naval and maritime strategy. Coupled with this, of course, would be the advent of nuclear propulsion, which gives these undersea warships the ability to submerge for long periods of time (months), limited only by food supplies on board—they can propel themselves and create both water and breathable air. And he would have been stunned at the size and capability of today's submarines—while some small diesel-powered boats were in existence by the end of his life, to think of a 19,000-ton, 560-foot-long warship with missiles capable of destroying large cities and creating nuclear killing zones around the world all while being under the water and essentially invisible would have been too much even for a man used to ranging freely across the oceans of the mind.

A second surprise: it would have been hard for him to conceive of the way in which warfare has gone from service-specific to joint, meaning highly integrated among the land, sea, and air components. The way in which the United States would fight a war today depends utterly on seamless command and control between the services (Army, Navy, Air Force, and Marine Corps), integrated munitions that can be shifted between them, and operations that use all branches to create shock and awe—missile strikes, aircraft attacks, naval gunfire, Marines landing and flying to an objective, heavy Army units right behind, all of it collectively creating a sense on the part of the enemy that defeat is inevitable. For Mahan, naval forces would have generally operated within their watery domain, fought a great battle with an enemy fleet, and been tasked with sea control, logistic resupply for forces ashore, and occasional power projection from cannons and Marines over a beachhead. But the essence of the fleet was to find and destroy the enemy fleet, thus ensuring control of the vital sea lanes of communication.

He also, naturally enough, would have had no conception of the importance of cyber. The world of information, command, communications, and cyberwarfare simply had no existence in the period of time in which he was writing. It is hard enough for us to keep up with the latest changes in information warfare, let alone expect Mahan to imagine them. Perhaps the biggest technological change on ships would have been the use of computational power to direct weapons, giving them a distance, accuracy, and lethality he could not have imagined. The major cultural change, of course, would have been the advent of instantaneous communications, meaning that a captain's decisions in battle are far more subject to "helpful advice" from a fully informed chain of command. I suspect the latter would not have been good news, as Mahan was someone who prized the initiative, verve, and confidence of the American naval commander at sea. But all good things must end, and in today's world a captain still maintains a certain amount of tactical control over operations, even if he (or she!) is receiving a great deal of broad operational and strategic guidance.

Additionally, it is hard to imagine that Mahan could have predicted the integration of space and unmanned systems into the nautical battle world. The vast expanses of the ocean always provided a sort of natural hiding place for ships, and the challenges of navigating across the track-less oceans challenged even the best of navigators. Electronic aids to navigation emerged in the middle of the twentieth century (radio beacons, for example), and radar deployed from aircraft began to shrink the unknown spaces of the sea. Once satellites were launched, and the Global Positioning System put in place, the world of the oceans was finally effectively mapped and tracked from on high. This has changed the character both of navigation itself and of how combat is conducted—virtually all naval weapons today depend on guidance obtained at least in part from GPS systems.

One final surprise for Rear Admiral Mahan would have been the emerging importance of undersea cables in linking the world together and creating a sort of undersea sea lane of communications (quite literally) upon which we all depend. One other important aspect of thinking through a maritime strategy for the twenty-first century is what lies at the *bottom* of the ocean. In addition to a formidable geography—just like the surface of the earth, with high mountain ranges, valleys, plateaus, plains, and on and on—there are critical cables, man-made of course, that carry much of the world's knowledge and commerce.

At the bottom of the world's oceans, like so many snakes surrounding the globe, are the standard commercial fiber optic cables that carry 99 percent of the world's international telecommunications daily. They move information at a brisk clip: two terabits of data every second, including nearly $5 trillion every twenty-four hours in financial transactions. About two hundred of them carry the vast majority of all that vital information.

As one observer recently commented, "Though often mentioned in passing, the fact that the overwhelming bulk of Internet activity travels along submarine cables fails to register with the public. High-flying satellites orbiting the crowded skies, continent-spanning microwave towers and a million miles of old 20th Century copper phone wire all carry but a fraction of the Earth's Internet traffic compared with deep-sea fiber-optic cables." As we consider the role they play today and what the potential might be for further enhancements, there is both promise and peril to consider.

First, the peril—as strategists are increasingly aware, these cables are vulnerable. While their extreme depth protects them up to a point, advanced industrial nations—including the United States, the Russian Federation, and China—all reportedly have significant ability to monitor, exploit, damage, and destroy the cables. During the cold war, both the USA and the USSR were believed to have attacked antisubmarine systems and arrays at similar depths.

As Steve Weintz wrote recently in the *National Observer*, "If you wish to practice hybrid warfare—disruption and degradation with little overt engagement—then the ability to cut submarine cables at will and at depth gives you a very powerful weapon. Cut up undersea hydrophone networks and you deafen your adversary. Cut Internet cables and you have the ultimate denial-of-service cyber weapon."

There have certainly been plenty of incidents of accidental cable cuttings and losses of data resulting from such activities. In 2006 and 2008, accidental destruction of cables effectively shut down Internet services to several large countries or parts thereof, including, among others, Egypt, India, China, and Pakistan. Fortunately, the cables are fairly substantial: typically, a couple of inches thick and well insulated with galvanic padding. But they are quite vulnerable, especially at cable heads when they emerge from the water. In Egypt just a couple of years ago, swimmers were caught while trying to cut through a major 12,500-mile cable. Internet speeds throughout Egypt plummeted by more than 60 percent.

Overall, the cable system is fairly robust in facing routine challenges—

accidents, anchors dragged over them, corrosion, low-level attacks. The challenge will come as nations and transnational groups (criminal cartels, terrorists) find ways to disrupt them on a massive scale. Even with the 285 cables on the bottom of the world today and the 22 "redundant" or "dark" cables in reserve, the vulnerabilities are clear. Both individual nations and international organizations should collectively be thinking through disaster scenarios and considering how best to use collective defense of these cables going forward.

So much for the peril; but what about the promise of this system? Are there new technologies coming that can leverage and improve this capability? The good news is a resounding yes.

First, the information technology itself is improving—and it has to. Just a couple of years ago, the Internet moved about five gigabytes per capita. It will hit fourteen gigabytes per capita in 2018. And with billions more devices connecting to the Internet in the next decade, the problem is obvious. Fortunately, we are able to use new phase modulation and also improve what is called submarine line terminal equipment (SLTE). This will boost capability by more than fifty times. Additionally, the prosaic ability to lay, adjust, repair, and maintain the cables is improving through the use of unmanned systems, big data analysis, and better materials.

Additionally, there are increasingly creative ideas about how to leverage the cable system to improve access to high-speed Internet around the world. Satellites—at least for now—are just not the answer. Their signals capacity is severely limited by latency and bit loss, whereas underwater fiber optic cables deliver signals at nearly the speed of light (they are optic, after all). So what can we do to amp up their contribution?

One idea is to create mobile networking hubs, both airborne and on the surface of the sea. The airborne vehicles could operate at forty to fifty thousand feet in altitude, which would enable broadcast to 250 nautical miles in all direction while receiving data from as far as 500 nautical miles. The surface hubs would be a system of "risers" above the cables to move the data to the surface and make it accessible to the mobile airborne hub.

Such a system could have serious commercial viability, of course. It could also be very advantageous to military planners seeking another means of moving data. The key is the relatively low cost of moving data compared with satellites—this system, even considering the added cost of the mobile airborne hubs and the risers, would be orders of magnitude less expensive than satellite systems, and vastly faster. From a military perspective, this would be a redundant system to the backbone satellite systems in use today. This is also an idea rife with potential for public-private partnerships, as the risers could be connected via the systems that oil and gas industry platforms are using today.

As with any system for communications, there is both risk and reward possible. In the case of submarine cables, we should increase our ability to protect this vital portion of the global communications grid and seek innovative ways to leverage its capability.

So if all of that reflects Mahanian thinking, where are we today? Are these classic ideas and principles important today, as well as the new technologies that are all part of our idea of twenty-first-century sea power? The short answer is yes—up to a point.

In March 2015, the chiefs of the nation's sea services—Navy, Marine Corps, and Coast Guard—unveiled "A Cooperative Strategy for 21st Century Seapower," charting a forward, engaged, ready course to meet the nation's global maritime strategic responsibilities. Then–chief of naval operations Admiral Jonathan W. Greenert, then–Marine commandant General Joseph F. Dunford Jr. (he has since been promoted to chairman of the Joint Chiefs of Staff), and Coast Guard commandant

Admiral Paul F. Zukunft underscored the growing importance of increasing cooperation among the services to achieve the maximum forward presence and war-fighting capabilities required for national defense and homeland security. I enjoyed leading a conversation among the three of them at the official rollout of the document in Washington in 2015.

This is *not* about diminishing the criticality of our nation's air and ground forces: far from it. The document is about how the maritime world fits into the broader geopolitical context out of efforts to create twenty-first-century security.

A bird's-eye view of the shipyards, port facilities, Navy ships, Marine Corps, Coast Guard, and Special Forces bases and stations in and around the nation certainly reminds us that the United States is a global maritime power. This is as true today as it has been since the beginning of the Republic. What is often forgotten is the critical importance of a *maritime strategy* to go with all that capability. The sea services have developed such strategies for three decades, and they have been largely successful in driving the size, deployment patterns, and impact of our maritime forces.

In 1986, with the fast-growing Soviet navy as the potential adversary, the U.S. Navy and Marine Corps published "The Maritime Strategy," aimed at using maritime power, in combination with the efforts of our sister services and forces of our allies, to bring about war termination on favorable terms. This flowed from presidential guidance. As then–secretary of the Navy John Lehman once reminded, President Ronald Reagan, when asked to summarize what his policy toward the cold war would be, replied: "We win and they lose." Pretty simple.

As a newly selected lieutenant commander (still a *very* junior officer), I was in the Pentagon as a special assistant to the chief of naval operations and had a chance to play a small role in the formation of "The Maritime Strategy." Because I had a brand-new PhD, it was assumed that I was at least marginally capable of thinking and writing. This translated mostly to getting coffee for the actual authors, senior captains not only with comparable degrees but in possession of actual experience as strategic planners. But in hanging around the process, I learned a great deal about how these strategies are put together that I was able to use when I was more senior.

In a nutshell, it begins with a political idea that "now is a good time" to put out a fresh strategy. This normally comes either when a high official (a secretary of defense or the Navy, or a chief of naval operations or Marine Corps commandant) comes into office. Or occasionally when a distraction is needed from the negative flow of events. A small team of bright officers is selected, several of whom will have had experience doing such work in the past. They will be given office space, a small support staff (such as Lieutenant Commander Stavridis), and will put together a draft concept.

This will then be vetted through the enormous staff groups in the Pentagon, a process that can take months. Various offices will attempt to drive their particular areas of emphasis to the top of the priority queue, for example subsurface warfare, the threat of cyber affecting seagoing operations, tactical strike operations with aircraft, unmanned vehicles, and so forth. Lots of horse trading goes back and forth at increasingly higher levels in the food chain, until the leader of the drafting group—having done his or her best to synthesize all the "helpful input"—will take the melded draft concept to the decision maker, say the chief of naval operations. This august leader will provide a blessing, and now the true hard work begins—writing the actual words that will be part of the strategy.

No one should ever underestimate the passion that goes into the heart and mind of a human being offered the chance to edit another's prose. Once the drafting team produces an actual draft—sentences, paragraphs, a title, and so on—it must be sent around not only to the Pentagon staff, but to the various fleet elements as well. *Lots* of "helpful input" comes back, and is again considered (and mostly rejected) at this point. Finally, a smooth draft is completed that can go "outside the life lines of the Navy (or Marines)" and be presented to the Department of Defense (the boss) and informally to think tanks, influential thinkers and writers, retired august figures, and the like.

All of this will typically have taken about nine to twelve months, but incredibly the product is usually pretty balanced and often contains some basic, useful guidance. "The Maritime Strategy" of 1986 was big and bold and really captured the imagination of the Naval Service. Subsequent strategic road maps would be published in 1992, 1994, and 2007. The massive blue-water threat of the USSR faded and the sea services became more skilled at littoral warfare as guided by the strategy titled ". . . From the Sea" in 1992. (Note: the three dots in front of the words "From the Sea" were intentional, meant to imply the flexibility of the Navy.) The world economy—largely dependent on sea transport of commerce—was becoming more interconnected. The challenges to national security were evolving to include wars between major powers, regional conflicts, international terrorism, piracy, and response to natural disasters. There was one constant. Whenever a new international crisis faced the nation, the president then in office would continue to ask, "Where are the carriers? Where are the Marines?" Why? Because they form the ready strike forces that are sustainable from the sea.

"A Cooperative Strategy for the 21st Century" addresses the challenges and opportunities before the sea services from 2015 to future horizons, framing the strategic discussion in terms of:

- Global security environment
- Forward presence and partnership

- Sea power in support of national security
- Force design: building the future force

World changes since 2007 are presented in summary and then examined in detail: "Today's global security environment is characterized by the rising importance of the Indo-Asia-Pacific region, the ongoing development and fielding of anti-access/area denial (A2/AD) capabilities that challenge our global maritime access, continued threats from expanding and evolving terrorist and criminal networks, the increasing frequency and intensity of maritime territorial disputes, and threats to maritime commerce, particularly the flow of energy."

Chinese naval capabilities, the longer reach of that navy into the Indian and Pacific oceans, and China's growing territorial claims are highlighted, as are China's participation in international exercises and disaster response missions. In the strategic context, these are understood as both challenges and opportunities. But of course it is not all about a Pacific pivot: Europe still matters deeply.

More U.S. ships, aircraft, and Marine Corps forces will be operating in the Indo-Asia-Pacific region. In broader terms, if the sea services' global forward presence is imperative, the expansion of naval and Marine Corps planning and operations with allies and other friendly nations on seas around the world goes hand in hand. Such partnerships provide increased international stability in peacetime and increased combined-force capability in time of conflict. In parallel, the Coast Guard, as a regulatory and law enforcement agency, and one of the nation's five armed services, is expanding combined operations—with more than sixty bilateral agreements already in place with foreign governments—countering international illegal operations and further enhancing maritime stability.

The sea power now required to protect the homeland, provide national security, and provide sea control includes:

- The Navy's powerful carrier strike groups, centered on a massive U.S. nuclear-powered carrier with its embarked air wing, accompanied by a brace of cruisers and destroyers
- Amphibious task forces with their embarked Marines
- Surface warships and submarines operating independently or in small tactical groups
- Cutters of the U.S. Coast Guard, which have reasonable warfighting capability

If the maritime strategy is to be implemented and succeed, it will be essential to have all-domain access—that is, access allowing both protection of U.S. operating forces wherever they may be and effective projection and mission completion by those forces in areas contested by foreign powers. In the words of the chief of naval operations, "We must be able to create access in any domain. That means altering how we plan and coordinate actions in the air, sea, land, space, and cyberspace domains, identifying and leveraging the right capability mix to assure access and freedom of action."

Against the current background of budget constraints, flexible, agile, and ready forces and the most highly trained and capable sailors, Marines, and Coast Guardsmen—"our greatest asymmetric advantage"—will be required. This will include a balanced force of submarines, aircraft carriers, amphibious ships, and surface combatants for deterrence, sea control and power projection, and maritime security needed to combat terrorism, illegal trafficking of people, drugs, and arms, piracy, and the safeguarding of freedom of navigation.

There is one top-priority, underlying message throughout the new maritime strategy: *the need for sea power is greater than ever.* Again, this does not diminish the need for other forms of national power—land, air, special operations, cyber. But make no mistake: there are extremely difficult international threats and challenges in the years ahead. It is essential that we provide the forces and the people the sea services require, and this new strategic vision does a commendable job articulating the case.

Throughout the nearly four decades of my long career on active service in our Navy, I worked on many strategic plans. The Navy, along with the other services, is constantly tinkering with a new version. Sometimes it truly laid out big visions ("The Maritime Strategy" and the associated six-hundred-ship Navy of the 1980s come to mind) and other times the "visions" are somewhat incremental and timid. As we head for the turn and conclude two decades of this incredibly turbulent twenty-first century, it is high time for some "blue sky" (some would say "blue water") thinking. The oceans remain largely ignored as much more than a convenient highway for our goods. If the United States is to prosper and lead in this century, we need a coherent national strategy, of which a significant component should be based on the timeless strategic principles of Mahan as adapted for today's world—the power of our geography, national character, and a keen sense of the potential of the oceans.

One final thought to consider is how we should look geographically at each of the world's oceans from a *strategic* sense. While the essence of sea power is the connective power of the unity of the oceans into a single global commons, there are historic, cultural, political, economic, and military reasons to think about each from a strategic perspective.

Let's begin with the "twin towers" of the world's oceans, the North Atlantic and Pacific. Like two massive guardians, they flank the continental United States, providing distance—which translates into time and insulation from the rest of the world. U.S. strategy throughout our history has been to ensure that we have benign neighbors to north and south, and we have achieved that, enjoying an excellent relationship with both Canada and Mexico. The Caribbean is largely harmless, and the prospects of war in the Americas are remote. All of this translates into three key strategic elements: maintaining a cordial relationship in the Americas, especially with Canada and Mexico; ensuring that we have sufficient sea power to maintain sea control in both the North Atlantic and North Pacific; and controlling the Panama Canal to provide the ability to "swing" the U.S. fleet as necessary. In practical terms this translates into approximately 350 significant battle force ships, divided into at least twelve carrier battle groups. There have been multiple studies over the past thirty years that have validated these numbers again and again. Time will tell whether the promised fleet-size increases under the Trump administration will come to be and, if so, whether they will meet the needs for our international interests.

During the 2012 election, President Obama mocked Republican presidential candidate Mitt Romney when Romney suggested that we needed a set minimum number of ships. Obama pointed out, correctly, that we don't need cavalry units anymore when Romney accurately said our fleet was the smallest in decades. Romney was right—quantity has a quality all its own when it comes to ships, and the enormous distances of the Atlantic and Pacific testify to the need for a formidable U.S. fleet. Events since 2012—the rise of China's navy, a much more assertive Russia with a significant naval building program, distributed threats around the world—make the argument for higher numbers of ships even more salient. U.S. maritime strategy must be built on an absolute ability to control the ocean approaches to our nation. We are not seriously challenged today, but if we neglect fleet size and military spending, the day will come when we cannot take for granted the sea lanes of communication to and from our continent. This is the basic building block of our strategy.

The Third Fleet in the Pacific is commanded by a three-star vice admiral reporting to the overall commander of the Pacific fleet. The old Second Fleet, which patrolled the East Coast, was decommissioned in 2011 and has been taken over by the four-star commander of the Atlantic fleet. Both fleets have two key missions: protecting the coasts of the United States and the territorial seas, as well as the high seas; and conducting training and exercising to prepare the Navy ships that will go forward and operate on deployments to the Sixth Fleet (Mediterranean), Fifth Fleet (Arabian/Persian Gulf), Seventh Fleet (western Pacific and Indian Ocean), and Fourth Fleet (Latin America and Caribbean). This structure remains viable at the moment, although over time the United States should consider an Eighth Fleet for the Indian Ocean as operations increase there. We do not need a fleet for the Arctic (yet), but we should reserve the number for a Ninth Fleet for the High North. Interestingly, the Navy has designated a numbered fleet for cyber operations, the Tenth Fleet.

After the North Atlantic and Pacific, the closest ocean space is, of course, the Caribbean. Not only is it the "soft underbelly" of the United States, but it is also the waterway that controls the Panama Canal. The vast majority of trade transiting the Americas goes through the canal, and we must control the approaches to its passage. In 1962, the United States almost went to war with the Soviet Union when it sought to emplace nuclear-tipped missiles on the island of Cuba. While there was legitimate concern about the presence of such weapons so close to U.S. borders, the geostrategic reason for the confrontation was simple: the United States cannot cede control of the Caribbean to anyone else. Today when I think about the Caribbean, it is even clearer than ever that we need to invest there in the broadest terms.

This region—the Caribbean and the waters of Latin America—is the purview of the Fourth Fleet. The newest of the modern U.S. fleets, it has its headquarters in northern Florida and reports to the combatant commander in Miami. When I arrived as commander of U.S. Southern Command in 2006, there was no designated fleet controlling the area. I had to requisition forces from the Atlantic Fleet commander, who had many missions of his own and was not always fully attentive to the needs of the region. Working with the chief of naval operations at the time, an old friend and fellow captain of destroyer *Barry*, Admiral Gary Roughead, we were able to stand up a small but symbolically important new command: the Fourth Fleet.

This was not without controversy in the region, and some of the nations perceived it as a return to U.S. imperialism. Cartoons of me appeared in various publications around the region in the left-leaning countries like Argentina, Nicaragua, and especially Cuba (of course) showing an admiral with a battle helmet and a long spear through the heart of South America. I kept making the point in all my visits that the Fourth Fleet was focused not on combat but on the real missions of the region: humanitarian assistance, disaster relief, medical diplomacy, training and exercises, protection of the Panama Canal from sabotage, and counternarcotics. Over the past decade, that message has landed and the protests have faded away. However, I still treasure the fact that I was personally condemned in *Granma*, the official publication of Cuba, on the front page by Fidel Castro himself.

This is why the naval station at Guantánamo Bay is a very important U.S. installation. We need to reimagine Guantánamo Bay in strategic terms, getting away from the idea of it as a prison colony for terrorists—a failed construct from a geopolitical perspective. The base serves today as the logistical, training, and naval hub of the Caribbean and South Atlantic. It is where the U.S. military stages and operates its extensive program of humanitarian activity, medical diplomacy, and disaster relief—swinging into action after the frequent hurricanes, earthquakes, and other natural disasters of the region. Guantánamo Bay is leased from Cuba (although the Castro regime disputes the legitimacy of the agreement and doesn't cash the rent checks).

The "normalization" of relations with Cuba is a good thing on balance, as it will probably end up creating more pressure for liberalization of the regime in Cuba than the embargo had accomplished across the decades. Over time, it will gradually have the effect of helping the people of Cuba achieve their potential. And—*ojalá*, as is said in Spanish, "God willing"—it will ultimately strengthen the democratic movement there and resolve the last remaining dictatorship in the Americas in a positive way.

Over the next five years, the United States will come under serious pressure from the Castro regime and its partners in the Americas (Venezuela, Nicaragua, Ecuador, Bolivia, and others) to close the naval station and return it to Cuban sovereignty. They will say: you gave back the Panama Canal, closed bases elsewhere (in Ecuador, for example), and generally do not deploy forces without the consent of a host government. If relations with Cuba are "normal," why would Cuba not get the same treatment?

One answer would be to begin using the base as the hub of a U.S.-led international effort to address the challenges of the region. Naval Station Guantánamo, with the cooperation of Cuba and the United States, could be used for:

- Large-scale disaster relief efforts as the inevitable hurricanes and earthquakes devastate the region
- Humanitarian relief work, cooperating to build clinics and schools and develop sources of clean drinking water
- Basing hospital ships and training vessels focused on civil improvement projects and education
- Storage of relief supplies—major facilities for this already exist

- Collective counternarcotics efforts, partnering with the Joint Interagency Task Force in Key West

All of this would require a delicate negotiation with the Cubans, agreement from the United States to continue providing the lion's share of the funding, and cooperation from other partners (Brazil, Colombia, and Mexico all have capacity). It would probably also require closing the detention facility as other nations are unlikely to participate without the departure of Joint Task Force Guantánamo (the detainee command). All very complicated.

But the idea of essentially internationalizing Naval Station Guantánamo has real possibilities and would allow the United States and Cuba to work together on a positive project going forward. The odds of the United States' needing the base for combat operations are essentially nil—luckily we enjoy peace here in the Americas. We should explore the possibilities for collective use of Naval Station Guantánamo in addressing the real problems in this hemisphere: poverty, natural disasters, development, and narcotics.

MOVING A BIT FARTHER AFIELD from the continental United States, it is the two "forward seas" that matter most: the Mediterranean Sea and the South China Sea. Each is ringed with U.S. allies and friends, and each faces a variety of challenges both internal and external.

For the Mediterranean, it is the pressure of violent extremists, at the moment surging principally from the so-called Islamic State, that is the most dangerous element, from the Syrian seacoast to the long stretch of Libya. Additionally, there is pressure from Russia, which seeks to maintain bases on the Mediterranean and continues to press south from its

Crimean bases in the recently annexed region of Ukraine. Our NATO friends and allies need our support and presence in the region.

The job of patrolling the Mediterranean falls to the Sixth Fleet, which is based out of Italy. It has a flagship and a handful of surface combatants (typically AEGIS guided missile destroyers and cruisers) and also can access aircraft carriers and amphibious readiness groups that are in transit or swung north through the Suez Canal from the Indian Ocean and the Gulf in times of need. As events over the past several years have demonstrated, the eastern Mediterranean is a zone of conflict akin to the South China Sea. We should therefore increase the size of the Sixth Fleet and have a permanently deployed flotilla of at least ten ships to the Mediterranean (today we typically have two or three).

In the South China Sea, we should likewise be working closely with allies (the Republic of Korea and the Philippines, as well as Japan just to the north of the region) as well as with friends (Vietnam, Taiwan, Malaysia, Singapore). We currently have an aircraft carrier strike group permanently stationed forward in Japan, and that should continue. We need to increase the number of our submarines in the region, basing them out of Guam or Japan. Forward naval presence in the South China Sea will be necessary to maintain a balance in the region.

North of the South China Sea, we will also need a maritime-based plan to deal with North Korea over time. Let's start with why we care. North Korea is arguably the most dangerous nation in the world—they have a small arsenal of nuclear weapons, a budding ballistic missile capability that will soon be able to deliver them at range (as evidenced by their November 2017 long-range missile test), and they have continually demonstrated the propensity to use military force while occasionally conducting an actual nuclear weapon test. The nation has significant malnutrition, a huge prison population on a per capita basis, no democratic means of succession, and territorial disputes with its southern neighbor, the

Republic of Korea. The North Koreans also regularly threaten the United States, Japan, and other countries that they perceive stand in the way of their economic and political objectives. Taken together, the pattern of behavior and basic fact pattern on the ground in North Korea demand a plan for dealing with this pariah state.

First, the international community should be increasing sanctions dramatically. Given the level of sanctions leveled on Iran for merely pursuing a nuclear weapon, why would there be any fewer sanctions applied to a state that has such weapons and detonates them in unnecessary tests? The U.S. Congress just passed a revised, tougher set of sanctions that will begin to go after international cash accounts and penalize banks that do any kind of business with North Korea—this is an important step that other nations should follow. Japan is likewise imposing new, stronger sanctions. Other nations in the region—especially China—should follow suit. Initial sanctions to North Korea's weapons tests in 2017 were a step in the right direction, but more action is needed to slow North Korea.

Another important element is preparing appropriate levels of missile defenses, especially in South Korea and Japan. For example, adding the state-of-the-art Terminal High Altitude Area Defense (THAAD) system to the arsenals of both countries. Given that there are tens of thousands of U.S. soldiers and their families in both countries, this is in the interest of both the host nations and the United States. The United States, South Korea, and Japan should work together to finance and put in place this highly capable system, which has a range well over two hundred kilometers and flies at Mach 8-plus to effect terminal kills of incoming ballistic missiles. China will not like this (seeing it as at least partially directed against Chinese systems), but will need to accept the need on the part of the other nations. Perhaps the Chinese concerns will lead to a more aggressive stance toward Pyongyang, which would be helpful.

Indeed, much depends on Beijing in terms of reining in Kim Jong-un. While the young leader's attitude toward China is ambivalent at best (he killed his uncle, the central interlocutor, early in his regime), the Chinese have real economic leverage. They should be encouraged to use it, and if necessary, the sanctions regime against North Korea should apply to Chinese banks and businesses conducting commerce there.

In addition to THAAD, more advanced Patriot Air Defense and AEGIS maritime-based air defense systems should be deployed to the defense of South Korea and Japan. Both nations have versions of Patriot, and Japan has AEGIS ships; but these systems can be modernized, and all three nations should conduct exercises and training together to link them into a coherent regional missile defense system.

Additionally, there is more that the United States and its allies can do in the cyber world. While North Korea is notoriously difficult to penetrate (because it carefully screens its links to the Internet), it does use portions of the Web for specialized security functions, and its military rides on a computer-based backbone that can be accessed, albeit with difficulty. Working closely with our South Korean and Japanese cyber counterparts, we should use cyber aggressively to sabotage the North Korean weapons programs, insert monitoring devices in their critical infrastructure, and generate the means to attack their electrical grid if necessary and in response to a North Korean attack against the South. The North Koreans have already lashed out at a U.S. company, Sony Pictures, over cyber circuits, destroying millions of dollars in equipment and doing significant business damage to Sony's interests by releasing thousands of embarrassing internal e-mails.

In terms of additional military preparations, the United States should do all it can to link South Korea and Japan in the air defense area, as well as in maritime cooperation. Working together in the air and at sea can help provide a deterrent effect on North Korea, balancing the strong

U.S. ground forces on the Korean Peninsula already. Conducting a large, annual, U.S. Joint Staff–sponsored exercise in the region specifically focused on North Korea and the danger it poses would make sense. It should have a strong cyber component as well.

Finally, despite all the frustrations and dangers, we need to do what we can to keep a means of communication open with North Korea. While fruitful negotiations seem unlikely, we should be generally open to dialogue—but careful not to fall into the familiar trap of North Korea: bad behavior, negotiations, concessions on food, fuel, and sanctions, and no change in overall behavior. It is a depressingly familiar cycle. This is where working with China over time might have a helpful effect— without Chinese engagement and economic clout, any attempt at negotiation will be unlikely to succeed.

As in the film *The Interview*, which mocked Kim Jong-un and was the motivation for the Sony Pictures attack, it is easy to laugh at the chubby young leader. But he is a clear and present danger to the region, and we will need determined collective action—economic, military, and diplomatic—to counter his growing potential to provoke a major crisis in the heart of the world's economy, East Asia.

ALL OF THIS WILL BE the purview of the U.S. Seventh Fleet, historically the largest and most capable. It will need the most advanced weapons systems, to include antimissile technology on AEGIS combatants, significant carrier presence (at least two, one permanently in Japan and the other roaming the Pacific), strong Marine Corps elements (on Okinawa and Guam), ballistic missile submarines as the most survivable leg of the triad to deter China, and strong special forces and cyber support. The Seventh Fleet should remain headquartered on the islands of Japan, our strongest ally in the region, and will also require a string of bases

around the Pacific. Some of the key nodes are on the home islands of
Japan, the South Korean Peninsula, and Okinawa. Additionally, we
should explore at least cooperative arrangements to base a light footprint
in the Philippines (the legislature there appears poised to approve a
return to historic Subic Bay), on northern Australia (probably in Darwin),
and—over time—in Vietnam. Access to bases in Singapore is essential,
and the defense relationship there is very strong.

The major body of water the greatest distance from the United
States, literally on the other side of the world, is the Indian Ocean. Here
our strategy must first and foremost take into account the emerging super-
power India. We should do all we can diplomatically, culturally, militarily,
politically, and diplomatically to strengthen our ties with India. This
should particularly include cooperating in the maritime realm, including a
new series of exercises and training with the Indian navy; promoting sales
of advanced naval hardware, notably the AEGIS combat system on surface
combatants; cooperating on operating nuclear submarines; working with
India and Japan on naval exercises focused on counterpiracy in and around
the approaches to the Indian Ocean; and developing a program of maritime science diplomacy for the Indian Ocean.

In addition to working closely with India, our two major Anglophone
allies New Zealand and Australia are important as well. Australia is of
major geostrategic importance given the size of its coastline, which includes a huge coastal "waterfront" on the Indian Ocean. Great Britain continues to own Diego Garcia and deploys internationally to the Arabian/
Persian Gulf as well, and our involvement there will be crucial.

The Arabian/Persian Gulf will continue to be a vitally important
waterway for the United States, and the linkages between the greater
Indian Ocean and the Gulf will be a "hot" seam in maritime affairs. The
United States must continue to maintain a significant naval fleet (numerically, the Fifth Fleet) in the region. It is mandatory to maintain a

carrier strike group (a nuclear-powered aircraft carrier and a handful of AEGIS guided missile escorts) in the region 24/7. Additionally, having a Marine Expeditionary Unit (also known as an Expeditionary Strike Group) in the area will be advisable. The latter consists of three large amphibious ships that carry a specially trained and reinforced Marine Expeditionary Unit (about two thousand Marines, aircraft, and the ability to move them with extreme speed). We should also have a strong minesweeping and special forces capability. Clearly the region will continue to be contentious, and given the high level of global hydrocarbons moving through it the United States will need to work with coalition partners to keep it open.

Finally, there is the Arctic. The strategic terrain at the top of the world will be increasingly important to U.S. strategy, and our approach in the High North must include first and foremost ensuring that we have sufficient icebreakers. This means a strategic program to purchase (or lease) icebreakers. At an absolute minimum, a coherent U.S. maritime strategy should have four heavy and four medium icebreakers. Fortunately, pretty much everyone in Washington agrees with the idea that we need icebreakers, and we need them now. Our global maritime strategy should have an icebreaker component built into it.

Additionally, we need more transportation and exploration infrastructure (roads as well as ports and airstrips) in the High North. While we have some in place and plans for others, the fall in oil prices in 2015–16 has slowed the pace of construction. In addition to shore-based infrastructure, we also need sea-based structures that can be used for emergency search and rescue, environmental disaster response, and scientific research. These can be built on the basic structures of offshore oil and gas platforms and—when hydrocarbon prices rise again—can be built into the tax base levied on the companies exploiting the natural resources of the region.

There is not a U.S. Navy fleet assigned to the Arctic, and at the moment one is not necessary. The best approach would be to make this an area of focus for the U.S. Coast Guard, with the Department of Defense acting in support.

What remains? Both the far South Atlantic and the South Pacific are relatively secure and can be considered theaters where an "economy of force strategy" can be used. This simply means that we do not need permanently deployed ships or permanent bases in either region. We will need to make occasional cruises to support presence and conduct basic military-to-military contacts, but no significant forces will be required.

Taken together, it is clear that many of the principles of Mahan apply—we still need forward bases, extended fleets, and secure logistics (although not so much coal anymore). But what we can add to the Mahanian construct is international (both alliances like NATO and informal coalition partners), interagency (especially with the Coast Guard), and private-public cooperation. This twenty-first-century global maritime strategy is the right one for our nation, requires a fleet of around 350 ships, is affordable, flexible, and provides the nation both hard-power and soft-power options—a smart-power approach for the seas.

THE UNITED STATES CONTINUES on a voyage that is both personal to the mariners who sail it and of vital geopolitical importance. In the end, we are an island nation, bounded by oceans and nurtured on the global commerce, international markets, fishing expeditions, hydrocarbon offshore rigs, and strategic waterways of the world's oceans. Without the oceans and our ability to sail them, we would be enormously diminished as a nation. Our ability to navigate, both literally and figuratively, through the oceans will be a determinative part of the voyage of our nation in this century. I began this volume with the thought that there is both a deeply individual component to sailing and understanding the oceans and a key geostrategic element to the idea that the sea is truly one. Taken together, it seems clear that the nautical character of our nation will continue to be vital, indeed essential, for all that the future promises to our country and the world. Let us continue to sail in our ships, which take our sailors daily out of sight of land, and leave us gazing at the eternal vista of the deep sea, where we stand on a narrow hull, rolling before the waves and the wind, knowing we are at heart a nation that will forever depend on sea power and our sailors for security and prosperity.

ACKNOWLEDGMENTS

First, my research assistants during academic year 2015–16, Matt Merighi and McKenzie Smith, contributed to chapters 1 and 2 on the Pacific and Atlantic, respectively. My research assistant for 2016–17, Colin Steele, added content and edits for this paperback volume, and Commander Jeremy Watkins helped with ideas for chapter 9 on strategy and contributed data for the arms race in the Pacific highlighted in chapter 1.

Some of this material was published in previous public writings of mine, mostly in *Foreign Policy, The Wall Street Journal, Nikkei Asian Review, Signal* magazine, and *Proceedings* (U.S. Naval Institute), and is reprinted with their permission. All of it is original work of mine, of course. In particular, some of the material at the end of chapter 1 on the Pacific is based on a column I wrote for *Nikkei/Financial Times Asia* in 2015. At the end of chapter 3 on the Indian Ocean is some material from a column in *Foreign Policy* written in 2014. The final paragraphs of chapter 4 on the Mediterranean are based on material published in *Foreign Policy* in 2015. Chapter 5 on the South China Sea has several paragraphs based on articles from *Foreign Policy* and

Nikkei Asian Review from 2015. Chapter 6 contains some material from a column in *Foreign Policy* in 2015. Chapter 9 includes material on undersea cables and the new maritime strategy that appeared in *Signal* magazine.

Captain Bill Harlow, a close friend and colleague of more than three decades, has been a superb supporter, adviser, and sharp-eyed editor of this manuscript.

My friend and agent Andrew Wylie supported this idea and helped persuade Penguin Random House to take the plunge (pun intended) to publish such a watery book.

Scott Moyers, a gifted agent and now an editor at Penguin Press, conceived the idea and persuaded me to take on the challenge of crafting this broad and deeply personal book.

My wife, Laura, as always, has been a stalwart and patient source of love and support, even when our weekends were a bit curtailed as deadlines loomed.

All errors of fact, content, or imagination are mine alone.

I dedicate this book to all the sailors at sea: Godspeed and open water to them all, wherever the wind and waves have taken them.

SOURCES AND RECOMMENDED READINGS
ON THE WORLD'S OCEANS

NONFICTION

Admiral Bill Halsey: A Naval Life by Thomas Alexander Hughes (Cambridge, Mass.: Harvard University Press, 2016)

America and the Sea: A Maritime History edited by Benjamin W. Labaree, et al. (Mystic, Conn.: Mystic Seaport Press, 1998)

The Anarchic Sea: Maritime Security in the 21st Century by Dave Sloggett (New York: Hurst, 2014)

Arctic Dreams by Barry Lopez (New York: Scribner, 1986)

Asia's Cauldron: The South China Sea and the End of a Stable Pacific by Robert D. Kaplan (New York: Random House, 2014)

Atlantic by Simon Winchester (New York: HarperCollins, 2013)

Atlantic History: Concept and Contours by Bernard Bailyn (Cambridge, Mass.: Harvard University Press, 2005) (Web)

Atlantic Ocean: The Illustrated History of the Ocean That Changed the World by Martin Sandler (New York: Sterling, 2008)

Bitter Ocean: The Battle of the Atlantic, 1939–1945 by David Fairbank White (New York: Simon & Schuster, 2006)

Black Sea by Neal Ascherson (London: Jonathan Cape, 1995)

Blue Latitudes: Boldly Going Where Captain Cook Went Before by Tony Horwitz (New York: Picador, 2003)

Box Boats: How Container Ships Changed the World by Brian Cudahy (New York: Fordham University Press, 2006)

"Charting a New Course for the Oceans: A Report on the State of the World's Oceans, Global Fisheries and Fisheries Treaties, and Potential Strategies for Reversing the Decline in Ocean Health and Productivity" by William Moomaw and Sara Blankenship (Medford, Mass.: The Center for International Environment and Resource Policy, The Fletcher School of Law and Diplomacy, Tufts University, 2014)

Cod: A Biography of the Fish That Changed the World by Mark Kurlansky (New York: Walker, 1997)

The Cruise of the Snark by Jack London (New York: Macmillan, reprint, 1961; 1939)

The Discoverers by Daniel Boorstin (New York: Vintage, 1983)

Dreadnought: Britain, Germany, and the Coming of the Great War by Robert K. Massie (New York: Random House, 1991)

Facing West by John C. Perry (Westport, Conn.: Praeger, 1994)

Gift from the Sea by Anne Morrow Lindbergh (New York: Pantheon, reprint, 1991; 1955)

Globalization and Maritime Power, edited by Sam J. Tangredi (Honolulu: University Press of the Pacific, 2011)

The Great Ocean: Pacific Worlds from Captain Cook to the Gold Rush by David Igler (New York: Oxford University Press, 2013)

The Great Pacific Victory from the Solomons to Tokyo by Gilbert Cant (New York: The John Day Company, 1946)

Great Wall at Sea: China's Navy Enters the 21st Century by Bernard Cole (Annapolis, Md.: USNI Press, 2011)

Guns, Germs, and Steel: The Fates of Human Societies by Jared Diamond (New York: Norton, 1999)

The Indian Ocean in World History by Edward A. Alpers (New York: Oxford University Press, 2014)

In the Heart of the Sea: The Tragedy of the Whaleship Essex by Nathaniel Philbrick (New York: Viking, 2000)

Inventing Grand Strategy and Teaching Command: The Classic Works of Alfred Thayer Mahan Reconsidered by Jon Sumida (Baltimore: Johns Hopkins University Press, 1997)

The Log from the Sea of Cortez by John Steinbeck (New York: Penguin Classics, reprint, 1995; 1951)

Longitude: The True Story of a Lone Genius Who Solved the Greatest Scientific Problem of His Time by Dava Sobel (New York: Walker, 1995)

Maritime Economics by Martin Stopford (New York: Routledge, 1997)

The Mediterranean and the Mediterranean World in the Age of Philip II, 2 vols., by Fernand Braudel (New York: Harper, 1972)

The Mediterranean in History, edited by David Abulafia (London: Thames and Hudson, 2003)

Mirror of Empire: Dutch Marine Art of the Seventeenth Century, edited by George Keyes (Cambridge: Cambridge University Press, 1990)

Monsoon: The Indian Ocean and the Future of American Power by Robert Kaplan (New York: Random House, 2010)

Ocean: An Illustrated Atlas by Sylvia Earl and Linda Glover (New York: National Geographic Press, 2008)

The Oxford Encyclopedia of Maritime History, edited by John Hattendorf (Oxford and New York: Oxford University Press, 2007)

Pacific Ocean, by Felix Riesenberg (New York and London: Whittlesey House, McGraw-Hill, 1940)

The Pacific Theater: Island Representations of World War II, 8 vols., by Geoffrey M. White and Lamont Lindstrom (Honolulu: University of Hawaii Press, 1989)

The Polynesian Journal of Captain Henry Byam Martin, R.N., by Henry Byam Martin (Salem, Mass.: Peabody Museum of Salem, 1981)

The Price of Admiralty by John Keegan (New York: Viking, 1983)

Principles of Maritime Strategy by Julian Corbett (Mineola, N.Y.: Dover Publications, 1911)

The Quiet Warrior: A Biography of Admiral Raymond Spruance, by Thomas Buell (Annapolis, Md.: USNI Press, reissued 2013)

The Rise and Fall of the Great Powers by Paul Kennedy (New York: Random House, 1987)

The Sea and Civilization: A Maritime History of the World by Lincoln Paine (New York: Alfred A. Knopf, 2013)

The Sea Around Us by Rachel Carson (Oxford and New York: Oxford University Press, reprint, 1991; 1951)

Seapower by E. B. Potter (Annapolis, Md.: USNI Press, 1972)

Seapower: A Guide for the Twenty-First Century by Geoffrey Till (New York: Routledge, 2013)

Seapower as Strategy: Navies and National Interests by Norman Friedman (Annapolis, Md.: Naval Institute Press, 2001)

The Sea Power of the State by S. Gorshkov (New York: Pergamon Press, 1979)

Sovereign of the Seas by David Howarth (New York: Atheneum, 1974)

Villains of All Nations: Atlantic Pirates in the Golden Age by Marcus Rediker (Boston: Beacon Press, 2004)

Voyage of the Beagle by Charles Darwin (New York: Penguin Classics, reprint, 1989; 1839)

FICTION AND LEGEND

The Caine Mutiny Court Martial by Herman Wouk—the stress of men at sea in a small minesweeper during World War II.

The Cruel Sea by Nicholas Monserrat—convoy duty in the North Atlantic during World War II, with lessons in leadership and coping with tragedy.

Lord Jim by Joseph Conrad—mistakes made at sea and their impact on a young life.

Master and Commander, the Novels of Patrick O'Brian by Patrick O'Brian—a series of twenty brilliant sea novels that take the reader deep into the lives of Captain Jack Aubrey and his seagoing surgeon, Stephen Maturin.

Moby-Dick by Herman Melville—in Captain Ahab's fevered search for the Great White Whale, we find the greatest sea story of all in the ill-fated voyage of the *Pequod*.

The Odyssey by Homer—a journey across the wine-dark sea from victory at Troy through a long decade returning home to Ithaca.

The Old Man and the Sea by Ernest Hemingway—Santiago the fisherman's fight with the huge fish and then the sharks is the stuff of legends, and a metaphor for life itself.

The Open Boat by Stephen Crane—survival at sea in the most challenging circumstances.

The Secret Sharer by Joseph Conrad—a sea captain's imaginary stowaway; or is he real? The sea can make men and women mad, especially those with the loneliness of command as part of their burden.

The Ship by C. S. Forester—a day in the life of a World War II destroyer in the
   Mediterranean, full of timeless observations of the sailor's life.

Toilers of the Sea by Victor Hugo—fishermen, salvage crews, battles with
   creatures of the deep.

Two Years Before the Mast by Richard Henry Dana Jr.—a weak-eyed college
   student ships out and discovers the life of a sailor in the nineteenth century.

INDEX

2034

A Novel of the Next World War

Elliot Ackerman and Admiral James Stavridis

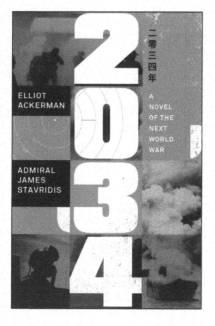

A chilling, authentic geopolitical thriller, *2034* imagines a naval clash between the United States and China in the South China Sea and takes us inside the minds of a global cast of characters—Americans, Chinese, Iranians, Russians, Indians—as a series of arrogant miscalculations on all sides leads the world into an intensifying international storm. In the end, China and the United States will have paid a staggering cost, one that forever alters the global balance of power.

"A rippingly good read." —*Wired*

 PENGUIN PRESS PENGUIN BOOKS

Sailing True North

Ten Admirals and the Voyage of Character

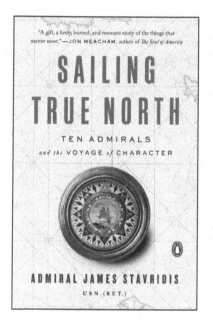

In *Sailing True North*, Admiral James Stavridis offers lessons of leadership and character from the lives and careers of history's most significant naval commanders. He also brings a lifetime of reflection to bear on the subjects of his study: naval history, the vocation of the admiral, and global geopolitics. Above all, this is a book that will help you navigate your own life's voyage—the voyage of leadership, of course, but more important, the voyage of character. *Sailing True North* helps us find the right course to chart.

"A lively, learned, and resonant study of the things that matter most." –Jon Meacham, author of *The Soul of America*

 PENGUIN PRESS

 PENGUIN BOOKS

Ready to find your next great read? Let us help. Visit prh.com/nextread